CREEKTOWN DISCOVERIES

The

Apple Creek

ANNOUNCEMENT

CREEKTOWN DISCOVERIES

The
Apple Creek
ANNOUNCEMENT

WANDA E
BRUNSTETTER

Guideposts

Published by Guideposts
100 Reserve Road, Suite E200
Danbury, CT 06810
Guideposts.org

This Guideposts edition is published by special arrangement with Barbour Books is a registered trademark of Barbour Publishing.

All scripture quotations are taken from the King James Version of the Bible.

All German-Dutch words are taken from the *Revised Pennsylvania German Dictionary* found in Lancaster County, Pennsylvania.

This book is a work of fiction. Names, characters, places, and incidents are either products of the author's imagination or used fictitiously. Any similarity to actual people, organizations, and/or events is purely coincidental.

Cover design: Buffy Cooper; cover model photography: Richard Brunstetter III; cover background photography: Doyle Yoder Photography

ISBN 978-1-961126-30-5 (softcover)
ISBN 978-1-961126-28-2 (epub)

Printed in the United States of America
10 9 8 7 6 5 4 3 2 1

Dedication

To Pastor Dan and Robyn:
Thank you for your ministry that
touches so many people's lives.

~

*This is the confidence that we
have in [God], that, if we ask anything
according to his will, he heareth us.*
1 JOHN 5:14

Prologue

Walnut Creek, Ohio

"Would ya look at this old chair? I think it's a beauty, don't you?" From his kneeling position, Orley Troyer pointed to the vintage oak office chair he'd purchased at a family-run estate sale he and his wife had visited earlier in the day.

"I'd say so, and it appears to be in quite good condition. Not only that, but you got the chair for a fair price," Lois responded. She held up an old washboard she had found at the sale. "But this is one of my favorite items. I don't know if you noticed, but the lettering on the backside of the board looks pretty clear."

Orley nodded. "Now we need to put these items on display in our store."

"I'll place the washboard with the kitchen items, and you can move the chair over with the furniture."

"No problem." Orley stood up and rubbed the small of his back, where a knot had begun to form. "Although business has been strong this spring and hopefully will continue to grow now that it's summer, it has been a while since anyone has come into Memory Keepers with some sort of problem they wanted to talk about." His eyes squinted as he pulled his fingers slowly through the end of his long, full beard. "I miss mentoring folks one-on-one."

"I do too," Lois agreed, "but I'm glad for the opportunity to advise people who contact me via the Dear Caroline column in the local newspaper."

"*Jah*, that must be a good feeling all right." Orley couldn't help feeling a bit envious that his wife had such a unique opportunity to help others. Even so, there were days when he wished Lois would quit the job and spend more time with him. He looked over at her and said, "Maybe the newspaper would be interested in hiring a man to write a Dear Samuel column just for men. Then we'd both be too busy to make popcorn and work on puzzles in the evenings." He jiggled his brows and gave her arm a playful poke. "What do you think, *Fraa?* Would it be a good idea if I went to the newspaper and suggested that they hire me for that job?"

Lois snickered as she rolled her eyes at him. "I think you'd better stick to selling antiques and stay ready for the day when the Lord sends another person into our store who needs some counseling from you."

Orley smiled. "You're right, and I hope that day will come soon."

Chapter 1

Click...click...click... Andrea cringed as her newest piano student's fingers hit the keys while she played the piece of music she'd been given last week. For some piano teachers, the sound of nails clicking on the keys was exasperating. Andrea was one of those teachers.

She waited until the fourteen-year-old girl had finished playing before speaking to her. "Peggy, you hit all the right notes, and your timing was good, but your fingernails are much too long, and I'd like you to cut them before your next lesson."

"But Miss Wagner, the teacher I had before my folks and I moved to Apple Creek never said anything about my nails." Peggy held out her hands. "I like 'em this way, and they don't look as pretty when they're short."

"Having shorter nails will help you maintain a relaxed, curved hand position," Andrea explained.

"Why do my fingers have to be curved?"

"By doing so, you will make them close to the same length, giving each finger equal playing ability. I'm sure your previous teacher must have told you that." Andrea paused to be sure that she had her student's full attention, but the girl merely sat with a glum expression.

"Being able to feel the keys with the pads of your fingers will give you a better touch on the keyboard, which in turn will allow you to play with greater control," Andrea continued. "You'll also have greater speed, because long nails could get in the way and might even cause you to make mistakes. And have you noticed how when your nails hit the keyboard they make clicking sounds?" Andrea placed her hand on the girl's shoulder. "During a recital, would you want the only thing your audience remembers from your performance to be the sound of your nails?"

Peggy lifted her shoulders in a brief shrug. "I guess not."

Believing she had gained a little headway, Andrea added one more thing. "Not only can long fingernails affect a pianist's performance, but they can also increase your chances of getting injured."

"What do you mean?"

"It may seem hard to imagine, but when I was a girl taking lessons, my teacher told me about one of her students who had refused to trim her fingernails and ended up catching one of them between keys, which caused the end of the nail to break and bleed."

Peggy's eyes widened. "Ouch!"

"I agree, but if the student had willingly trimmed her nails, the breakage could have been avoided." She looked directly at Peggy and spoke kindly but firmly. "So what do you say—are you willing to trim your fingernails before your next lesson?"

To Andrea's surprise, the girl shook her head. "After today's lesson is done, I'm goin' home and tell Mom and Dad that I want 'em to find another teacher who isn't picky about my nails. Either that or I'm gonna quit taking piano lessons."

"It's up to you, Peggy, but your folks might not be happy about it—especially since they've paid me in advance for your next eight lessons."

"Okay, whatever. I'll wait and see what Mom and Dad have to say." The girl lifted her chin in a defiant pose. "'Cause I don't think cutting my nails will make me play one bit better."

"You don't have to cut them really short, just short enough so you can easily feel the keys with the entire fleshy part of your fingers."

"All right, I'll do it—but only if my mother won't look for another teacher."

Andrea's toes curled inside her shoes. At a moment like this, she wondered why she had decided to teach private piano lessons when she could be painting pictures full-time. Of course, her artwork didn't sell on a regular basis, making it difficult to pay the bills with what her father had often referred to as "a nice hobby."

With cautious hope, Andrea moistened her lips using the tip of her tongue. *Maybe tomorrow at the open-air market, several of my paintings will sell.*

Andrea pulled her minivan into the parking area, noticing several horses and buggies at the hitching rails on the other side of the lot. Andrea wished she could set up her easel right now and paint the appealing scene set before her, but there was no time for that. She'd arrived at the Farmstead Vintage Market, located on the Pine Hill Farm, later than she'd planned and needed to get to her open-air booth so she could display her paintings before the crowds poured in.

Andrea looked in the rearview mirror to check her hair. She'd showered this morning, but with trying to hurry out the door, she hadn't done much to style her chin-length auburn bob. Andrea pulled out a lip color from her small cross-body bag and applied it with care. Grabbing her purse, she got out of the minivan.

Andrea had no more than opened the back hatch of her van when her best friend, Colleen Jones, showed up. "Oh good, you're just in time." She hugged Colleen and gestured to the items inside her vehicle. "I was afraid I'd have to lug all this stuff over to the booth by myself."

Colleen shook her head. "Promised I'd be here, didn't I?"

"Yes, but I wasn't sure if you'd be able to find a sitter for Tyler."

Colleen offered Andrea one of her usual easygoing smiles. "My mother was more than willing to watch him for me this morning. Of course," she quickly added, "by the time I pick up my active two-year-old, he will no doubt be ready for a nap, and so will Mom."

"I hope if I ever have any children that my mother will be willing to watch them." Andrea reached inside the van and slid out the folding table she'd brought to display some of her smaller paintings.

"I'm sure she'd be willing, and if that good-looking veterinarian you've been dating for two years would get down on one knee and ask you to marry him, there might be a few kids in your future." Colleen grabbed the other end of the table.

"Maybe." Andrea started walking in the direction of the market. Truthfully, she wasn't sure Brandon Prentice would ever propose. If he was as committed to her as he was to his profession, he would have proposed by now. Brandon was a popular vet in their area, and his business was expanding, which meant longer hours for him. He worked at the clinic Monday through Friday, and sometimes on Saturdays when there was an emergency. Brandon also doctored large animals such as horses and livestock outside of the clinic. Andrea had heard from many sources that his animal patients and their owners liked Dr. Prentice, and it wasn't hard to realize that he liked them too. Brandon's kindness and gentle ways were two of the things that had drawn her to him, as well as his six-foot stature and those piercing blue eyes. *I have to agree with Colleen—my boyfriend is good-looking.*

The tantalizing aroma and sounds of caramel-flavored popcorn being made near the entrance of the market drove Andrea's dreamy thoughts aside. The sweet and salty treat was almost addictive, and she felt tempted to stop and buy some right now. But it would have to wait, at least until she'd set up her booth. And it was definitely time to quit thinking about the man she'd fallen in love with and hoped to marry, because she needed to focus on the day ahead.

After they'd found Andrea's booth space and set up the table, she glanced down the aisle where several other vendors were busy setting their items out. Wind chimes tinkled in the gentle breeze, drawing attention to displays of baked goods, honey, homemade candles and soaps, pottery, jewelry, birdhouses, and various other rustic gifts. So much to look at but no time to do it now. Andrea wished she had time to browse and maybe buy a few items, but she needed to get the rest of her things out of the van and finish setting up.

"It sure would be nice to do some shopping here today," Andrea commented as she and Colleen made their way back to the parking area. "But I guess that's the price I must pay for renting a space to hopefully sell some of my paintings."

"I'll stay with your booth whenever you feel like browsing," Colleen responded. "I want to do some shopping too, so we can take turns."

Andrea put her hand in the small of her friend's back and gave it a few tender pats. "That's nice of you, but I didn't think you'd be staying very long today. Figured you came just to help me unload and set up."

Colleen shook her head. "Nope. I'm here for the duration or until you kick me out."

"Not a chance of that." Andrea opened the van's hatch and reached inside to grab a box filled with some of her larger paintings. "I appreciate the time you're giving up to help me when you could be spending the day with your family."

"I don't mind." Colleen tucked one of her blond curls behind her ear. "It's good for Tyler to bond with his grandparents, and my husband needs a day off to spend with his golfing buddies."

"Guess it worked out well for everyone." Andrea waited until Colleen had picked up a second box, and then they started back toward the market. They hadn't gone very far when she noticed two more Amish buggies pull into the parking lot.

"I wonder what it'd be like to be Amish," she whispered to her friend.

"I don't know, but I can't imagine giving up my car for a horse and black carriage."

Andrea chuckled. "It would be pretty hard to imagine either of us dressed in Amish clothes, not to mention having long hair pulled up in a bun, or being seen in public with no makeup to hide our imperfections."

Colleen shook her head. "Nope, not for me. I'm a city gal, even if I do live in a rural community."

At noon, Andrea left her booth in the capable hands of her friend. She would check out a few of the booths on the other side of the market and stop by the food truck to get them something to eat. Of course, she wouldn't go back to her booth without picking up two large bags of kettle corn.

Andrea was pleased that she'd sold two paintings this morning—both images from Amish country. The larger one was of a black buggy parked near a red barn. The second painting featured a clothesline with several Amish quilts flapping in the breeze. That had been one of Andrea's favorites, and she'd hated to part with it, but the money she'd earned had made it worth the sacrifice. Besides, living so close to an Amish community made it easy for her to paint more pictures of quilts and other Amish backgrounds that appealed to her. Rural scenes, especially anything depicting the Plain people's way of life, were Andrea's favorite subjects. Those seemed to be the ones that sold quickly and for more money.

Andrea wandered up and down a few aisles, stopping to smell some lavender-fragranced products. She'd also been invited to sample some mild-tasting herbal tea and had even paused to try a bit of salsa—although it had proven to be a bit too spicy for her taste.

I bet Brandon would have liked it, Andrea thought as she approached the next stand. An assortment of items, most of them appearing to be secondhand or of vintage quality had been spread out on two large tables. She felt the urge to check out the display.

Andrea had picked through a few of the items when her gaze came to rest on an old quilt that looked like it had seen better days. Something about the faded quilt drew Andrea. She pursed her lips. *Perhaps this would be an interesting piece to drape over a quilt rack and hang in my house so I could paint a picture of it.* She fingered a fraying patch on the quilt.

Andrea noticed a small piece of paper pinned to one corner of the quilt and blinked when she saw the price. *Twenty-five dollars?*

Could that be right?

Andrea picked up the quilt and headed over to where a teenage girl, her arms crossed, sat in a metal chair behind a small table that held the cash box.

"Excuse me, but is this the right price?" She pointed to the place where the square piece of paper had been pinned.

The girl nodded. "Yep. My aunt Nicki—she's the one who rented this booth—said everything had been priced."

"Where is your aunt now? Could I talk to her?"

The girl shook her head. "She had to go home 'cause her baby got sick, so she left me in charge. Aunt Nicki said she'd send my uncle to come help me. He should be showing up here pretty soon, so if you have any questions about the quilt, he might be able to help you."

"I can't wait around because I have my own booth and need to get back there soon. Do you know anything about this quilt—how old it is or who it used to belong to?" Andrea questioned.

"Nope."

Continuing to hold the item, Andrea couldn't help feeling the lure of the soft fabric in her hands. "And you're sure it's only twenty-five dollars?"

The girl bobbed her head. "If I remember right, my aunt said she found it at a yard sale a few years ago, and she only paid five dollars for it. She was hoping to make a profit, so if you're interested. . ."

"Yes, I'm definitely interested." Andrea reached into her purse and took out her wallet. After she'd paid for the quilt, the girl put it in a cardboard box and handed it to Andrea. "I don't know what you're gonna do with that old thing, but it's the first sale I've made since Aunt Nicki left, so thank you."

Andrea smiled. "You're welcome." *I'm glad I stopped by this booth. I can't wait to get this quilt home and set out for display.*

Andrea had blanked out all thoughts of getting lunch or even grabbing a couple sacks of the tasty kettle corn she'd been craving all morning. She headed straight back to her booth, feeling like a child who'd opened a favored gift on Christmas morning.

Chapter 2

When Andrea returned to her booth and saw Colleen on her cell phone, she set the cardboard box with the quilt inside under the table and waited near the entrance of her vendor's stand.

"Is everything all right?" Andrea asked when her friend ended the phone call and looked at her with a pinched expression.

"That was my mom, and it's nothing serious," Colleen replied. "She's having a hard time getting Tyler to eat his lunch. He's kind of a picky eater." She patted her stomach. "And speaking of food. . . what took you so long? I'm hungry."

"Sorry," Andrea apologized. "One of the vendors had an old quilt for sale, which I ended up buying." She gestured to the box under the table. "So I set getting lunch aside and hurried back here with the quilt. If you don't mind keeping an eye on things here a little longer, I can get us something to eat right now."

"Maybe it would be better if I go to the food truck," Colleen said. "That way you'll be here to answer any customers' questions. You might have lost a few sales while I was in charge, because a couple of people came by and wanted to know if you would lower the price on some of your paintings."

Andrea groaned. "Oh great. I really hadn't planned on lowering any prices."

"Not to worry—if the potential customers come back, you can let them know that your prices are firm."

"Yeah, I suppose, but I have already lowered the prices a bit on some of the paintings so I can't go too much lower. Did anything sell in my absence?"

"Just one small painting of Lady sleeping on top of your piano."

"Guess that's better than nothing." Andrea smiled. "It was a cute cat pose."

"I agree, but I'm surprised she stayed there long enough for you to paint her portrait."

"Lady's good at sleeping in obscure places, and she usually remains in one position for quite a while."

Colleen smiled and reached for her purse. "I'd better head out to get us some lunch, or the food truck won't have anything left to offer."

"Let me give you the cash to buy my food." Andrea opened her bag. "Here you go. It's much easier to use cash at these places or write a check than try to pay with a card."

"That's true. Some of the vendors are old-school." Colleen slipped the money into her purse.

"Oh, before you go, would you like to see the quilt I purchased? I'd like your opinion."

"Sure, let's see it."

Andrea pulled the box out and removed the quilt. "What do you think?"

Colleen stepped closer and looked it over, rubbing her fingers slowly against the fabric. "Looks like an old one, but it's not in the best condition. I hope you didn't pay much for it."

"It was only twenty-five dollars."

"That was a bargain, even with it being old and not in the best condition. What are you planning to do with the quilt?"

Andrea shrugged. "I'm not sure yet. I'll probably see about getting it repaired, and then I might display it in my house somewhere."

Colleen chuckled. "Here I thought I was the one interested in antiques."

"Normally I'm not, but this quilt is different. I'm curious to know how old it is and find out what it's worth."

"You could take it to one of the quilt shops in our area."

"Would they do an appraisal?"

"Maybe. Or you could take it to an antique store." Colleen looked down at the quilt and snapped her fingers. "Hey, I think I know just the one too. There's an antique store called Memory Keepers in Walnut Creek, and it's owned by an Amish couple. I've been there a few times and was impressed with the variety of vintage things in their store. And who better to ask about an Amish quilt than a member of the Plain community?"

"Would you be willing to go with me—maybe one day next week?"

"Sure. How about Monday? We could have lunch at Boyd and Wurthmann's either before or after we visit the antique shop."

Andrea smiled. "I don't have any piano lessons to teach on Monday, so that'd be great."

"I'll see if Mom can watch Tyler again, because taking a two-year-old into an antique store would not be a good thing." Colleen spoke rapidly. "Even eating out at a restaurant with my active little boy can be a challenge."

"Speaking of eating," Andrea interjected, "the two of us still have not had any lunch."

"Right." Colleen lifted her purse straps over one shoulder. "I'll take care of that problem right now."

Walnut Creek

Lois sat behind the checkout counter, watching Orley across the room, talking with an Amish man from their church district. She couldn't hear what they were saying and wondered if their discussion pertained to antiques or some other topic. For all she knew, they could be talking about the hot, humid weather they'd been having so far this summer. Or maybe this man had a problem he wanted to discuss with Orley.

I'm sure my husband would like that, Lois thought. It wasn't that Orley wanted people to be faced with problems. Certainly not. But he, like Lois, felt blessed whenever they were given the opportunity to minister to someone who was hurting emotionally or needed advice. It seemed that God had given Orley and Lois the desire to help others, along with the gift of knowing what to say and which scriptures to share.

Lois thought about a recent letter that had been sent to her Dear Caroline column. The woman who'd written had stated that she and her husband were having marital problems. It reminded Lois of Jeff and Rhonda Davis, whom she and Orley had mentored almost two years ago. The couple had a little girl now, and they were doing quite well with the inn they'd bought in the area. The answer to Jeff and Rhonda's marriage problems had been finding a personal relationship with the Lord. That's what Lois hoped for anyone who hadn't accepted Jesus as their personal Savior.

Her thoughts turned inward as she reflected on the day she'd asked God to forgive her sins and had acknowledged His Son as her Lord and Savior. She also remembered the feeling of peace and joy she'd felt as she stood with several other young people her age to acknowledge Christ, receive baptism, and join the church. She'd gone home that afternoon with a spring in her step and the determination to remain firm in her faith. Lois had also resolved to try and set a good example and minister to anyone she met whom she felt had a spiritual or emotional need, although there were times when she felt inadequate.

The bell above the front door jingled, pushing Lois's musings aside. The Amish man Orley had been talking to left the store a few seconds before Paul and Lisa Herschberger stepped in.

Lois left her place behind the counter to greet them, and Orley hurried across the room. Handshakes were shared between the men, and the women hugged each other.

"It's wonderful to see you both. How have you been?" Lois questioned.

"Real well," Paul replied. "We just came from a celebration lunch and wanted to stop by here to give you and Orley our good news."

"We're always open to good news." Orley looked at Lois and grinned. "Isn't that right, Fraa?"

She nodded and turned her attention to the happy-looking couple. "What's your good news?"

Lisa placed both hands against her stomach. "We're expecting a baby."

"That's right. He or she will arrive sometime in early February," Paul added.

"Congratulations." Lois gave them both a hug, and Orley followed suit.

Lois would never have let on, but she couldn't help feeling a bit of sadness because she and Orley had never been blessed with a child. She certainly would not want to dampen Paul and Lisa's joy or hurt Orley's feelings because of his inability to father a child. Although Lois loved her husband dearly and would not allow herself to dwell on being childless, there were moments, like now, when she had to be mindful not to let envy take over. Instead, Lois would continue to thank the Lord for the loving husband she had married.

Apple Creek

Andrea curled up on the sofa, petting Lady's soft white fur as the cat stretched out in her lap. Her cat's soothing purr always helped Andrea to relax after a long or stressful day. She hadn't taken time to unload her vehicle yet because she was tired and decided it could wait until she'd fixed something to eat and rested awhile. At the end of a busy or hectic day, she liked to sit quietly in a darkened room and let her mind go blank.

When the bell rang, Andrea lifted Lady off her lap, turned on a light, and went to see who it was. Upon opening the door, she was surprised to see Brandon on the porch with a smile on his face and a pizza box in his hands.

"I brought supper." He leaned in to give her a sweet, gentle kiss.

Had it not been for the box between them, she would have melted into his arms. "Oh, thank you so much. I'm exhausted and dreaded having to fix anything for supper." She stepped back so Brandon could enter.

"I was thinking about you and thought you might have had an exhausting day at the market. Should I put this on the dining room table or in the kitchen?" he asked.

"Let's eat in the dining room. I'll turn some music on, and we can pretend we're on a dinner date."

He kissed her forehead. "We are. We're just not going out to a crowded, noisy restaurant. By eating here, I'll have you all to myself and won't have to shout to be heard."

She nodded. "Good point. I'll go to the kitchen and get some paper plates and napkins. Oh, and what would you like to drink? I have iced tea, lemonade, and grape juice."

"Iced tea is fine for me."

While Brandon headed for the dining room, Andrea went to the kitchen. A short while later, they were both seated at the table with the Italian-style cheese and pepperoni pizza between them. After saying grace, Brandon pushed the pizza toward Andrea and told her to dig in.

"I should make a tossed green salad to go with this, but I'm hungry and don't want to take the time," she said, reaching for a piece of pizza and putting it on her plate.

"That's okay." Brandon smiled. "This is a family-style pizza, so there's more than enough for us to eat, and I'm sure you'll have leftovers."

"Maybe you'd like to take them home."

He shook his head. "This is my treat, and whatever's left will be yours."

Andrea didn't argue; she just smiled and said, "Thank you." She figured with Brandon's hearty appetite, there might not be anything left.

"How'd your day at the open-air market go?" he asked.

"Not too bad. I sold a few of my smaller paintings, and I appreciated Colleen being there to help me load and unload things as well as set up my booth."

"I wish it could have been me who had helped you, but I had an emergency at the clinic this morning and several farm stops to care for people's horses and livestock." Brandon paused to drink some iced tea. "It was a tiring day, but yours probably was too."

"Yes, especially toward the end of the day as the crowds thinned out. By then there wasn't much left to do except wait for four o'clock, when we could start packing things up."

"If you didn't sell much, do you feel like it was worth your effort and the money you spent to rent a booth?"

"I did hand out several of my business cards, so it's possible that I'll get a few calls from interested buyers." Andrea picked a piece of pepperoni off her slice of pizza and ate it. "I probably missed a few sales when I left Colleen at my booth to go get us some lunch. When I got back—without any food—she said a few people had stopped by the booth and were interested but wanted to offer less for the paintings. I may have taken their offers if they hadn't been too much less than what I was asking."

"Sorry you didn't make many sales. I'm curious, though—how come you returned to your booth without anything for lunch? Did the food truck run out of food?"

"No, it was my fault. I stopped by one of the vendor's stands and ended up buying an old quilt that I'm quite sure is Amish. I was so excited and wanted to get it back to my booth, so I kind of forgot about getting lunch."

"Where is this old quilt that you chose over eating?"

"It's in the back of my van, along with the table I took to the market and all my paintings that didn't sell."

"I'll help you take everything out when we finish eating."

"Thanks. When I first got home, I was too tired to bring everything in." Andrea glanced at her cat, lying on the floor a few feet from the table. "Besides, Lady missed me while I was gone, and she needed some attention."

Brandon chuckled. "I know how that is. When I got home this afternoon, Duke was so eager to see me that he tried climbing his way out of the pen."

"Pets are great, but they're a lot of work, and they demand plenty of attention from their owners."

"My dog is worth it, though, and I'm sure you feel the same way about your cat."

"Most definitely."

"It's too bad Duke's scared to death of Lady. That might cause a problem when we get married."

Andrea nearly choked on the piece of pizza she'd put in her mouth. "Are—are you asking me to marry you?"

Brandon's eyes appeared even bluer than usual as he looked deeply into Andrea's eyes. "I realize this isn't the most romantic setting, and I probably should be down on one knee right now, but the answer is yes, I am asking you to be my wife."

Andrea felt a sense of weightlessness as she moved her head up and down. "Yes, Brandon, a thousand times, yes. I will marry you."

He left the table so quickly that his chair nearly toppled over and was swiftly at her side. Andrea stood, and they sealed their commitment to each other with a kiss that took Andrea's breath away. She wanted to ask what had taken him so long but figured that question was best left unspoken. The last thing she wanted to do was say anything that might ruin this special moment between them.

Chapter 3

Berlin, Ohio

Andrea glanced at her gold-toned watch. It was one thirty, and she'd been sitting at a table inside Boyd and Wurthmann Restaurant for half an hour, waiting for Colleen. At least she had her guest list to work on and at times would take little breaks, browsing on her phone at different sights of interest. The restaurant was active with the steady hum of conversations going on around her, and the waitresses worked busily, seeing to their customers.

Andrea kept looking toward the entrance for Colleen, but so far only strangers were coming in to sit down for a nice meal.

She picked up her water glass and took a drink. *I wonder what's taking her so long.* It wasn't like her friend to be late for anything. In fact, Colleen prided herself on being punctual, and she usually was.

Maybe they got behind at the dental clinic and she didn't get off at noon like she normally does on Mondays. Brandon's father was a dentist, and Colleen, along with one other dental hygienist, worked for him. Colleen had been working part-time: half days on Mondays and Fridays and full days on Tuesdays and Thursdays. The schedule gave her more time to be at home with Tyler.

Andrea stared down at the paper and thought back to the day at the market and all the Plain people there. It amazed her how they could continue to live such a simple lifestyle and not have electricity.

They're a unique kind of people in the way they dress and their old-fashioned mode of transportation, she thought. *And the Pennsylvania Dutch language they speak to their children and to each other seems strange to me.*

Andrea mulled over how much work it would take to be a Plain person. Without electricity and many modern conveniences, it would be difficult at best. Andrea couldn't imagine doing without her dishwasher, computer, and even the heated styling tools she used on her hair. *How do the Amish function without all the nice comforts I'm used to? I can't help feeling intrigued and wondering why they choose their way of life.*

Andrea looked up from the list she'd been creating and glanced toward the door. Colleen was just entering the restaurant. She wore a soft pink blouse and a pair of gray slacks, which was the style she'd said she liked to work in. On the days she wasn't working, Colleen usually pulled on a T-shirt and blue jeans.

When Andrea noticed Colleen's pinched, tension-filled expression, she wondered if something had gone wrong.

"Sorry I'm late." Colleen paused and swiped a hand across her forehead before taking a seat across from Andrea. "I got off work on time, but the traffic was crazy, plus I needed to stop and fill my gas tank."

"It's okay. I had plenty of time to work on my guest list."

"Are you planning a party?"

Andrea shook her head. "Not exactly. It's my wedding guest list."

Colleen blinked rapidly as she stared at Andrea with her mouth slightly open. "Brandon finally proposed?"

"Yes. Saturday evening he came by my place with pizza, and during our meal he asked me to marry him." Feeling somewhat breathless herself, Andrea picked up the menu in front of her and fanned her face, unable to hide the excitement she felt.

Colleen gave her two thumbs-up. "Well, congratulations, and it's about time. When's the wedding going to be?"

"We haven't set a date yet."

Colleen pointed to Andrea's left hand. "Apparently your future groom didn't give you an engagement ring either."

"We're going to pick it out together one night this week."

"Have you both told your parents?"

Andrea shook her head. "Not yet. We thought it would be nice to take the four of them out to dinner this weekend and share the good news." She put a finger to her lips. "So if you should see my folks or Brandon's mother anytime this week, please don't say anything—especially to Brandon's dad, since you work for him."

Colleen drew a finger across her mouth. "My lips are sealed."

"Thank you. Now are you ready to take a look at the menu so we can order? I'm starving."

"Same here." Colleen picked up her menu and looked it over. When a waitress came to the table, they placed their orders.

"Did you bring the quilt with you?" Colleen asked after their server walked away.

"I sure did, and I'm anxious to see if we can find out anything about the time period it was made, as well as the value of it now."

"After lunch we can head over to Helping Hands quilt shop and see if they can give you any information." Colleen smiled. "If we don't find out what you want to know there, we'll head for Memory Keepers in Walnut Creek."

When Andrea entered the quilt shop with Colleen, she sucked in a quick breath as her eyes feasted on the amazing array of quilted items. Numerous long table runners had been stacked on display tables, along with lovely coverings of several shapes and colors for smaller tables. On the opposite side of the room, a huge collection of quilted bed coverings had been draped over wooden racks. The walls were adorned with a variety of wall hangings in so many different patterns it nearly made Andrea's head spin. The quilt she'd brought inside the cardboard box she held looked inferior to all these newly made quilted items. Even so, Andrea had already developed a fondness for her old quilt, and it wasn't fair to compare old to new.

"Wow! Did you ever see such a variety of quilts? This place is amazing." Colleen made a sweeping gesture with her hand.

"Haven't you been in this quilt shop before?" Andrea shifted the box in her hands.

Colleen shook her head. "I've known about it for some time but have never come in until today."

A young woman dressed in conservative Mennonite attire stepped up to Andrea and Colleen. "May I help either of you with something?"

"I bought an old quilt recently, and I'm wondering about the age of it as well as the pattern and current price." Andrea set the box on the floor and reached in to retrieve the quilt.

The woman spread the quilt out on an empty table and looked it over. "It's in pretty rough shape, isn't it?"

Andrea nodded. "Do you know the name of the pattern?"

"Yes, it's a Fan quilt."

"How much is it worth?" Colleen interjected.

The young woman shrugged. "I'm not sure how old it is or what the current value would be. If you're interested in having the quilt restored, I know someone who does that kind of thing. Would you like her phone number?"

Andrea tilted her head as she weighed her choices. "Maybe, but I'd like to find out more about the quilt before I have anything done to it. Right now I mainly want to find out the age and value of the quilt."

"Perhaps you should take it to an antique dealer," the clerk suggested.

"Yes, our next stop is Memory Keepers antique store in Walnut Creek." Andrea refolded the quilt and put it back in the box. "Thanks for your time. If I decide to get it restored, I'll call your store for the number."

"You're welcome. I'm sorry I couldn't give you more information.

The other woman who works here is on her lunch break, but we're both new, and I doubt she would know much more than I do regarding the value." She shrugged her slender shoulders. "If I gave you a number, I'd only be guessing."

Andrea smiled. "No problem. I'm just glad to know the name of the quilt pattern."

After Andrea and Colleen left the store, she looked over at her friend and said, "Since I've never been to Memory Keepers and you have, you can lead the way and I'll follow in my car."

~

Walnut Creek

There were no customers in the store, so Lois left Orley up front and went to the office near the back of their building. Unless they got busy, she would spend the next hour or so getting caught up on some paperwork and reading a few of the letters addressed to Dear Caroline she'd picked up at the post office this morning.

Lois had only been sitting at her desk a few minutes when Orley entered the room. "Two English women just came in, asking about an old Amish quilt," he announced.

Lois touched the base of her neck and lowered her brows. "Didn't you tell them that we don't have any old quilts for sale in the store at this time?"

"I did, but the one lady said she wasn't looking to buy a quilt. She brought one in and would like information on the age and value of the quilt." He moved closer and placed a hand on the desk. "My knowledge of old quilts is limited. That's your area of expertise."

Lois nodded slowly. "All right then, please let them know that I'll be right out."

"Will do." Orley kissed her cheek and hurried from the room.

Lois arranged the letters she'd received, checked to make sure her head covering wasn't askew, and left the office. When she approached the front of the store, she saw two women—one with auburn hair and the other a blond—talking to Orley near the checkout counter.

"Hello, I'm Lois Troyer," she said. "My husband, Orley, informed me that you brought in an old quilt for appraisal."

The young woman with auburn hair bobbed her head. "My name is Andrea Wagner, and this is my friend, Colleen Jones. We're from Apple Creek."

"It's nice to meet you both."

"How much would you charge to look at the quilt and give me an estimate of its age and value?" Andrea asked.

"There'll be no charge for that." Lois smiled. "I'd be happy to take a look at your quilt and offer my opinion."

"Oh, thank you so much." Andrea bent down and lifted an older-looking quilt from the box at her feet. "Is there a table where I can lay it out so you can have a better look?"

"All our tables are filled with antiques right now," Lois replied. "But there's a quilt rack in our storage room that we can drape it over." She looked at Orley. "Would you mind getting it for me?"

"Not at all." He headed off in the opposite direction.

Andrea glanced around the antique store as she and Colleen waited for the man's return. Although there were no quilts for sale, she saw plenty of vintage items.

It would be fun to set a few of the old kitchen items on an antique table and paint a picture of them, she thought. *Maybe I'll come back sometime and buy a couple of things.* Her gaze came to rest on a small vintage office chair that appeared to be made of oak. *That would look good somewhere in my home. It'd be a real conversation piece.*

Andrea was on the verge of going over to take a seat in the old chair, when Orley returned with the quilt rack. In no time, he had it set up, and Lois helped Andrea drape it over the wooden rails. Holding the corners of the bed covering, she inspected it carefully. "This is a vintage Fan quilt, probably made in the early 1950s. The design was also quite popular in colonial days."

"It's a simple pattern yet quite intricate." Andrea pointed to the stitching on one of the fans decorating the quilt. "Is there anything you can tell us about how a hand-stitched covering like this would be made?" she asked the Amish woman.

"Why yes. The fan patches are sometimes placed with each of them sitting the same way. It is a simple design that resembles plants tilting toward the sun." Lois gestured to the quilt. "The fans might also be placed against each other in a variety of different ways, which creates rolling lines or colorful circles."

"You certainly seem to know a lot about quilts," Andrea commented. "Are you a quilter?"

"No, but one of my aunts certainly was. I stayed with her for a while when I was a teenager. During that time, she taught me a lot about quilts, but I never tried making one myself." Lois had a far-off look in her eyes as she stood for several seconds with her arms crossed.

"How much would a quilt like this sell for in today's market?" The question came from Colleen.

"Since it's not in the best condition, the bed covering isn't worth anywhere near what a new quilt of this size and pattern would be," Lois responded.

The bell over the door tinkled. When another customer came in, Lois looked that way. "If you have any questions, sir, my husband over there can help you," she called before pointing in the direction where Orley stood.

"Thanks." The man headed in the direction of Lois's husband.

"If Andrea wanted to sell the quilt, how much do you think it would go for?" Colleen questioned.

Lois shifted her stance. "Probably not more than three hundred dollars."

Colleen looked at Andrea with her head slightly tipped. "That's not even close to the high price of newer Amish quilts."

"Three hundred dollars is still quite a bit more than I paid for it." Andrea fingered one corner of the aging quilt.

"Are you going to sell it?" Colleen gave Andrea's arm a little nudge.

"I don't think so. For some reason, I feel drawn to this quilt." Andrea lifted the item off the rack and put it back in the box. "I may drop by some other time," she said, looking at Lois. "I'd like to browse a bit and see what all you have for sale."

"That would be nice." Lois offered her a friendly smile. "I hope you do stop by."

Andrea glanced at the office chair. *If that's still here when I return and isn't too expensive, I may take it home.*

Chapter 4

Lois watched Orley from across the supper table, wondering why he'd barely touched her baked chicken and mashed potatoes, having eaten only a few bites. Even the pickled beets went untouched. Normally, her husband would have finished them and asked for seconds by now. Of course, she would have encouraged him to be satisfied with only one helping so he wouldn't start gaining weight, which was a concern due to his hypothyroidism. But it bothered her to see Orley pushing food around his plate instead of eating.

"Is something wrong with your appetite this evening, Husband?" Lois asked. "Or is the *hinkel* not baked to your liking or the *gemaeschde grummbiere* not creamy enough?"

Orley looked up and shook his head. "There's nothing wrong with the chicken or the mashed potatoes. My mind's been filled with questions this evening."

"Is it something you'd like to talk about?" Lois took a delicate bite from the serving of potatoes on her plate. She noticed his brow lines deepening before he spoke again.

"I'm still disappointed that no one has come into our store for a good many months with a problem they wanted to share." His shoulders slumped. "Am I getting too old? Maybe God doesn't want to use me as a mentor anymore."

"I can't imagine where you got such a notion." She gave a slow shake of her head. "According to the Bible, the good Lord wants every believer to minister to others in need. No matter how old we are, as long as we're able and willing to serve Him, He will allow us to be His servants. Although lately God hasn't sent anyone who has a need we can help with, I'm confident that at the correct time, the right person will walk into our store and share something that will let us know they need a bit of counseling."

Orley sat silently for a time, as though considering her words. He stroked the salt-and-pepper hairs in his beard before he spoke again.

"I suppose you're right, but I can't help feeling a bit envious of you getting to reach out to people through your Dear Caroline column."

Lois liked how open her husband was, but hearing that he felt envy over her newspaper column wasn't easy. *I hope what I say next will be helpful and make my dear husband feel better.*

"Remember, Orley, I never meet the people who write me letters, so I don't know whether they take my advice or not. It's a lot different than mentoring people one-on-one the way we have done when they come into our store and we sense there's a need." Lois lifted her shoulders in a brief shrug. "For all I know, the ones who write to me might choose to ignore my suggestions."

"I can't argue with that." He pulled a finger down the side of his nose. "Guess there must be some reason the opportunity to mentor someone again hasn't happened yet." Orley picked up his fork and took a bite of the chicken. He looked at Lois. "Maybe the Lord is trying to teach me to have more *geduld.*"

"Learning patience can be difficult, but at times we all need to be taught that lesson."

Wooster, Ohio

"Dinner's on me tonight," Brandon said after he, Andrea, and their parents were seated at the City Square Steakhouse. Several years ago, this upscale restaurant had been located inside the historic Germania

Hall building, which was built in 1878. Back in its day, it had been known as the "skyscraper." The charming establishment had even been recognized as one of the "Top 100 Steakhouses in America."

Brandon looked at his folks and then at Andrea's parents. *I wonder if I'll be the one telling them the good news about our engagement or if my fiancée will want to do the honors.* Brandon was fine with whatever Andrea wanted to do. And he hoped this evening would go smoothly for him and the sweet woman he looked forward to making his wife.

"Paying for our meals is very generous," Andrea's mother, Evelyn, said. She smiled and gestured to the linen cloth and napkins on their table. "This is such a lovely place to eat."

"I agree," Brandon's mother, Jennifer, said. "And even though the inside of the restaurant is nice, I've always enjoyed eating out here on the covered patio."

The weather was just right for their little evening celebration. The outside dining area had been nicely decorated, and pots brimmed with colorful summer foliage. The view from their table was pleasant.

A waiter arrived at the table and asked if anyone would like an appetizer.

"How about the baked spinach artichoke dip with crispy pita chips?" Brandon's gaze went to each person at the table. "I can get an order for each couple. How's that sound?"

"Sounds good to me," his dad was quick to respond. "Is everyone else okay with that?"

When they all nodded, Brandon looked at the waiter and said: "Three orders of baked spinach artichoke dip, please."

Everyone placed their beverage orders, and then the well-groomed waiter said he would be back with their drinks and appetizers, at which time everyone could order their entrées if they were ready.

After the young man left the table, Brandon's father, Larry, spoke up. "Did you invite us here for some special occasion, or was it simply because it's been a while since we've all gotten together for a meal?"

"Both." Brandon leaned close to Andrea and whispered, "Should we share our good news now or wait till after our meal?"

"I think we should make the announcement now," she murmured quietly.

"Okay. Do you want to tell them, or shall I?"

"Why don't you go ahead?"

"What's all the whispering about?" Andrea's father, Ray, questioned. "Are you two sharing a secret?"

"It is now, but it won't be in a few seconds." Brandon's gaze took them all in. "Andrea and I have an announcement to make." After a brief pause, he continued. "I asked her to marry me, and she said yes."

Both sets of parents applauded and said, "Congratulations." Everyone began talking at once.

"Have you set the date?"

"I don't see an engagement ring on Andrea's finger."

"Where will the wedding be held?"

"Have you made plans for a honeymoon yet?"

Brandon held up his hand. "Andrea and I will be happy to answer all of your questions, but please, just one at a time."

"I'm surprised you're not wearing an engagement ring." A flush of red erupted on Evelyn's cheeks as she looked at her daughter. "Sorry, honey. It's really none of my business."

"After Brandon left his clinic Thursday evening, we went to the House of Silva Jewelry store here in Wooster to pick out our rings," Andrea said. "We found the perfect set, but they needed resizing, so I won't have my beautiful diamond, yellow-gold engagement ring until sometime next week."

Her mother nodded. "That makes perfect sense."

"Have you set a date for the wedding?" Brandon's mother asked.

He shook his head. "Not yet, but we'll let you all know as soon as we do."

Andrea's mother, Evelyn, smiled. "That's good, because we'll have a lot of planning to do, and that will take time."

"I'd like to keep things simple," Andrea said. "Just a nice church wedding with our close friends and relatives will be fine."

"And we'll have a reception in the church fellowship hall afterward," Brandon interjected.

"What?" Jennifer's brown eyes widened. "I understand the church wedding, but our fellowship hall is rather small and kind of plain. Wouldn't you rather have the reception someplace where you can invite more people and celebrate in style?"

"I—I don't know. Brandon and I just got engaged, and we haven't had time to count the number of people we want to invite." Andrea looked at Brandon as though for confirmation.

He gave a decisive nod. "My future wife is right, Mom. We've really made no plans at all."

"Say, I have an idea," Brandon's father put in. "Why don't you have the wedding at Peacock Ridge in North Lawrence? You could make it an all-day event. The grounds are secluded, in the middle of rolling hills with beautiful views. My friend Randy's daughter, Nicole, got married there." He looked over at Brandon's mother. "Remember, Jennifer, how much you raved about that outdoor wedding held by the pond?"

"Oh yes, Larry. And the two geese swimming in the pond gave it such a special touch. Not only that, but the barn, where the reception was held, had been decorated so beautifully with thousands of lights, draped ceilings, and some unique custom-looking chandeliers." She spoke rapidly, with obvious enthusiasm. "There were so many wonderful places for photos to be taken too."

Leaning slightly forward, Andrea opened her mouth like she was about to say something, but Brandon's mother cut her off.

"There's also the lovely Pineview Acres in Massilon." She reached up and touched the bun at the back of her head, as if worried that a hair might be out of place. "I've heard that's a lovely setting for both indoor and outdoor weddings and receptions."

"And don't forget about the Barn at the Meadows in Orrville.

The historic barn dates back to the 1820s," Andrea's father spoke up. "That one is closer to home, so there'd be less of a commute, and it even has a hay wagon." He nudged his wife's arm. "Now how fun is that?"

"I suppose it would be, Ray," she responded, "but I wonder how expensive it would be."

"Well, let's keep in mind that Andrea is our only daughter, and we love her very much, so we won't worry about the cost."

"You're right," Evelyn said. "I think we can all agree that we want Andrea and Brandon's wedding to be a day they'll always remember."

Andrea's chin trembled, and Brandon figured she might be close to tears. It was time to call a halt to this whole pre-wedding planning discussion.

And just in time too, he thought, when their waiter came to the table with their orders of baked spinach artichoke dip and crispy pita chips.

———

Andrea swallowed against the constriction that had formed in her throat. Even though she had twin center-cut filet mignon medallions on her plate, along with rice pilaf and asparagus, she had no appetite. How could she, when it had become obvious that Brandon's parents, as well as her own, wanted to plan her and Brandon's wedding? Even now, as they all ate their meal, the conversation continued to be centered on Andrea and Brandon's upcoming wedding. Didn't any of them realize that the decision as to where and when the ceremony and reception would be held was up to the bride and groom? Didn't she and Brandon have the right to choose? It wasn't that Andrea did not want their parents' help. She just didn't like the idea of allowing any of them to choose the wedding venue.

Andrea felt certain that Brandon's parents would host a lavish rehearsal dinner and no doubt want to pay for all the flowers. Her parents would most likely want to foot the bill for the wedding venue, photographer, catering service, bride's gown, and wedding invitations. Andrea would not feel right asking them to dip into their savings and put out a large sum of money for the use of a wedding venue that they really couldn't afford. Besides, she wanted to get married in their church and felt sure that Brandon did too. Perhaps if they got married during one of the warm weather months, they could have their reception in Brandon's parents' lovely, well-appointed backyard. It was definitely large enough to accommodate their guests.

Andrea made a mental note to speak to Brandon about the possibility. In fact, there were a lot of wedding details they needed to discuss. And they ought to do it soon, before their parents completely took over. Andrea had read once that planning a wedding could be stressful, and now she knew it was true. By simply making the announcement to their parents, her stomach already felt like it was tied in knots. Was it any wonder she had no appetite?

Take a deep breath and remember to pray, she told herself. *Maybe someday I'll look back on this evening and think it was silly to feel so stressed out over a few suggestions about the wedding venue.*

"I'm sorry our meal this evening didn't go better." Brandon reached across the seat in his SUV and took Andrea's hand.

"The atmosphere and food were good," she murmured.

"I can't imagine that you'd know how the food tasted. You didn't even finish your meal."

Andrea looked down at the box filled with her leftover food. "I didn't have much of an appetite."

"And for good reason. When we decided to tell our folks about our engagement, I expected they'd be happy for us and offer congratulations, but I wasn't prepared for them trying to take over and make our plans." Brandon paused to turn on the wipers as rain began to fall. "I realized right away that you were upset, and even though I tried several times to steer our conversation in another direction, someone always brought it back to the wedding plans."

"I know." She sniffed, trying to hold back tears. "At some point, we may have to be firm and let our parents know that this is our wedding, and we need to be the ones to choose where and when we get married."

"Agreed. And speaking of that... We still need to choose a date for the wedding. Any thoughts?"

"We do need several months to make plans and take care of all the arrangements. How about February? Maybe we could get married on Valentine's Day."

"Hearts and flowers for the decorations?"

"Yes. And I definitely want to be married in our church, with Pastor Rawlings officiating."

"I want that too." Brandon took hold of her hand again. "Let's get together one night next week and start making plans. Why don't you come over to my place Friday evening, and I'll barbecue some bison burgers."

"Sounds good. By then my appetite should be back, so you may have to fix me two."

He chuckled. "That can be arranged."

Andrea smiled. How thankful she felt for the relationship she and Brandon had. He was always so kind and supportive. She looked forward to becoming his wife and hoped the next seven months would go by in a hurry.

Chapter 5

Apple Creek

Andrea was about to step out the door when her cell phone rang. Checking the caller ID, she saw that it was her mother. Here it was Friday, and Mom had called nearly every day this week. Each time she'd brought up the wedding, asking questions and making suggestions. She wanted her mother to listen to what she desired to do and to have Mom's total support throughout the entire planning of the wedding. In all of her thirty-two years, Andrea had never known her mother to be pushy or controlling.

So why now? she wondered. *Is Mom that eager to see me get married? Or could she be trying to make up for the extravagant, fancy wedding that she and Dad never had?*

Andrea had tried to be patient and polite, but with each conversation, she'd become more frustrated. Andrea considered letting Mom's call go to voice mail but decided it was best to answer.

"Hi, Mom. I've only got a minute, so unless this is important, I'll have to call you back later."

"Are you teaching a piano lesson this late in the day?"

"No, I'll be on my way to Brandon's place soon, and I don't want to keep him waiting."

"I remember the last time we talked you mentioned that the two of you would be making some wedding plans this evening. Is that the reason you're going there?"

"Yes. . .that and to enjoy a meal together. He's planning to grill some bison burgers."

"That sounds good." There was a short pause, then Andrea's mother spoke again. "The reason I called is to tell you that I spoke with Brandon's mother this morning, and Jennifer said she had talked to her husband about them paying half the cost for one of those wedding venues we'd talked about at the restaurant last week."

"Oh well, Mom—"

"We'll need to get one of the places reserved as soon as possible because well-appointed venues like that book up quickly."

Andrea's jaw clenched. "An outdoor wedding would not be good in the middle of February."

"I thought you and Brandon hadn't set a date yet."

"When he drove me home from the City Square Steakhouse last week, we decided on February fourteenth."

"Valentine's Day?"

"Yes, but we've made no plans beyond setting the date and deciding that the wedding will be held in our church's sanctuary."

"Oh, but Andrea—"

"I really have to leave now, Mom. Brandon will be worried if I'm late. Once he and I have made some definite plans, I'll fill you in, and then we can talk about who would like to do what. I'm sure to need your help with many things."

"I hope so, because your father and I want to do everything we can to make yours and Brandon's wedding day special."

"I know, Mom, and I'll talk to you soon."

"Okay, hon. I hope you and Brandon have a good evening."

"You too. Bye for now." When Andrea clicked off her phone and headed out the door, she breathed a sigh of relief. *Hopefully Mom has accepted the fact that Brandon and I will be getting married at church, and she won't bring up any of those venues again.*

~

"Yum." Andrea smacked her lips. "This bison burger is delicious. Did you buy the meat somewhere locally?"

Brandon shook his head. "I got it via the internet from a business in Nebraska. I ordered several boxes, and they came frozen, packed well with dry ice. I was pleased to see that none of the meat had thawed, so it went right into my freezer."

Arf! Arf! Arf!

Andrea looked down at Brandon's rusty-colored Brittany spaniel, Duke. The dog had inched his way to the table and sat looking up at them as though desperate for food. "I think Duke's hoping we might share some of our burgers with him."

Brandon laughed. "Yeah. He started begging the minute I put the patties on the grill." His face sobered. "In addition to wedding planning, we need to talk about the situation between my dog and your cat and how we are going to work things out once we're married."

Andrea blotted her lips with a napkin. "Oh, you mean the fact that Duke is scared of Lady?"

"Yeah. He's a good dog, and I don't want to get rid of him. I'm sure you feel the same way about Lady."

"You're right about that, but we can't let those two come between us or put a damper on our marriage. Maybe you can figure out some way to teach Duke not to be so intimidated by my cat's presence." Andrea paused to add another scoop of potato salad to her plate. "And I'll work on the problem of getting Lady to approach Duke in such a way that he won't be afraid."

"Sounds like a plan. I hope we can make it work. Otherwise, my poor pooch will spend most of his time in hiding once we are married." Brandon reached over and placed his hand on Andrea's arm, giving it a few tender pats. "We'll work it out. Lady's not a mean cat. Duke's just a big baby. I remember the day you first came to my clinic when Lady had a nasty thorn in her paw. Even though the poor thing was hurting, she remained calm and didn't try to scratch or bite me."

Andrea smiled. "That's because she sensed your gentle, caring spirit, just as I did."

"I sensed that about you too, sweetie." He finished what was on his plate and pushed back his chair. "How about we clear these dishes, and then we can go into the living room and make some plans for our wedding."

"Sounds good to me."

Brandon took a seat on the couch beside Andrea and kissed her cheek. "Ready to talk about our wedding?"

She held up the notebook in her hand. "Definitely. I just hope my mother is still speaking to me when I tell her whatever decisions we've made." Andrea tapped her pen against the notebook. "She called me before I came over here and said she had talked to your mom this morning. I believe they both want us to get married at one of the venues that were brought up during our meal at the restaurant in Wooster last week."

"I know they do." Brandon frowned. "I'd barely gotten home this evening and was about to heat up the grill, when my mom called. I told her I was expecting you soon, but she went on and on about the one venue with peacocks and swans, and I could barely get a word in edgewise." Brandon's brows lowered. "I don't want to hurt their feelings, but we're going to have to be firm and let them know that it's our wedding we're planning and it's our right to make all the final decisions."

"I agree." Andrea held her pen against the notebook. "So let's begin at the beginning."

Walnut Creek

The following day, Andrea decided to visit Memory Keepers again to see if the vintage oak desk chair was still there.

I should have bought it the day Colleen and I went to the antique store, Andrea thought as she searched for a parking spot near the store. *If it's gone, I'll have no one to blame but myself.*

Sometimes, like when Andrea had bought the old quilt, she

made hasty decisions. Other times, such as last night at Brandon's, Andrea couldn't decide what she wanted. She and Brandon had worked on their wedding plans for several hours, going over the pros and cons of each detail. They'd definitely decided that their wedding ceremony would be held at the church, but to make their parents happy, they'd agreed that it might be nice to have the reception at one of the venues they'd talked about. Andrea would ask her father to take care of the arrangements. That way he could choose the one he felt would fit his budget. Brandon had said his parents would no doubt be willing to help with the cost too. Andrea would ask Colleen to be her maid of honor, and Brandon wanted his brother, Joe, to be his best man.

When someone pulled out of the parking spot in front of the antique store, Andrea pulled her minivan in. It was time to set wedding plans aside and see if that old chair was still available.

~

Lois had been washing a streak off the front window when she spotted the auburn-haired woman who had visited the store previously asking about an old quilt she'd bought. When the young woman entered the store, Lois set her cleaning supplies aside and went to greet her.

"Well, hello. . . It's Andrea, right?"

"Yes, I'm surprised you remembered."

"My wife has a great memory—especially for people's names," Orley called from across the room, where he'd been hanging a few vintage signs he'd picked up at a yard sale that week. "It's a lot of work to pick through other people's things, but we nearly always find some old item, and it feels like we've unearthed a piece of history."

Andrea looked at Lois and smiled. "I came by to see if you still had that old oak desk chair for sale. I looked at it when I was here the last time and wished I'd bought it."

"Yes, we still have it. The chair is over there by that old desk." Lois pointed.

"I'll take another look," Andrea said, "but I'm almost certain that I still want it."

Lois led the way. When they stood next to the chair, Andrea bent down and rubbed her hand across the seat. It was then that Lois noticed a sparkly diamond ring on the young woman's left hand. She did not recall seeing it the last time Andrea was here. *But then*, she reasoned, *my concentration was on the vintage quilt not Andrea's hand.* Although Lois and other Amish church members did not wear jewelry, she knew that when a single English woman wore a diamond ring on her left hand, it meant she was engaged to be married. A second ring—a wedding band—would mean she was already married.

"This is really a nice chair, and I'll take it." Andrea stood and reached into her purse. "Will you accept a credit card for payment?"

Lois gave a slow shake of her head. "I'm sorry, but we're not set up for that. We only take cash or checks."

Andrea's cheeks turned rosy as she rubbed the bridge of her nose. "Oh, that's right. I noticed your sign by the cash register when I was here before. Sorry, I'm a bit stressed out right now, and my brain feels kind of fuzzy."

With no other customers in the store, Lois felt it was safe to speak to her openly. "I'm sorry to hear that. Is it anything you'd like to talk about? My husband and I are pretty good listeners."

"And sometimes we offer advice," Orley added after he'd gotten down from the ladder and walked over to them.

Lois couldn't believe he had blurted that out. To Andrea, it might seem as though he was sticking his nose in her business.

She briefly closed her eyes and said a little prayer inwardly before she spoke. "We don't wish to pry, and if you'd rather not talk about whatever is bothering you, that's fine."

Andrea leaned against another desk that sat behind her and released a lingering sigh. "It might actually feel good to talk about it with someone who isn't biased. So if you have the time, I'll tell you what's been happening since my boyfriend, Brandon, and I told our parents that we were engaged."

For the next twenty minutes or so, Lois and Orley listened while Andrea told them about hers and Brandon's parents—especially their mothers, who seemed to want to take charge of the wedding plans. "So now you know why I'm feeling so stressed out."

Orley spoke first. "Planning for a wedding, whether it be English or Amish, can be a hectic time for any engaged couple, so it's important to remain calm and avoid conflict as much as possible." He stopped talking long enough to give his earlobe a tug. "Sometimes parents may feel insecure due to the fact that they're losing a child. They want to feel important and appreciated."

Using her fingertips, Andrea made little circles across her forehead. "I hadn't thought of that. Since I'm an only child, Mom and Dad probably feel a sense of loss even though I've been living out on my own in a small rented home for some time."

"Your parents might feel neglected if they are not involved in your wedding plans, which is not to say that you and your fiancé shouldn't be the ones to decide where and when you'll get married," Lois interjected. "I think it would be helpful if you stay in communication with your parents about each aspect of the wedding."

"Asking for their help and communicating your ideas to them would be good, in addition to updating them on any decisions you and your groom-to-be make," Orley added.

Lois placed a hand on Andrea's arm and gave it a pat. "Your wedding should be a joyous occasion, without the added stress of tension between family members, so try to be patient with them and understanding."

"Thank you for your kind words and sound advice. It helped to talk about this with someone who isn't involved, and the things you've said make good sense." Andrea reached up and wiped away a few tears that had slipped down her cheeks. "I feel better already."

"We're glad we could help, and feel free to come by anytime if other things regarding your wedding plans come up and you need to talk more about them." Orley picked up the oak chair. "Should I take this to the front of the store for you?"

"Yes, thank you."

A short time later, Andrea left with the chair, and Orley turned to Lois with a wide smile. "Well, that was her."

She tipped her head and looked at him with eyes squinted. "What do you mean?"

"I believe God sent that young woman with the pretty auburn hair into our store today so we could mentor her." He slipped his arm around Lois's waist. "Aren't you excited? He's using our willingness to serve Him again. And maybe this won't be the end of it either. Andrea might come back here again, and if she does, we need to be ready to listen and offer more sound advice."

Lois nodded and smiled. It was nice to see her husband's enthusiastic grin. If by some chance Andrea did return to Memory Keepers, she hoped they would have the opportunity to share Jesus with her, because at this point, they really didn't know where she stood spiritually.

Chapter 6

Before heading out on her drive home from Walnut Creek, Andrea took out her cell phone and called Brandon's number. All she got was his voice mail, so she left him a message: "Hi, Brandon. It's Andrea. I'm in Walnut Creek, and I visited Memory Keepers antique store where I'd taken my vintage quilt for an estimate. I went there to look at an old oak desk chair that I'd seen on my first visit to the Troyers' store. The chair was still there, so I bought it." Andrea shifted the phone to her other ear. "The real reason I'm calling, though, is to tell you that I shared with the Amish couple who own the store a couple of things about the situation we've had with our parents wanting to take over our wedding plans, and they offered some good advice. I'll be heading back to Apple Creek soon and plan to stop at my folks' house to bring them up to date on the wedding plans you and I made last night. I also want them to know that any help they'd like to give us will be appreciated. If I don't talk to you this evening, I'll see you at church tomorrow. Love you. Bye for now."

Andrea put her phone away and pulled out into traffic. As she drove in the direction of Apple Creek, she reflected on all the things Lois and Orley had said to her. Andrea felt guilty for being short with her mother yesterday and needed to apologize. Since her parents would be paying for a good portion of the wedding, they needed to be involved in many areas of the planning. Even so, the final decisions, especially where the wedding and reception should take place, ought to be up to Andrea and her groom.

Glancing in the rearview mirror, Andrea spoke out loud. "I need to express that to my parents in a better way." She tapped the steering wheel. "I hope they'll both be home when I get there so we can work things out."

Apple Creek

"I need to ask you something, Ray." Evelyn stepped up to her husband's reclining chair and nudged his arm, but with him focused on the newspaper in his hands, he barely acknowledged her presence.

Evelyn frowned. Ray loved his hobbies, and golf was a big one. He indulged in it at least once a week, weather permitting. Another guilty pleasure of his was being an avid reader of books and the daily news. It wasn't hard for him to become engrossed in either one. If the material was good, Ray's eyes appeared locked on whatever he read, and when that happened, he was determined to finish it. Other times, when news items were deficient to him, Ray would scan through the paper or even fall asleep. Either way, it could be difficult to get or keep his attention.

She nudged him again. "Ray, did you hear what I said?"

He set aside the newspaper and looked up at her. "Umm. . .no, sorry, guess I didn't because I was focused on the newspaper."

"I would have never guessed." She placed both hands firmly against her hips. "When I talked to our daughter yesterday, even though she spoke kindly to me, I felt a bit of an undercurrent when we discussed her wedding plans."

"Could you be making a mountain out of a molehill?"

Evelyn was well aware that her husband was a bit disgruntled because she'd interrupted his reading. Ray's unenthused tone about her concern seemed to say it all. Basically, he didn't want to be bothered right now.

She sometimes felt that her opinion didn't matter to him. *Why can't my husband be more supportive of my feelings? Is it too much to ask?* She looked at him, wishing he'd get a clue, but unfortunately, Ray obviously lacked interest in the topic at hand.

"Maybe you should back off and let Andrea make her own wedding plans." Ray's unexpected comment caused Evelyn to bristle.

"What are you talking about, Ray? You were in on the discussion we all had at the restaurant in Wooster. As I recall, you were in favor of the wedding being held at one of the venues that was mentioned."

"I was, but I've thought it through since then, and I have come to the conclusion that since it's not our wedding being planned, Andrea and Brandon have the right to choose their own venue along with many other things that will be involved in their wedding."

"I agree." Evelyn took a seat in the chair beside him and heaved an audible sigh just as her fox terrier, Frisky, leaped up and tried to squeeze in beside her. "I just don't understand why they want to get married in the dead of winter," she said, moving over a bit so the dog could lie down. "If the weather is bad, some people they've invited might not be able to attend. And of course, an outdoor reception would be out of the question."

Ray's facial features softened, along with his tone, as he reached over and patted her arm. "Let's allow the bride and groom to worry about all those things, okay?"

Maybe my husband is right. I might be making a mountain out of a molehill. Slowly, she nodded. "I just hope—"

The melodic chiming of their doorbell interrupted Evelyn's sentence, and she rose from her seat. "Guess I'd better go see who that is."

~⁓~

When the front door opened, Andrea stepped in and greeted her mother with a hug. Mom smelled of her favorite cologne, and not one light brown hair was out of place from where it had been pulled back into a smooth ponytail. Mom's terrier stood by her feet.

"This is a pleasant surprise. Your dad's in the living room, and we were just talking about you."

"Uh-oh. Should my ears have been ringing?"

Mom shook her head. "It was nothing bad. Now let's go into the living room so you can say hello to your father."

Andrea followed her mother and found her dad sitting in his easy chair, holding the newspaper. "Hey, Dad. Did you make it to the golf course this morning?"

He grinned up at her. "Sure did. I played a pretty good game too."

Andrea smiled in response. "That must have felt good."

"Yep." He gestured to the chair beside him, which was where Andrea's mother usually sat. "Take a seat."

She glanced at her mother, and when Mom gave a nod and took a seat on the couch, Andrea seated herself in the comfortable chair. She'd barely sat down when Mom's terrier darted into the room, leaped onto her lap, and began slurping Andrea's cheeks.

"For goodness' sakes, Frisky, get down! I'm sure Andrea doesn't want your kisses." Mom clapped her hands. "Come here, you naughty little boy."

"You've got it right. That mutt is always getting into some kind of trouble." Dad's brows drew together, and he pointed at Frisky, who had settled down in Andrea's lap instead of obeying Mom's command. "This morning, before I left to play golf, I found him digging in the yard again." He grimaced. "That sure didn't set well with me. I've gone to a lot of trouble to find a reliable lawn care business here in Apple Creek. Those fellows have done an excellent job keeping the yard looking as neat as the greens at the local golf course."

"He didn't dig up any of our plants though, did he?" Mom asked.

"No, but he could have if I hadn't caught him in time." He looked at Mom over the top of his reading glasses. "You oughta put that dog in obedience school."

Mom shrugged. "I'm working with him on my own, and I

believe we're making some progress."

"Really? My suggestion is that you need to buy a book on how to train that mutt to behave."

Andrea couldn't miss Dad's sarcastic tone, and she figured it was time for a topic change, so she gave Frisky's head a brief pat and said, "The reason I stopped by is to tell you about the wedding plans Brandon and I made last night."

Mom and Dad turned their heads in her direction.

"I've already told your father that you plan to be married next year, on Valentine's Day," Mom responded.

Andrea nodded. "And we want our ceremony to be at the church."

"We understand," Dad interjected. "You had also previously stated that you wanted the reception to be held there as well."

"We've changed our minds about that. Brandon and I think having the reception at one of the venues you and Brandon's parents mentioned the other day might be a good idea." Andrea paused to give Frisky another pat. "If you feel it won't put a strain on your budget, that is."

"I think we can manage." Dad looked at Mom. "Right, Evelyn?"

"Yes, of course. Andrea, do you have any particular venue in mind?"

"Not really, but we'd be happy with the least expensive one that has adequate indoor seating. There's no point putting out a large sum of money for a few hours of celebration."

"You're so very special to us, and we want you to have a memorable wedding and reception." Mom's voice faltered on the last word.

"I appreciate that," Andrea responded. "And I don't want you and Dad to feel left out, so we'll leave most of the reception planning in your capable hands. For other things pertaining to the wedding, Brandon and I will also keep you, as well as his parents, in the loop and ask for help as needed."

Mom smiled and wiped a few tears from her cheeks. Dad reached over and placed his hand on Andrea's arm, which caused

Frisky to jump down to the floor and give a few loud barks. Everyone laughed.

Andrea let her head fall back against the chair. She felt a sense of peace about things now and was hopeful that, from this point on, all the wedding plans would go smoothly.

Walnut Creek

Lois stood at the living room window, watching her husband make his way down their driveway.

The neighbor's dog met Orley, wagging its tail, and he reached down, giving the friendly yellow Lab a few pets. Then the animal walked alongside her husband as though they were the best of friends. She couldn't help but notice the spring in Orley's step as he and the dog headed out to the phone shack, where Orley would make a few phone calls and check for any messages that may have come in while they'd been at their store.

Orley had been full of enthusiasm ever since the young auburn-haired woman had come into the store and shared with them about the situation she'd been having with her parents concerning her upcoming wedding. Lois had to admit that being able to offer some advice had given both her and Orley a sense of satisfaction. She hoped, however, that Orley wouldn't be too disappointed if Andrea never returned to the store or sought their counsel. Surely, in God's time, some other person would show up who needed guidance—perhaps of a spiritual nature, which would be the most rewarding, like it had been in the past with several other people Orley and Lois had mentored. Sometimes the ones they'd helped would move on and wouldn't be seen again. There were some, though, who continued to stop by their antique store to catch up and visit, just like family.

Lois smiled as she reflected on this. *It does my heart good to see the positive outcomes of the Lord's work when we were obedient to His call upon our lives.*

She moved away from the window and headed for the kitchen to start supper. Her first thought was to heat some frozen broccoli and creamy cheddar soup, but it might take a while. Lois wasn't in the mood to cook a big meal this evening and hoped Orley would be okay with a tossed green salad and a bowl of egg drop soup, which was a favorite of hers and easy to make.

Lois opened the refrigerator and took out the ingredients for the salad as well as a carton of eggs, some green onions, and a bottle of soy sauce. Next, she removed a large can of chicken broth, salt, and garlic powder from the cupboard. She'd just taken out a kettle for the soup when Orley came in through the back door with downturned facial features. "I'm sorry to have to tell you this, but I have some bad news," he announced.

"What's wrong?" Lois's chest tightened as she held her breath, waiting for his response.

"There was a message from your stepmother, letting us know that your *daed* had a heart attack this afternoon and is in the hospital. She sounded quite upset and said that his heart is very weak and it doesn't look good." Orley moved toward Lois and placed his arm around her waist.

She set the kettle down and stood with one arm holding the other at the elbow. "We need to go to Kentucky, Orley. If my dad should die before I've had a chance to make things right between us, I'll never forgive myself."

"I understand. I will go back out to the phone shack and call one of our drivers. Hopefully, we can head out within the next few hours, so I think you should go ahead and put whatever we'll need in our suitcase."

"Wh–what about supper?" Lois gestured to all the items she'd put on the counter.

"You may as well put everything away. We can stop somewhere along the road to eat." Orley gave her a comforting hug before going hastily out the back door.

Truth was, she had lost her appetite after hearing the news

about Dad. Lois worried about her father's condition. With every fiber of her being, she hoped he would receive the best of care. Time was truly of the essence if she was to get to the hospital, which was many hours from here.

Lois hurried to put all the food items away. She leaned against the counter and closed her eyes. *Dear Lord, if it is Your will to take my father, please don't do it until I've had a chance to see him and make sure he knows that I love him.* Tears coursed down Lois's cheeks as she finished her prayer. *Dad needs to know that even though I still feel that some of the things he did and said when I was a girl were wrong, with Your help, I have forgiven him.*

Turning toward the door, Lois left the kitchen and made her way down the hall to their room, continuing to pray with each step she took. It would take them at least nine hours, allowing for stops, to reach Hopkinsville, Kentucky. She could only hope and pray that they would make it in time.

Chapter 7

Hopkinsville, Kentucky

At three o'clock the next morning, Lois sat in a chair beside her father's hospital bed, holding his wrinkled hand. His wife, Sarah, sat in another chair next to her, and Orley stood off to one side. Lois's sisters, Rebekah and Elizabeth, lived in Wisconsin, and her half-brothers, Benjamin and Jacob, had settled in Oklahoma, so none of them had arrived yet. It didn't look good for their father, and Lois hoped the rest of the family would make it to the hospital in time to say their last goodbyes.

Because she'd been up for almost twenty-four hours, Lois was having a hard time staying awake. Orley also showed signs of fatigue with his stifled yawns and tired eyes. She couldn't help feeling sorry for keeping him here, but Orley wouldn't be anywhere else when he felt needed by her, and she knew it.

Lois looked through blurring eyes at her father. *Besides being here with you and praying, I wish there was something else I could do for you, Dad.* "Has he opened his eyes or said anything to you?" Lois looked over at Sarah.

The silver-haired woman shook her head. "Not since a few minutes before he collapsed at home. I could see that he wasn't feeling well, and when I asked him what was wrong, he said his chest pained him and he felt kind of dizzy." Sarah drew in a shuddering breath. "The next thing I knew, your daed collapsed onto the floor. His breathing was shallow, and when I couldn't rouse him, I made a beeline for the phone shack we share with our closest neighbors."

Unable to speak around the lump in her throat, Lois let go of her father's hand and reached over to clasp Sarah's trembling hand.

At the same time, Orley moved closer and put both of his hands on the women's shoulders. "You must have been terribly frightened, Sarah."

"*Jah*, very much so, and I still am. I don't think my dear husband is going to make it. The doctors said Jeremiah's heart is very weak—too much so for any kind of surgery." Sarah drew in another breath and released it slowly. "Guess that's what happens when old age creeps in."

"We need to pray," Lois murmured. "We can ask God for a miracle."

Apple Creek

The shrill sound of the alarm clock ringing near her head pulled Andrea out of a deep sleep. She rolled over, clicked it off, and sat up on the edge of her bed. Once the cobwebs of sleep cleared, she reached for her cell phone to check for messages. Brandon hadn't returned her call last night before she'd gone to bed, and there were no new messages from him. A sense of dread welled in her chest. It wasn't like him not to call. They talked to each other nearly every day. Could he have been involved in an accident, become ill, or been too busy to check his phone for messages? If it was the latter, that wasn't like him either. Brandon had always been good about returning her calls. Something had to be wrong.

Andrea rose and cleared her throat. She took a drink from the glass of water sitting on the nightstand, closed her eyes, and prayed that Brandon was all right. Afterward, Andrea tried his number in hopes of reaching him and hearing that things were okay, but Brandon's phone rang until it went into voice mail again. She left him another message, asking that he call her back as soon as possible and telling him she loved him before hanging up. *I hope he's okay.* She picked up her phone again. *I'll try his parents. Maybe they've heard from him.*

Andrea punched in his folk's number and felt relieved when his mother answered. "Sorry to bother you, Jennifer, but I can't get a hold of Brandon. Have you talked to him lately?"

"You sound worried, but I think he's okay." Her soothing tone came through clearly. "He called and left a message yesterday shortly before 8 a.m., saying he had a full schedule at the clinic, along with a couple of rural calls, and that he wouldn't have time to join his dad and me for supper, like we had hoped. He also said he would see us at church this morning and that maybe the four of us could go out for dinner after the service."

"I called Brandon yesterday afternoon and left a message, but he never returned my call." Andrea pulled her fingers through the ends of her hair. "A few minutes ago, I tried calling again, but all I got was his voice mail. I'm worried something might be wrong."

"I'm sure it's nothing to be concerned about. Maybe he's in the shower and didn't hear the phone ring." Jennifer's tone sounded hopeful, but Andrea wasn't convinced. She could not believe how unconcerned his mother seemed. Andrea had a sick feeling in the pit of her stomach that something was wrong.

———

Brandon woke up to the sound of his alarm and padded over to the window to look out. He pulled up the blinds and smiled when he saw the sunshine and blue skies. *What a nice Sunday morning greeting*, he thought. Then, remembering to look for his cell phone, which he had carelessly left someplace at home yesterday and been too tired to search for last night, Brandon put on a T-shirt and a pair of jeans and went looking. *There's still plenty of time before church, and it shouldn't take me long to find it.*

After searching through every pair of pants in his closet and coming up empty-handed, he ambled out of the room and headed for the kitchen to look around. Brandon frowned. *This is strange. Where on earth did I leave it?*

He searched every nook and cranny and even looked in the refrigerator, but there was no sign of his phone. Brandon paused to rub his forehead and think. *When and where did I last use my cell?* He felt frustrated with himself for not keeping better track of the device, but with his hectic lifestyle, Brandon was glad he didn't have to go through this kind of issue often. He always tried to keep all his ducks in a row to avoid forgetting things. Yesterday had been pretty crazy, and he hadn't had time to make a trip back home to look for his phone. At the clinic, it wasn't a problem because there was a landline. But out on the road, heading to the farms he'd been called to, Brandon needed his cell phone and would normally have had it with him.

His brain raced with other ideas as to where the phone could be. He was so desperate at the end of looking in the kitchen that he opened the cookie jar and peered in. All he found were a few stale-looking cookies that had been in there too long. *I think I've checked out this room long enough.*

Brandon moved into the living room and looked under the couch, behind the cushions, on the coffee table and each of the end tables, but there was no sign of his phone. He couldn't take too much more time looking or he'd be late for church.

I hope Andrea's not worried about me. I bet she's tried calling several times. He sat down and thumped the arm of his favorite chair. *Guess I could just go on over to Andrea's place and pick her up for church, but I'd rather call first, if I can find my phone.*

Brandon leaned his head back and closed his eyes as he tried to visually retrace his steps from yesterday morning. *Let's see now. . . . I fixed a cup of coffee and was about to step outside to get the newspaper when my cell phone rang. It was Mom, but I couldn't talk long, so I said I'd see her and Dad tomorrow and hung up. Then with my phone still in my hand, I let Duke out and went to the paper box. After I grabbed the paper, Duke started barking and ran out of the yard. I hollered at him, but he wouldn't come back.*

Brandon's eyes came open and he sat up straight. *Oh brother! I remember putting the phone inside the newspaper box and chasing after my disobedient dog. Sure hope it's still there.*

Brandon made a dash for the front door, and Duke was right behind him. Once outside, he picked up a stick and threw it across the yard, figuring that would keep the dog occupied while he went out the front gate and checked the box.

When Brandon reached his hand inside the box and touched his cell phone, he heaved a sigh of relief. Now he could take it inside, make sure it was charged, and give Andrea a call.

Hopkinsville

Lois had been sitting for several hours beside her father's bed, leaving only once to use the restroom. Orley had stayed by her side, giving all the support she needed. During the wee hours before daybreak, she and Orley had managed to get short catnaps while lounging in their chairs. Lois was concerned for her father and wanted to support Sarah with all the energy she could muster.

Toward daybreak, Rebekah and Elizabeth entered the room. They exchanged tearful hugs and greetings before going over to Dad's bedside. It was a bittersweet moment for Lois. They talked and cried as they remained near their father's bed.

Sometime later, Orley asked if anyone was hungry and volunteered to find food. Sarah informed him that the cafeteria wouldn't be open for another two hours, but she volunteered to go with Rebekah and Elizabeth down the hall for coffee or juice and some kind of a snack from the vending machine.

Orley sprang into action, retrieving some money from his wallet to give the women.

Soon after they left the room, Lois looked at her husband, who sat in the chair beside her. "Would you mind leaving me alone with my daed for a few minutes? I don't think he's going to make it, and I'd like the chance to say a private goodbye."

"Okay." Orley rose to his feet. "I'll join the others. Is there something you'd like me to bring back for you to eat or drink?"

She shook her head. "I'll get something later if I'm hungry."

He gave Lois's shoulder a gentle squeeze and left the room.

She scooted her chair a bit closer to her father's bed. "I forgive you, *Daadi*, for being so harsh with me when I was a girl," she whispered. "I know that I disappointed you many times, and I'm sorry I could never measure up—was not the kind of daughter you wanted me to be." She blinked as hot tears rolled down her cheeks. "I've told God that I'm sorry too, Daadi. I'm sure He's forgiven me. Will you do the same?"

Lois's father opened his eyes briefly, murmured a few words she couldn't understand, and then his breathing stopped. Lois had no idea whether her dad had heard anything she'd said to him or not, but even in her sadness, a sense of peace settled over her like a soft blanket. She felt God's presence, whispering in her ear, *"My grace is sufficient for thee."*

Chapter 8

As the warm August sun beat down on her head, Lois teared up while she stood with her family and other mourners, watching her father's casket be lowered into the ground. Although she and her father had never been close, she'd felt a great loss since his passing three days ago. From the solemn expressions on her four siblings' faces, Lois knew they did as well.

She glanced at her stepmother, shoulders hunched and eyes staring at the ground. When she looked up briefly, Lois saw the wrinkles around the elderly woman's mouth and eyes sag. Although she couldn't comprehend losing a spouse, Lois understood the loss of her father. At moments, the wave of missing him would hit, and Lois's heart ached for what she wished she could've had. *If only my dad and I could have had a closer bond in this life. But for reasons beyond my understanding, it didn't happen.*

Lois's father had been widowed twice, and Sarah was his third wife. He'd met her five years ago while visiting an Amish community in Colorado. After getting married, they'd remained in Colorado two years; then Dad had gotten the notion that they should move to Kentucky. Lois had never understood why he'd chosen that state, since he'd had no family or close friends there, but she'd been glad he wasn't living alone and had Sarah by his side. Lois figured with Dad gone now, Sarah would most likely return to Colorado to live with her oldest son, Henry. He and his wife, Caroline, had hired a driver to bring them to Hopkinsville for the funeral. It was good that Sarah had some of her immediate family's support today, although Lois felt sure Sarah appreciated her stepdaughters and sons being with her as well.

And why wouldn't we be? Lois thought. *Even though we were all married and out on our own by the time Dad married Sarah, she's still our stepmother and we care about her welfare.*

Lois was ever so grateful for Orley's moral support as they stood shoulder to shoulder while the coffin was buried and the minister read the Lord's Prayer.

She glanced over at Sarah, dabbing her eyes. *I can't imagine how much her life will change.* Lois tried to hold it together as she shifted her stance and turned to look at Orley. Their eyes connected for a moment, and he gave her a tender, consoling smile. She couldn't comprehend what her life would be like without her dear husband by her side. Lois hoped that when it was their time to go, the Lord would take them both together.

~

It tore at Orley's heartstrings to see how hard Lois was taking her father's death. Although she was trying to be strong, the way her lips pressed together and her body trembled indicated the extent of Lois's grief. He wanted to give his wife all the support needed during her time of sorrow. Orley had mentioned to Lois that if she wanted to linger for a few days beyond what they'd intended, he was fine with that. It was obvious to him that his wife and siblings needed this time together, as they shared things about the past—sometimes laughing and at other times shedding more tears. It was a shame Jeremiah hadn't been able to say a proper goodbye to his children. As far as Orley knew, the dying man hadn't opened his eyes or uttered a single word to his wife or daughters. And by the time Benjamin and Jacob had arrived, their father had passed from this world into another.

Once the graveside service was over, Orley put his hand against the small of Lois's back as they walked solemnly with the others toward the waiting horses and buggies. After leaving the Amish cemetery, they would go to Sarah's house for a light meal provided by some of the women in her church district. Once they finished eating, Orley hoped Lois might be able to lie down for a while. She'd only slept a few hours last night and was exhausted. Lois and her sisters had helped Sarah with the preparations for the funeral. Orley had noticed that his wife's appetite had declined, but whose wouldn't under these circumstances? He assumed that being in unfamiliar territory, sleeping in a strange bed, and eating meals at unusual times contributed to his wife's behavior. Hopefully, she would feel better once they returned to Ohio and opened their store for business again.

Apple Creek

Andrea smiled as she stood in an empty field across from an Amish farm, painting a picture of the barn and a black buggy. The weather was lovely, and the temperature felt pleasant to her. Andrea had driven by this place before, and it had inspired her to return. Of all the rural settings where she often set up her easel and canvas, anything that depicted the Amish lifestyle was her favorite thing to paint. Sometimes she became so absorbed in the scene, she almost felt as if she were Amish.

I wonder if other non-Amish people ever feel like that, she thought. Andrea didn't know anyone personally who had left their English world and joined the Amish faith, but she'd read about a few who had made the transition.

Andrea pursed her lips as she dabbed white paint on the barn in her picture. *That must have been difficult. I might be able to dress plainly, go without makeup, and let my hair grow long, but I can't imagine having to give up my car, cell phone, laptop, or anything that needs electricity. Although their life seems unique and interesting, I am glad I wasn't born Amish, because then I'd have no choice in the matter, unless I left my Amish home and upbringing and became part of the modern world.*

In an attempt to refocus, Andrea stopped painting and glanced across the road once more. Setting down the paintbrush for a moment, she reached for her water bottle nearby and took some sips. *It's so peaceful out here. This open country, fresh air, and beautiful scenery has a way of calming my nerves.*

As Andrea set her water aside, she spotted two teenage girls dressed in Plain clothes, walking toward the Amish carriage by the barn. A few minutes later, an Amish man wearing a straw hat came out of the barn, leading a beautiful, dark-colored horse up to the buggy. Andrea didn't want them to see her staring, so she quickly picked up her brush and turned back to face the canvas.

Her thoughts went to Brandon and how things had gone when he showed up at her home Sunday morning. She'd been relieved, seeing that he was okay and learning why he hadn't returned her calls the day before.

She smiled. The dinner with Brandon's parents after church had gone well too. Jennifer and Larry had obviously been relieved when Brandon announced that he and Andrea had made some definite plans and wanted both sets of parents to be included in various aspects of the wedding preparations.

So everything is back on track. Andrea added a little more color to the barn in her painting. *Now we can move forward with the details for the wedding, knowing our parents are happy and nobody feels left out.*

At the *clip-clop, clip-clop* sound of a horse's hooves, Andrea's thoughts were pulled aside once more. She turned to watch the proud-looking horse pulling the buggy, and she lifted her hand when the Amish girls smiled and waved. *That looks like fun, and I bet it's a peaceful mode of transportation. Wish I had the opportunity to ride in an Amish buggy. I'll have to try to make that happen someday.* She dabbed her brush into the paint again. *Right now, though, I have plenty of other things to think about.*

~

Hopkinsville

"I checked on Sarah, and she's resting in her room." Lois's sister Rebekah took a seat on the dilapidated couch next to Lois. Even the two overstuffed chairs in the living room looked like they had seen better days.

While Orley and the spouses of Jeremiah's children had gone to the kitchen to put away the leftovers from their recent meal, Lois and her siblings had gathered in this sparsely decorated living room to visit. Lois, Elizabeth, and Rebekah sat on the couch, and their half-brothers had taken the two chairs.

Lois gave a nod in response to Rebekah's declaration that Sarah was resting. "That's good. She needs to get caught up on her rest. When Dad was in the hospital, Sarah stayed by his bed much of the time and got very little sleep. With the funeral and graveside service, today has been a long day for her. I'm sure she must be exhausted." Truthfully, Lois had felt like taking a nap too, but being with her siblings was more important than sleep right now. She would go to bed early tonight if necessary.

For a few minutes, Lois sat silently, reflecting on how she had kept quiet about Dad murmuring something when she was alone in his hospital room. Since she hadn't been able to understand what he'd said, she saw no reason to mention it to anyone.

"I think we're all tired and feeling the effects of the day," Elizabeth said, stifling a yawn with the palm of her hand.

Everyone nodded.

"We need to talk about Sarah and what's going to happen to her now that our daed is gone," Benjamin, the oldest half-brother, spoke up. "I thought her son and his fraa would take her in, but as far as I know, they have not extended an invitation."

Shifting on the faded couch and feeling the need to defend Sarah's son and his wife, Lois spoke up. "I'm sure they will want Sarah to move back to Colorado and live with them. It would certainly not be good for her to stay here all alone."

"I agree," Elizabeth said. "I don't believe she would want to remain here, where she has no family and lives in a house that is quite primitive compared to what the rest of us have. Not to mention how isolated she is out here with no close neighbors."

"Maybe Sarah likes Kentucky," Jacob, who was thirty-eight and the youngest of Lois's half-brothers, commented. "I know Daed sure did."

"That may be true, and it might be hard for Sarah to leave this area since she's lived here for a while with Daed. Even so, it wouldn't be good for her to be left alone." Lois looked at each of her siblings.

"There are enough of us here who I'm sure would be willing to take Sarah in, but whatever she does, it will have to be her decision." Rebekah readjusted her head covering that was slightly askew.

Everyone nodded.

"It's nice for us to all be together like this, discussing things in person, but it's too bad we're all so busy and live in different states. Unfortunately, we only see each other on rare occasions like weddings and funerals," Rebekah observed.

"That is so true." Benjamin looked at them with a sober expression. "We need to make an effort to get together more often."

"Jah," Lois agreed. "Letters and phone calls are fine, but it's more personal when we're in the same room, spending time together like this."

A few minutes of silence passed, interrupted when Sarah entered the room with a cardboard box. She placed it on the coffee table and lifted the flaps. "I have some things that belonged to your daed in here, and I'd like each of you to have one." She reached inside and handed Benjamin his father's gold-plated pocket watch. "Since you are his oldest son, I'm sure your daed would want you to have this."

"Danki." Benjamin choked up, and it took him several seconds to say anything more. "Receiving this item that Daed carried on him most of the time means a lot to me."

Sarah reached into the box again. This time she removed a wooden case that Lois recognized as her father's set of woodcarving tools. She gave it to Jacob.

Sagging against the chair he sat on, Jacob stared at the item with his lips slightly parted. "I—I will put this to good use, and someday I'll hand it down to one of my sons."

Sarah nodded before pulling the next item from the box. "This is for you, Elizabeth." She placed Daed's harmonica on Lois's youngest sister's lap. "Your daed knew how much you enjoyed music, so I'm sure he would want you to have it."

"Danki. I will treasure this and remember Daed when I play it." Elizabeth's hand trembled a bit as she picked up the mouth harp their father had played many evenings after supper when Lois and her siblings were growing up. She held it close to her mouth without playing it.

Sarah took two Bibles from the box. One she handed to Rebekah, stating that it was her father's. The other she gave to Lois. "This was your mother's *Biewel*. Even though she's been gone a good many years, your daed had fond memories of her, which is why I'm sure he kept her Bible."

Rebekah and Lois said danki. Lois held her dear mother's Bible close to her chest. Although it was not one of her father's personal possessions, knowing that it was her mother's and Dad had kept it all this time made it more special.

Tears seeped from Lois's eyes and ran down her warm cheeks. *Oh, Mama, even after all these years, I still miss you. If you hadn't died when I was eight years old, maybe Daadi would have been kinder to me when I did things that were wrong and displeased him.* Lois's throat tightened so that she could barely swallow. *If I could go back and change the past, I would try to be a better daughter so he would not be disappointed. Maybe then Daadi would have loved me as much as he did my siblings.*

Chapter 9

Walnut Creek

"It's good to be back home and open for business again," Orley said after he'd put up the OPEN sign in their antique store's front window. "It seems like we've been gone for a lot longer than two weeks." He looked over at Lois, surprised to see her standing in front of the checkout counter with a blank expression. Orley hoped his wife wouldn't feel as troubled being in familiar territory now. *I suppose we can't leave our troubles behind*, he thought. *I'll need to continue to help Lois through this and offer all the support my dear wife needs.*

Orley walked across the room to stand beside her. "Are you all right?" He slipped his arm around her waist. "Is it too soon for you to come back to work? If so, I'm sure I can manage the store on my own until you feel ready."

She gave a slow shake of her head. "It's not that. Keeping busy will be good for me. I'm just thinking about Sarah and wishing she would have accepted her son's invitation to live with him and his wife in Colorado. At her age, she shouldn't be living by herself with no family close by."

"I agree. She turned down all the other offers too, including ours. But if Sarah doesn't want to leave Kentucky, it wouldn't do for anyone to make her go. And remember, she does have friends in the Hopkinsville area." Orley rubbed Lois's back with the same arm he had put around her waist.

"I'm aware, but living near friends is not the same as being close to family."

Orley finished the rub and rested his hand on the countertop. "I'm sure Sarah will relocate when she feels the need."

"I hope so." Lois released a deep sigh and moved away from the counter. "Guess I should get busy and do something constructive. There's some dusting that needs to be done and a box of vintage clothes in the back room that needs to be gone through. Then when we get home this evening, I have some Dear Caroline letters that need answering." With shoulders slumped, she shuffled off to the back of the store as though the weight of world rested upon her shoulders.

Orley gave his beard a tug as he mulled things over. *I know my fraa is concerned about her stepmother, but I think her melancholy mood has more to do with losing her daed.* Lois hadn't told Orley much about her childhood other than that her mother had died at a young age, and her father had been overly strict and often critical. This, he assumed, was the reason Lois had not been close to her father all these years.

Orley went around to the other side of the counter and took a seat on the stool. *Perhaps when the time is right, my dear wife will share more about her childhood and Jeremiah. I just can't relate to what she is going through right now, but the Lord knows.*

Orley leaned closer to the counter with his right hand on his knee. *I need to help Lois deal with this and be more sensitive to her needs.* Orley closed his eyes and prayed, *Lord, please help Lois through her time of grieving. She needs Your comfort and strength right now. And show me how I can help my dear wife get through this difficult time.*

Lois knelt in front of the box, pulling out each piece of the vintage clothes and inspecting them for wear and tear. They had been fortunate to find the clothing at a rummage sale a few days before they'd gotten news of her father's heart attack, so this was the first chance she'd had to go through them. Most of the items were from the early 1900s, but a few had been worn during the late 1800s. It wasn't hard to see how modest the period clothing looked at that time. The fabrics had heft, they weren't see-through, and the dresses went to the floor.

She smiled. *I can't help thinking how similar this fashion is to our Plain dresses.* Lois laid the dark brown dress she held on top of one that was deep blue. Some of the pieces would need to be mended, but other than a musty odor, most were in surprisingly good condition. She sniffed deeply and grimaced. A few of the blouses smelled of perfume, so Lois would spray those lightly with a white vinegar solution, which should lift the odor from the material, leveling out the perfume. Lois knew that the pungent vinegar smell would dissipate in a short time, so she wouldn't need to worry about the clothes smelling like salad dressing.

Lois's mind switched gears as an image of her father came to mind. She cringed at the thought of seeing him lying in that hospital bed and not being sure if he'd heard anything she'd said. The emotion of the memory surged through her soul. Oh, how she wished she could have understood the words he had mumbled before succumbing to death. Had he known she was beside his bed and tried to respond to what she'd said? She felt powerless over the past, present, and future. *I'm not even sure about my father's salvation.* Lois looked away from the clothing. *If only I had thought to ask Sarah.* The idea hadn't crossed her mind while everything was going on. *Does this really matter, since my father is gone now?*

Lois's chin trembled as she resigned herself to the fact that she would never know what her dad had said or where he stood spiritually before his death.

She glanced back at the stack of old clothes and whispered, "I need to quit thinking about this and stay busy with the project before me until it's done."

Brandon sucked in some air through his nose and blew out a long breath from his mouth as he started his rig, eager to head for home. Things had been busier and more hectic than usual at the clinic, and he looked forward to relaxing and spending the evening with Andrea over a nice home-cooked supper. His first stop, though, would be his home to take a shower and change. Then he and his faithful dog would head over to Andrea's place in the hope of getting Duke to accept Lady and not cower and whine whenever the cat came near him. Brandon hoped things would go well this time because he and Andrea's wedding would take place in six months, and the problem needed to be resolved by then.

Brandon gripped the steering wheel as he pulled out of the clinic's parking lot and onto the road. *I can't imagine what life will be like for me and my future wife if we can't get Lady and Duke to get along. I sure hope my dog and her cat won't cause a conflict between us. I can't imagine us breaking up over something like this or feeling forced to get rid of our well-liked pets.*

When Andrea heard a horn honk outside, she looked out the front window and saw Brandon pull his SUV in front of her rental. She turned to Lady, draped over the back of the couch, and stroked the cat's silky head. "Our company is here, and you'd better be nice and not tease my fiancé's dog. We need Duke to accept you."

Lady responded with a quiet *meow* and burrowed her head between her dainty white paws.

Andrea gave the cat's head a couple of gentle pats. "Of course you'll be nice, you pretty little thing. You're the best cat I've ever had."

When Lady closed her eyes and began to purr, Andrea smiled. "How can Brandon's dog be afraid of you? I bet you wouldn't harm a mouse if one got into the house."

She'd had other cats while growing up but hadn't bonded with any of them the way she had with Lady. They were usually outdoor cats that were good at keeping mice away and weren't spoiled or fussed over much.

A knock sounded on the door, and Andrea went to open it. A few seconds later, Brandon entered, leading Duke on a leash.

Brandon hugged Andrea and gave her a kiss. "Well, here we are. Now let's hope things go well this evening between your cat and my dog."

Andrea bent down and gave Duke's head a few pats. "Let's go into the living room. Lady's sleeping right now, so that might help. We can sit and visit awhile before it's time to eat supper."

"Okay, but I'm going to keep Duke on his leash just in case the cat wakes up and he catches sight of her."

When they entered the living room, the wavy-coated spaniel put his nose to the floor and started sniffing as he tugged against the restraint. Brandon allowed the dog to take the lead and followed as Duke made his way around the entire room. As they neared the couch, Lady woke up and jumped down, just missing Duke's back.

Waiting for the dog to react, Andrea held her breath. She figured Duke might growl and chase after the cat. Instead, the frightened animal, cowering against Brandon's leg, alternated between whining and panting.

Brandon rolled his eyes and gave a disgusted-sounding grunt. "I can't believe what a wimp my dog turns into whenever he's around Lady. And don't take it personally, Andrea," he added. "Duke freaks out every time he sees any cat, making it hard sometimes when we go beyond my yard for walks." He pressed his free hand against his chest and frowned. "This type of behavior might be common for some dog breeds, but until I got Duke, I'd never heard of it happening with a Brittany spaniel."

Lady, seemingly oblivious to the fearful dog, pranced back and forth across the room with her tail in the air, which only brought more whimpering noises from Brandon's poor trembling dog. Was she deliberately taunting him or just letting Duke know that this home was her territory?

Andrea made a dash and scooped Lady into her arms. "I think we'd better separate these two," she said, looking at Brandon.

He nodded. "Either that or Duke and I are gonna have to go home."

Andrea shook her head. "Please don't do that. I have a chicken in the oven for our supper, and I fixed that tangy potato salad you like so much."

"Okay, then I'll put Duke in your backyard till it's time for us to leave. Since it's fully fenced at least there's no worry of him getting out."

"That's probably for the best all right. Sorry I can't put Lady outside, but she's an indoor cat and would most likely run off."

"Duke will be fine. He's used to roaming around in my yard." Brandon picked his dog up and turned to face Andrea. "Next time we try getting our pets together, maybe it should be at my place. Since that's Duke's territory, he might not be so intimidated by Lady."

"That's a good idea," Andrea agreed. "I just hope my cat doesn't react negatively to being in strange surroundings."

Chapter 10

Apple Creek

Brandon took a seat in his favorite leather recliner and picked up the magazine he had noticed in his clinic's waiting room before he'd left for home. It had been lying there, wide open on one of the small tables, but he'd never noticed it before and didn't know where it had come from. Brandon assumed his receptionist, Connie, must have brought it in. She was good about putting new reading material in place for people while they waited. This magazine was focused on the unusual habits of dogs and cats. One article discussed what a person should do if they owned a cat and dog who didn't get along. Brandon hoped the article would include an answer to fixing Duke's cowardliness around cats. He felt bad for his faithful companion and wondered if there were other dog owners dealing with a similar issue. Brandon needed to find a way to get his dog to have courage and friendliness around his future wife's cat.

He opened the magazine and thumbed his way to the right page. *I can't help feeling that Duke is just a big baby when it comes to cats, but on the other hand, he's always been fine around children.*

Last week, Andrea had brought Lady over to Brandon's house to see if it would make a difference in the way Duke reacted. It hadn't. In fact, as soon as Duke caught sight of Lady, he'd made a beeline for the primary bedroom, jumped on the bed, and refused to come out. So much for thinking it would make a difference if his and Andrea's pets met in Duke's territory. Poor Lady had spent that evening in her cage, while Andrea and Brandon shared a pizza, both feeling very discouraged but agreeing to try again soon.

Now, as Brandon read the magazine article, a bit of hope welled in his chest.

"If your dog has been socialized with a cat, he won't have a fearful response," he read out loud. "But if he hasn't spent time with cats, he will either chase or fear them."

Brandon looked down at Duke, sleeping on the floor near his chair. "That would be you, little buddy. You're scared to death of Andrea's cat, and I hope there's something we can do about it, because it's not good for you to be quaking and quivering like a cat afraid of water every time Lady's around."

Brandon read on, noting that all dogs can experience and exhibit signs of fear over specific things. *Some dogs are afraid of thunder, children, fireworks, or going to a vet.* Brandon had witnessed many times in his practice when a frightened dog or cat shivered, howled, and sometimes became combative in a desperate attempt to escape what they feared. He remembered the bite he'd received from a frightened poodle when he'd let his guard down. Although the wound was deep and hurt a lot, it hadn't been bad enough for stitches.

Brandon put his concentration back on the article and continued to read. *Rather than consoling your dog, it's best to teach him to remain calm in the presence of a cat. This can be done through a combination of counterconditioning and desensitization. The ultimate goal is to decrease your dog's reaction to the cat to enable him to be around the feline.*

Brandon looked at Duke again, thankful that he was still sleeping and didn't demand his attention. He then turned his focus back to the article.

To desensitize your dog, he must be exposed to the cat several times in a controlled environment.

"Yeah, right—we've tried that already, and it didn't make a bit of difference." Brandon's jaw clenched. "Guess I'd better finish the article before I give up on Duke and Lady becoming friends, or at least Duke being able to be in the same space with her without whimpering, whining, or racing out of the room."

The last part of the article listed a few other suggestions, such as training the dog to sit beside you or lie at your feet when the cat is in the room. As a reward, a treat should be given, which would countercondition the dog to perform a positive behavior in place of fear. The article ended by saying that if none of the above worked, it would be best to find an experienced trainer skilled at working with pets that exhibited fears.

Brandon closed the magazine and tossed it on the coffee table near the couch. "If I'd known this would be such a problem, I never would have gotten a dog. Maybe I'll buy a child's stuffed kitten and introduce it to Duke. If he can adjust to that, maybe there'll be some hope for him to accept Andrea's cat." He frowned. "Of course, a stuffed animal wouldn't smell or act like a real cat."

This situation needed to be dealt with, but for now, after a hectic day, Brandon's eyes felt heavy. He brought up the leg rest of his recliner and felt the tension in his muscles begin to release.

Andrea had said goodbye to one of her piano students and shut the front door when her cell phone rang. She figured it might be Brandon, but it turned out to be Colleen.

"Hey, good friend and future maid of honor, how are you doing?" Andrea took a seat on the couch, and a few seconds later, Lady jumped into her lap.

"I'm good. How 'bout you? Still busy making plans for your wedding?"

Andrea stroked her hand gently over Lady's back and felt a bit of tension release in her shoulders when the cat began to purr. "Yes, but Brandon and I have run into a little snag."

"What's wrong? The church is still available on Valentine's Day, I hope."

"Yes, and we're still planning to have the ceremony there. It's after the wedding that I'm worried about."

"You mean the honeymoon?"

"No, we haven't made any definite plans for that yet. The problem we're faced with is Brandon's dog and my cat. The way things are now, they could never live in the same house together."

"Is Lady freaked out by Duke?"

"It's the other way around." Andrea continued to stroke her cat's head as the tension in her shoulders had returned. "We've tried getting them together a few times, and Duke either hides or sits close to Brandon, trembling and whining the whole time. Meanwhile, Lady acts aloof, like she doesn't know or even care that he's there."

"Did the meeting take place at your house or Brandon's?"

"We've tried both, but it made no difference." Andrea sighed deeply. "If we can't figure out a way for Lady and Duke to get along, one of us will have to get rid of our pet. Either that, or we won't be able to get married."

"Oh, don't say that. Don't even think about the possibility." Colleen spoke with conviction. "There has to be way to train Duke so he's not afraid of your cat."

Andrea sat quietly, feeling the vibration of Lady's body as her purring grew louder. "Brandon did mention that he might have to hire a dog trainer to help with the problem. But there's no guarantee it would work."

"Have you done an internet search on the topic of a dog being afraid of a cat?"

"No, I never thought about that."

"It's worth a try, don't you think? Maybe someone else who has dealt with the same problem and been successful in solving it has posted ideas on a blog or some special web page."

"That's a great idea. Don't know why I didn't think of it myself. I'll boot up my laptop and start searching for answers as soon as we hang up."

"I should probably let you go now so you can begin. I'm sure you'd like to get this situation resolved ASAP, and for sure before you and Brandon get married."

Andrea's hand moved to the back of her neck, where a knot had formed. "I agree. It could be a real problem for us."

"I can hear the concern in your voice," Colleen said. "Are you worried that Brandon might break off your engagement if Duke won't accept Lady?"

Andrea sucked in her lower lip. "I hope not, but I suppose it could come to that if neither of us is willing to get rid of our pet."

"That would be terrible. You and Brandon are in love, and I'm sure you'll figure out an answer or at least a compromise concerning your pets."

Andrea wished she felt as confident as her friend sounded. Unless she could find something helpful on the internet and it worked for Duke, giving up Lady might be her only recourse, because she couldn't stand the thought of breaking up with the man she loved.

Andrea sat in front of her computer, reading the second article she'd pulled up. This one had some suggestions she thought might work, so she wrote the ideas on a piece of paper to share with Brandon. The one suggestion she thought might work best was to allow the cat and dog to smell some item that belonged to the other while keeping the animals separated. Once the two animals appeared to be relaxed in the same room, the dog's leash could be dropped. Another suggestion was to feed both pets at the same time but on opposite sides of a closed door. The cat and dog would be able to smell each other while eating and begin to associate the smell with food. One final suggestion was to let the cat roam around several rooms of the house while the dog was outside in the yard. Then when the dog came back in, the cat should be put in its carrier behind a closed door, which would allow the dog the freedom to roam around to explore and smell the scent of the cat. When the dog seemed more comfortable, the cat carrier should be brought in, and if things were going well, the carrier door should be opened to allow the cat to come out. Once the dog showed no signs of fear, he could be let off the leash.

Andrea wrote down each idea and reached for her phone to call Brandon. It was time to schedule another meeting so they could try some of these ideas.

~

Walnut Creek

Lois was wearing one of her older work frocks and had tied a black scarf on her head to do her chores. Earlier that morning, she had done a few loads of laundry and hung all the wet clothing outside on the line to dry. Then she had come back inside to dust in the living room. She liked to keep her home clean and orderly.

Lois worked steadily until all the surfaces had been wiped off and everything looked spotless. Keeping busy was good for her. She welcomed the minor distractions that kept her from thinking about her father's death.

Feeling ready to switch gears from cleaning to answering letters from readers with problems, she put the dustrag away. Lois first heated up some water for a cup of tea to enjoy while tackling the letters.

A short time later, Lois sat at the kitchen table, reading the recent letters she'd received for her Dear Caroline page.

After having been in Kentucky for two weeks, she'd gotten behind on her work for the newspaper. Fortunately, Lois had turned in enough copy so that the paper had plenty to publish in the last two issues, but it was definitely time to do a little catching up.

The first letter she opened had been written by a widowed woman whose children wanted her to sell the home she'd lived in for forty years and relocate to another state to be close to family. The woman stated that while she knew she would enjoy living near her grown children and their families, it would be difficult to leave her friends, knowing she may never see any of them again. The letter was signed "Wondering What to Do."

Lois tapped her pen against the writing tablet, contemplating her response. It was a challenge to think of anything right now, when her mind kept replaying the scene in the hospital when she'd said her final words to Dad before he died. It was hard not to dwell on this when she should be focusing on other things.

Lois said a quick prayer and began to write on her tablet:

> Dear Wondering What to Do:
> Moving from one place to another can be stressful, and leaving friends behind makes a person feel sad. But if you keep your focus on the family you'll be living near, it will make the move easier. You can keep in touch with friends through letters and phone calls and maybe visit them on occasion. Or perhaps some of your friends will come to see you. It should be comforting to know that your family wants you to move close to them.

Lois swallowed hard as tears formed in her eyes. *Maybe if my daed had been living closer to Orley and me, our relationship could have been restored before he died.*

"Your shoulders are shaking. Are you crying, Lois?"

Lois felt her husband's strong hands on her shoulders. All she could do was nod.

"What's wrong? Does it have something to do with one of the Dear Caroline letters you've been reading?" he questioned.

She shook her head and pushed her chair away from the table. "It's hard for me to concentrate on answering these letters. All I can think about is my daed."

Orley pulled Lois gently to her feet and wrapped his strong, comforting arms around her. "It's always difficult when we lose someone we love, but the pain will lessen with the passage of time."

She listened and stayed in his reassuring embrace. *I missed so many years of trying to reconcile with Dad. I shouldn't have waited so near to the end of his life to openly forgive him.*

Lois wasn't sure if she regretted the timing of bearing her heart to Dad or if she wished she knew if his heart had changed and he wanted to make things right between them. Each day since he died had been a challenge for Lois, and she was ever so grateful for Orley and his comforting hugs.

Lois leaned her head against her dear husband and let the tears flow freely. The truth was, she hadn't realized how much she loved her father until it was too late. Now her heart ached for all that she'd lost, and she wasn't sure it would ever completely heal.

Chapter 11

Apple Creek

Andrea pulled her car up the driveway in front of Brandon's house and turned off the ignition. She sat there a moment, looking forward. It had been a week since she and Brandon had met at his place in hopes of getting their pets together without Duke being fearful of Lady. They'd talked on the phone a few times, going over the things they had both learned since their last meeting and deciding which ones they might want to try. Now it was time to see how one of those ideas might work.

Andrea hoped something would change, because this problem with their pets was exasperating and took some of the excitement out of wedding planning. It would be nice if Duke could at least learn to tolerate Lady.

Andrea got out of the car and opened the back door to retrieve Lady in her carrier. The cat let out a couple of noisy meows as Andrea gathered her things from the back seat and made her way up to the house. Lady had never been fond of being cooped up in her carrier for long.

"It's okay, pretty Lady. You're going to see Duke again, and you'd better be on your best behavior, because we really need him to accept you this time."

Andrea glanced at the freshly mowed lawn and beautiful flowering shrubs in Brandon's yard. She looked forward to living in this house and spending time in the lovely yard after they were married.

Due to Brandon's work schedule, he was too busy to keep the yard up, but he'd hired a landscaping service in the area, which was the reason it looked so nice.

Once her feet touched the welcome mat, Andrea fumbled for the doorbell button as Lady bumped around inside of her cage. "Settle down, pretty kitty."

When Brandon opened the door to let her in, she heard Duke barking but saw no sign of him. "Where's your dog?" Andrea asked after she'd set Lady's carrier down and Brandon had greeted her with a kiss.

"He's in the kitchen with the door shut, waiting to be fed."

She set down her purse and a brown paper bag she'd brought in with the items needed to try out their experiment. "Should I leave Lady in the carrier or take her out?" Andrea noticed her cat pawing at the bars of the cage.

He gave her a thumbs up and a comforting smile. "You can let her out when we try feeding them while they're on opposite sides of the kitchen door. But first, you'd better give me a few minutes to get into the kitchen, put food in Duke's bowl, and set it by the door."

"Okay." Andrea waited until Brandon had gone to the kitchen and let her know that Duke was eating from his bowl. Then she poured some dry cat food into the small dish she'd brought along in the paper bag. As soon as Lady's carrier door opened, the cat sprang from her cage and began chomping on the food. Andrea didn't know if the cat and dog could smell each other or the other pet's food with the closed door between them, but she heard Brandon say that Duke was doing fine with no apparent fear.

At least it's a start, she thought. *But things might change as soon as Brandon opens the kitchen door.*

Brandon stood off to one side, watching his hungry dog chow down on the crunchy food. If Duke had any awareness of Lady's presence on the other side of the door, he gave no indication.

"One small step for mankind." Brandon chuckled. "Sure hope the next step goes as well."

When Duke had finished his meal, Brandon clipped the leash to the dog's collar in preparation for taking Duke outside to do his business.

"I'm taking Duke out back for a few minutes," Brandon called through the door. "I'll bring his favorite ball in with me for your cat to sniff. While she's doing that, Duke can take a whiff of whatever toy you brought of Lady's."

"Sounds good," Andrea responded. "I'll have it out of the paper sack and ready for Duke's sniffing pleasure."

When Brandon came back into the kitchen with Duke, he told the dog to lie down, then he opened the door to the living room just wide enough to hand Andrea Duke's well-used tennis ball. In turn, she gave him a fuzzy, gray stuffed mouse.

Brandon was tempted to give Andrea a kiss, but he didn't want to take the chance of the cat getting into the kitchen, where his dog lay calm and unsuspecting. "Let's give our pets ten or fifteen minutes to get acquainted with each other's toys before we proceed to the next step," he said.

"Okay. I sure hope this works," Andrea responded.

"Same here." Brandon shut the door between them and dropped the stuffed mouse on the floor, close to Duke's nose. Instead of sniffing the item, like Brandon had hoped, his dog pounced on the toy and quickly tore it to shreds.

Brandon groaned. In addition to the fact that no sniffing had been done, he would now have to buy Lady a new toy mouse.

After Andrea put Lady's food dish away, she rolled Duke's ball across the floor and waited to see what would happen. Lady meandered over to it, took a few dainty sniffs, and walked away. Apparently, the old tennis ball held no interest for her.

Andrea gave the ball a gentle kick and watched as it rolled in another direction. This time the cat pranced across the room, heading toward the small round object. Although Lady didn't sniff the ball, she gave it a good whack with her paw, sending it into the dining room and under the table. Andrea expected the cat would go after it, but Lady went and sat next to her carrier instead.

Andrea released an exasperated breath. *When I let her out to eat, I'd hoped she would be more interested in the dog's toy, but I sure didn't expect her to just sit there—especially since she's usually eager to get out and explore.*

"Come on, Lady," Andrea coaxed. "Come and play with the tennis ball, or at least act like you're curious enough to smell the item real good." She picked up the ball and placed it in front of the cat's nose.

Lady gave it a couple of sniffs and curled up with her nose between her paws.

Andrea lifted her gaze toward the ceiling. *At least she showed enough interest this time to check out the odor of the dog's ball.*

"We're coming in now," Brandon called. A few seconds later, the kitchen door opened, and he entered the living room with his dog on a leash.

"How'd it go in there?" Andrea asked. "Did Duke get a good whiff of Lady's toy mouse?"

Brandon's brows furrowed as he glared at the dog. "I'm not really sure how much he actually smelled, but he went a little crazy and chewed up Lady's toy."

"What?" Andrea's mouth dropped open. "Oh my!"

"Unfortunately, this is all that's left." He showed her the item. "Sorry about that. I'll buy a new one to replace it. In fact, I think we still have some cat toys at the clinic. I'll check on it when I go to work tomorrow morning." Brandon took a step closer to Andrea, giving a tug on Duke's leash. The dog whimpered, dropped to the floor, and rolled over. Meanwhile, Lady remained in the same position, with her eyes closed and purring like a motorboat.

"Didn't Lady respond to Duke's tennis ball?" Brandon asked with lowered brows.

"She batted it around a few times and then headed over to her carrier. I put the ball in front of her nose, and she took a few sniffs, but then she closed her eyes and fell asleep." Andrea sighed. "I don't think we've accomplished much here this evening. Maybe I should take Lady home and call it a night."

Brandon's gaze darted from her cat to his dog, then back to Andrea. "You're not giving up on our quest to get our pets to accept each other, I hope."

She gave a noncommittal shrug. Truth was, Andrea figured it might be a hopeless situation. She worried that their wedding may not take place. What if their animals could not get along? Andrea wasn't ready to give Lady away, and Brandon liked Duke as well. She looked at her cat and heaved a sigh. *What are we going to do?*

Brandon stuffed what was left of Lady's mouse in his pocket and placed his hand on Andrea's shoulder. "We can do this, Andrea. There has to be a way. We just need to keep working at it and be willing to try some new things." He gave her shoulder a tender squeeze. "This is an important issue, and I refuse to give up. In the meantime, let's concentrate on our wedding plans and try not to worry about Duke's reaction to Lady, because I'm sure it'll work out."

Andrea rubbed her forehead and gave a slow nod. "Not tonight, though. I've developed a headache, so I'd better go home and sleep it off."

"Okay, sweetie. I hope you feel better soon." Brandon gave her a gentle kiss.

Andrea put Lady in her carrier, closed the door, and picked it up by the handle. "I'll talk to you sometime tomorrow, Brandon."

"Sounds good. I hope you sleep well tonight."

I'd sleep a lot better if my head wasn't pounding and I wasn't worried about the problem we have with our pets, Andrea thought as she went out his front door. She had a sick feeling in the pit of her stomach that if Duke didn't get over his fear of her cat, Brandon might ask her to find another home for Lady.

Walnut Creek

After tossing and turning for a few hours and not being able to sleep, Lois slipped quietly out of bed, being careful not to wake Orley. Maybe a cup of herbal tea would help her relax and allow her to sleep.

Downstairs in the kitchen, she filled the tea kettle with water, and while she waited for it to heat, she sat at the table with her mother's Bible. The feel of the soft leather beneath her fingers gave Lois an unexpected sense of peace. She opened the Bible to a page that had been marked with a pale blue ribbon and was surprised to see that one of the verses had been underlined: "Humble yourselves in the sight of the Lord, and he shall lift you up" (James 4:10).

That's a good verse, Lois thought. Although she had known her mother for only eight years and her early childhood was a distant memory, she still recalled how sweet and humble Mama was and how she could often be found sitting in her wooden rocking chair, reading God's Word or with her eyes closed in prayer.

Lois turned to another section that had been marked in her mother's Bible with a ribbon—this one was green. "Thy word is a lamp unto my feet, and a light unto my path" (Psalm 119:105). *Another good reminder from God's Holy Bible*, she thought.

A bit later, a page had been marked with a yellow ribbon. "I wait for the LORD, my soul doth wait, and in his word do I hope" (Psalm 130:5).

A red ribbon revealed another verse her mother had underlined. "This is the confidence that we have in [God], that, if we ask anything according to his will, he heareth us" (1 John 5:14). The last verse spoke to Lois's heart. "Whatever I pray for needs to be according to God's will, not mine," she whispered. "Because He knows what is best for me and every believer."

Lois tipped her head back and closed her eyes, feeling a sense of gratitude well in her soul. It was a wonderful gesture for Sarah to have given her this special Bible. It gave Lois a small connection to her mother, knowing Mama's fingers had touched the same pages as she was doing now, and reading the special verses that had been underlined in her mother's Bible. For the moment, the peace of God prevailed, and Lois knew that she could rest in Him. *I'm so glad to have the honor of possessing Mama's Bible.*

The silence in the room was interrupted by the whistle of the tea kettle. Lois opened her eyes and got up to fix a cup of chamomile tea. Returning to the table, she searched through the Bible for more ribbons and underlined verses.

On a page marked with a white ribbon, Lois found this verse underlined: "And as ye would that men should do to you, do ye also to them likewise" (Luke 6:31).

Lois wiped tears from her cheeks. Oh, how she wished she had gotten to know her mother better, but now, as she continued reading verses from this special Bible, Lois felt as if Mama was right there beside her, offering encouragement, wisdom, and comfort. Lois determined that she would keep Mama's Bible where it could be seen and wouldn't let a day pass without reading a few passages of scripture from it.

Chapter 12

Apple Creek

The next Saturday night, Brandon let Duke outside before getting ready for bed. The dog had been kind of hyper all evening, running through the house and barking a lot, which had tried Brandon's patience. He'd had another hectic day making farm animal calls and looked forward to getting a good night's sleep.

Brandon had made himself a frozen pizza for supper and needed to put away the leftovers, which only amounted to a few slices that he placed in a plastic container and set inside the refrigerator.

He grabbed the sponge and wiped down the counters and table. Content with the results, he thought about having more to drink.

After filling a glass with ice and water, Brandon took a seat at the kitchen table to wait for Duke to scratch at the door to come back in. He sat there thinking about how nice it would be to have all of the wedding details planned. The day when he and Andrea would be married was always at the forefront of his mind. He loved Andrea so much and couldn't imagine spending the rest of his life with anyone but her.

He drank some of his water, then closed his eyes. *I can't wait for the day I get to introduce her as Mrs. Brandon Prentice. It has a nice ring to it.* Brandon's eyes opened, and he couldn't help but smile. After they were married, they'd be living together here. Brandon was well aware that his bachelor pad would go through some changes. No doubt Andrea would want to add some of the furniture from her rental, and his closet space would shrink with the addition of her clothing.

Brandon looked around his kitchen, wondering what changes she might make to this space. *I'm not into decorating, and it does look a little barren in here. I'm sure in time Andrea will make some changes, and it will probably look much nicer.*

His thoughts scattered when he heard several shrill *yip-yips* coming from the backyard. Brandon left his seat in a hurry and went to see what was up with his dog.

When Brandon opened the door and turned on the porch light, he saw no sign of Duke. He cupped his hands around his mouth and hollered, "Where are ya, Duke? Come here, boy!"

A whimper came forth, and a few seconds later, the dog came out from behind a bush, whining and limping toward the porch steps. Brandon's adrenaline flowed as he looked in expectation about the yard. Could there be another animal around that might have provoked this situation? He didn't see anything out of the ordinary. All was quiet except when his dog let out another pathetic whine.

Filled with concern, Brandon picked up Duke and carried him up the stairs and into the house. Once inside, he put the dog down and looked him over thoroughly, touching and pressing on certain points to see if they were warm, swollen, or out of place. Each time Duke tried to walk, he would limp and yip. Brandon had no idea what the dog may have done to injure himself, but he figured Duke must have somehow sprained or strained his left front leg. He wouldn't know for sure until he'd taken an X-ray, which was important in order to rule out a broken bone. Despite the lateness of the hour, Brandon decided it would be best to take Duke to his clinic right away.

By the time Brandon returned from his veterinary clinic with Duke, it was well past midnight. This wasn't the peaceful evening he'd planned for himself. Brandon's idea was that after his pizza, he'd relax in his easy chair, maybe fix some popcorn to munch on, and watch a good movie, featuring one of his favorite actors. Now it was late, and he'd run out of steam to do anything but call it a night.

After a thorough examination and X-ray of Duke's leg while at the clinic, Brandon had determined that his dog's leg had been sprained, but thankfully, there were no broken bones or dislocations. He'd given Duke a nonsteroidal anti-inflammatory drug to ease the inflammation and applied an ice pack for the drive home. Now Brandon needed to make sure the dog rested and didn't jump or run. When he took Duke outside, he'd need to be on a leash and walk slowly. If Duke continued to limp and whine, Brandon would use a brace or some other support to hold the dog's muscle in place. He would also gently massage the injured area and make sure Duke didn't eat too much, which might cause him to gain weight. Since it could take several weeks for the sprain to heal, Brandon would not leave the dog alone in his pen outside or even in the house. He planned to ask his mother to sit with Duke while he was at work next week because he couldn't take the chance of the dog reinjuring himself when no one was at home.

The drug he'd given Duke seemed to make his faithful companion more comfortable. Duke sat on an area rug in the living room while Brandon gathered a couple of things for the dog. He couldn't wait to get Duke and himself settled in after such a long day.

Brandon placed Duke's doggie bed next to the couch, and then he flopped onto the soft cushions, thankful for his training as a veterinarian, which gave him the knowledge of what to do for his dog in a situation such as this. At the moment, Brandon was too tired to go down the hall and get ready for bed, so he figured he may as well sleep on the couch. He wouldn't bother to set an alarm because he'd have to skip church in the morning to take care of Duke. He would explain things to Andrea when she came over in the afternoon, like they'd planned, and would leave a message on her cell phone saying he wouldn't be at church.

With one arm dangling over the edge of the couch, Brandon stroked his dog's silky head. "Goodnight, Duke." He gave in to a noisy yawn. "Sleep well, and I hope you feel better in the morning."

The dog gave a quiet whimper and put his head between his paws. Brandon closed his eyes and succumbed to sleep.

~

Andrea loaded Lady into her carrier and carried it out to the car. She had listened to Brandon's voice mail this morning, saying he wouldn't make it to church and would explain things later. Since they'd agreed upon sharing a meal this afternoon and getting their pets together again, she assumed that was still in the plans. If it wasn't, surely Brandon would have said so in his message.

Lady let out a pathetic *meow* and scratched at the front of the cage when Andrea set the carrier on the back seat. "Hush, sweet kitty; you won't be cooped up long because we don't have far to go."

She shut the back door, took her place in the driver's seat, and turned on the ignition. When Lady continued to carry on, Andrea put a CD in and turned up the volume so she could drown out the cat's noise and listen to one of her favorite Christian artists.

A short time later, she pulled into Brandon's driveway and turned off the engine, pleased that her cat had finally settled down. It was short-lived, however, because as soon as Andrea carried Lady's carrier up the sidewalk and stepped onto the porch, the boisterous meowing began again.

Andrea glanced at the living room window and noticed that the drapes were drawn. Her forehead wrinkled. *That's odd. Why would Brandon have the curtains closed in the middle of the day?*

She rang the doorbell and waited, trying to hush her determined cat. Several minutes passed before the door opened. She was surprised to see Brandon looking at her through half-closed eyes. His clothes were wrinkled like he'd slept in them, and the top of his hair stood straight up. "Were you sleeping?" she asked.

He gave a nod. "Duke kept me up half the night, and the couch I slept on was not nearly as comfortable as my bed would have been."

"What do you mean? What happened that kept you up and caused you to sleep on the couch?"

She set Lady's cage on the floor and listened while Brandon explained what had transpired the night before.

"I'm sorry to hear about Duke's leg." To be heard, Andrea spoke loudly, above Lady's incessant meows.

"You can let her out if you want to," Brandon said. "I'll close the door to the living room, where Duke's lying on his doggie bed."

Andrea looked down at the carrier and back at Brandon. "It might be best if I take Lady and go home. This is obviously not a good time to try and get our pets together in a friendly manner."

"You're right, but I'd like to spend some time with you today, and I did promise to fix something for our Sunday dinner."

Andrea shook her head. "If anyone's going to cook dinner, it should be me." She reached up and smoothed his rumpled hair. "What were you planning to have?"

"Grilled sausages, sauerkraut, three-bean salad, and potato salad. The makings for most of it is in the refrigerator, including some boiled eggs." He gave her a sheepish-looking grin. "Of course, the potatoes would need to be cooked."

"No problem. I'll get started on it right now. I know how much you like my tangy potato salad."

He gave her a hug. "You've got that right. It's one of my favorites."

~

While Andrea made a potato salad and set the table, Brandon went out back to grill the sausages. He felt bad that he'd missed sitting beside Andrea during church today, but at least they could enjoy a nice meal together this afternoon.

When the sausages were fully cooked, he put them in a pan and carried it inside. "Should we eat in the kitchen or dining room?" he asked, seeing that Andrea had the potato salad almost done.

"How about the dining room? That's where I left Lady after I let her out of the carrier." Andrea laughed. "She quickly found a spot under the table to take a nap."

Brandon placed the pan of meat on the table. "Speaking of

pets... I'd better go check on Duke. He may be awake by now and need to go outside."

"Okay. While you're doing that, I'll finish up the potato salad and bring the food into the dining room."

Brandon passed through the dining room and was surprised to see that the door to the living room was slightly ajar. He thought he had shut it when he'd left his sleeping dog to answer the front door.

Brandon took a few steps toward Duke's doggie bed and halted. There lay Andrea's cat right next to Duke, with her head nestled close to his. Their eyes were closed, and Duke breathed in and out, while soft purring came from Lady. Brandon could hardly believe the scene set before him. It seemed as though Lady might be offering comfort to Duke, and the amazing thing was, Duke had apparently accepted her sympathetic gesture. Maybe something good had come from Duke's accident. Perhaps the animals could be friends after all.

Brandon went back to the kitchen. "You'll never guess what's going on in the living room."

She turned away from her job at the counter. "What is it?"

"Your cat and my dog are sleeping next to each other." Brandon swiped a hand through the back of his thick hair. "I could hardly believe my eyes."

Andrea's brows lifted. "They're both in the living room?"

"Yeah."

"How did Lady get in there?"

"The door was slightly open, so I must not have closed it tightly when I left Duke to answer the door when you arrived." He took hold of Andrea's hand. "Come on. You need to see this for yourself."

When they entered the living room, Brandon pointed at the sleeping duo. "What do you think of that?" he whispered.

Her lips parted slightly as she stared at their contented-looking pets. "I think it's a miracle. A definite answer to prayer."

He nodded and slipped his arm around Andrea's waist. "Wouldn't it be great if these two actually became friends?"

"It sure would, but I wonder what prompted Lady to approach

Duke and lie down beside him."

"I'm thinking she might have detected that he'd been hurt and needed comforting. Some animals have a sixth sense about things like that."

"That could be, but why would Duke have tolerated Lady lying down beside him when he's been so frightened of her?"

"I can't be sure, but with the need for sympathy, he must have set his fears aside."

"Well, whatever the case, let's go eat and not disturb their peaceful sleep."

"Sounds good to me. I'm eager to sink my teeth into the sausages I grilled, not to mention eat your tangy potato salad."

The two of them quietly left the room, and Brandon left the door open slightly so that if Lady and Duke woke up, he could hear if there were any problems.

Before they ate their meal, Brandon prayed, asking God to bless the food, as well as his and Andrea's relationship. He ended the prayer by giving thanks for what he and Andrea had witnessed with their pets in the next room.

When they'd both finished eating, Andrea suggested that they take a peek to see if anything had changed between Duke and Lady. She was pleasantly surprised to find them both awake and even more pleased to see that her cat was now licking the dog's injured leg while Duke laid there calmly, as though enjoying the attention.

Brandon smiled. "Looks like my dog has gotten over his fear of your cat. I sure never expected to see this, did you?"

"No, but as I said earlier, it's an answer to prayer." She clasped his arm. "Now that we don't have to worry about either of us feeling the need to get rid of our pet, there's nothing standing in the way of us getting married."

"That's right," he agreed. "It's going to be clear sailing from here on."

Chapter 13

Walnut Creek

"I can't believe it's the middle of October already." Orley eyed the perpetual calendar sitting on the kitchen windowsill.

Lois nodded as she filled the sink with warm water and detergent. "Time marches on, that's for sure."

"Indeed it does." Orley moved to stand beside her. "How about if I dry the dishes while you wash this morning?"

Lois looked over at him and smiled. "Danki, I'd appreciate that." She glanced out the window. "I'm surprised that fellow you talked to the other day hasn't come by like he said to give us a bid on taking down the old dying maple tree in our backyard."

Orley picked up the dish towel and dried the first dish Lois had washed. "He said he would be here by eight o'clock Monday morning, and here it is nine thirty already. Something must have happened to detain him."

"I hope he didn't forget—especially since we took today off from working at the store to see what it would cost to take down the tree." She gestured to the back door. "Maybe you should go out to the phone shed and call the man to see if he's on his way."

Orley set the dish towel aside. "Good idea. I'll do it now and finish drying the dishes when I get back to the house." He grabbed his hat and went out the door.

Upon entering the phone shed, Orley saw the blinking light on the answering machine, indicating that one or more messages had come in. He took a seat on the stool and punched the correct button to listen.

"Hey, Mr. Troyer—it's Eddie Bunker here. I hate to tell ya this, but I'm stuck out on the main highway, and thanks to the broken gauge, my truck's outta gas. Could ya bring me some?"

Orley scratched behind one ear, then gave his earlobe a tug. The only thing he used gasoline for was his lawnmower, and he had used the last of that Saturday evening when he'd mowed the lawn. He had plans to get the gas can filled sometime this week, but that was no help at the moment.

Even if I did have any gas, he thought, *I'd have to take it to him by horse and buggy or hire a driver to pick me up, which could take hours if none of our regular drivers are available.*

Orley shut off the answering machine and dialed the man's number, which went to voice mail. He left a short message explaining that he had no gas to bring the English man. Orley had just hung up when the phone rang.

"Hey, Mr. Troyer, it's Eddie Bunker. I called one of the guys who works for me, and he's bringing me some gas, so I should be there in the next half hour or so." There was a pause, then he added, "One of these days, I'm gonna get the gas gauge on my truck replaced."

Orley figured it might be a while before Eddie made it to his house. He was tempted to tell the man not to bother coming but figured he may as well hear his bid, so he responded with "Okay." At three o'clock, another man would be coming to look at the tree. Once that was done, Orley and Lois would make the decision on whose bid to choose.

After Lois finished washing the dishes, she gathered up some scraps to take out to the compost. Orley had come in ten minutes ago and told her about the message he'd received from the man giving them a bid on their tree. After he'd finished drying the dishes, Orley had gone outside to wait for Eddie Bunker, who was already two hours late.

Lois slipped into a pair of old sneakers, and since she was in a hurry to get busy answering some Dear Caroline letters, she didn't bother to tie the laces, just hurried out the back door. She noticed the man had finally arrived as she plodded across the slippery grass, still wet from yesterday's rains, and sidestepped a few mud puddles on her way to the compost pile. Lois was almost there when her shoestrings tangled, causing her to wobble in several directions before making a crash landing.

Lois's face heated as she scrambled to her feet and glanced around, hoping Orley and the man hadn't seen her fall and scatter all the scraps on the ground. They continued talking while looking at the pathetic old tree and didn't give a glance her way.

At least they didn't see me make a fool of myself, Lois thought as she brushed some dried mud and food scraps off her dress. *Guess that's what I get for not taking the time to tie my shoes. Sure won't make that mistake again.*

Once she had tied her shoes properly, Lois eyed their pumpkin patch. The bold, orange squashes poked out between the big green leaves. *I think some of those pumpkins would look nice on the front porch.* Lois stepped up to them and selected the ones she liked best. She carried two of the medium-sized pumpkins across the yard and placed them on the porch. After two more trips from the garden and back, she had enough pumpkins for her liking.

After Lois finished arranging them, she noticed quite a bit of mud from the garden had been tracked all over the porch from her grimy shoes. With a sigh, she went to get the outdoor broom they kept in the barn. The tree guy and Orley were over by the picnic table, and she noticed the man writing something on a piece of paper, which he handed to Orley.

Back on the porch, Lois used the broom to brush the caked mud from her sneakers. Then she swept the porch and even went after the cobwebs. She stepped down into the yard again and looked back at her finished work. *I think all those pumpkins look kind of cute. I wonder if Orley will notice and say something to me when he's done outside.*

Eager to get back into the warmth of the house, Lois hurried up the porch steps, leaving the broom propped near the door.

———

Apple Creek

Brandon entered his office at the veterinarian clinic and took a seat at his desk. He'd been busy all morning, and now it was time to take a brief lunch break. He had considered hiring another vet to help with the workload because at times his schedule was so tight, he had to work right through his lunch hour. He knew of other veterinary clinics that had more staff, and it probably made things easier. *I sure wouldn't mind being able to take vacations, sick leave, and even have the ability to come into work late or leave early when needed.*

He opened his insulated lunch bag and took out the ham and cheese sandwich he'd put together. He said a silent prayer before taking his first bite, thanking God for the meal set before him. He also asked the Lord's blessings on his family and friends. Brandon ended the prayer, thanking God for the sweet Christian woman who had come into his life. He looked forward to Andrea becoming his wife in four months. Things were going well with the wedding plans, and he felt relieved that Duke had accepted Lady. Now that the dog's leg injury was fully healed, Brandon felt comfortable leaving Duke at home without supervision while he was at the clinic. Of course, Brandon kept his pooch barricaded in the laundry room so he couldn't roam the house and potentially get into trouble. About a year ago, he had made the mistake of giving Duke free run of the house unattended, and he'd come home to a couple of messes. Not only had the dog gone to the bathroom where he shouldn't have, but Duke had gnawed a hole in one of Brandon's bedroom slippers, which he'd left on the floor by his recliner. Those things were nothing, though, compared to what one pet owner who'd come to the clinic had told Brandon. The owner's dog was blind in one eye and had been born deaf. Training the animal had been a challenge, and on one occasion after leaving the dog alone in the house for a few hours, the man and his wife had returned home to find the cushions on their couch torn to shreds. The couch looked so bad, the man had hauled it outside until he could dispose of it. Needless to say, his wife had been quite upset, especially since they'd had the couch only a little over a year.

Focusing once again on his lunch, Brandon tore open the bag of potato chips and ate a few. Not too long after, he heard a couple of raps on his office door. "Come in," he called.

His assistant, Fran, entered. "We have someone on the phone whose dog has quills from a porcupine and needs to have them removed." She paused. "Do you think we can squeeze the poor animal in to be seen today?"

"I believe so. We'll just need to work it into the schedule."

"All right, I'll let the caller know and let you go back to your lunch. Thank you, Dr. Prentice."

"You're welcome." He watched the door shut behind her and continued to eat his lunch. It would be a busy afternoon, and he'd possibly end up going home later than normal, but that was just part of the job.

I hope Duke's doing okay today. It was good of my mom to volunteer to come over to the house and check on him while I'm here at work. Brandon had always been able to count on his mother when he needed help, and this situation was no exception. He picked up his bottle of water and took a drink. Brandon was glad he'd become a vet, even though it had taken four years of undergrad school and an additional four years of veterinary school. He'd had a way with animals since he was a boy and cared about the welfare of people's pets. It was always difficult when a person had a pet with an incurable illness that needed to be put down. But being a vet had many benefits, such as seeing a dog, cat, or some other animal recover from an illness or injury, and those were the things Brandon liked to focus on.

Andrea closed the door behind her last piano student of the day and sank onto the couch with a groan. There were days when things went really well with her students and other times, like today, when everyone seemed to think they should play the piano their own way. Peggy still wasn't keeping her nails trimmed as short as they should be, but at least her parents hadn't found another teacher for her. Another girl, Anna, played with flat hands instead of curving her fingers as Andrea had asked. Then there was Todd, her only boy student, who played by ear and didn't want to learn the notes. Even her adult student, Kara, who had taken a few lessons as a child, could be a challenge because she lacked self-confidence. There were times, such as now, when Andrea wished she could quit teaching piano and concentrate fully on her artwork.

"Maybe after Brandon and I are married, I can do that."

Lady leaped into Andrea's lap and began to purr.

"Did you think I was talking to you, pretty Lady? Did you believe I was inviting you up?" Andrea gently rubbed the cat's back, which brought on more vibrations.

She smiled at the contented cat while thinking about the last few weeks and how well Lady and Duke had been getting along during their scheduled visits. It was a relief, knowing that neither she nor Brandon would have to part with their pet when they got married.

Andrea sighed. *Things are back on track and going well again. All I need to do now is concentrate on making all the final plans for Brandon's and my wedding. I can hardly wait for the big day.*

Andrea's cell phone rang from across the room, where she'd left it on an end table, so she moved a disgruntled Lady to the sofa cushion and went to see who was calling. Her mother's number showed on the screen, so Andrea quickly responded to the call.

"Hi, Mom. How's your day been so far?"

"Not well, Andrea." Mom's voice faltered, and Andrea heard a muffled sob.

"What's wrong? Has something bad happened?"

"Yes. I—I just got a call from your cousin, Vincent, saying his dad had been killed in a motorcycle accident around noon today. His mother was too upset to let anyone know. Vincent said Karen passed out when she got the news." Mom paused and sniffed deeply. "Oh, Andrea, I can hardly believe my brother is gone. I wish he and his family lived closer and we could have seen them more often. With them living out west in Idaho, our visits have been far and few between, and because of it, you never got to know your uncle Dave or any of his family very well."

Andrea sat quietly, breathing in and out. The pain she heard in her mother's voice brought tears to Andrea's eyes. "When is Uncle Dave's funeral service?"

"The family hasn't made any final arrangements yet, but Vincent said he would let us know." There was a short pause. "Will you be able to go with me and your dad? It would mean a lot to me if you could."

Andrea didn't hesitate to answer. "Of course I will go with you. Let me know as soon as you find out when the service will be, and I'll rearrange my teaching schedule."

"Thank you, sweet daughter. I don't think I could get through this without your support, and, of course, I'll have your father's also."

"Absolutely."

When Andrea hung up the phone a few minutes later, she returned to the couch where Lady lay curled into a ball as if she didn't have a care in the world.

Oh, the life of a cat, Andrea mused. *No schedules to keep or funerals to attend—all they have to worry about is where their next meal will be coming from.*

She leaned her head against the back of the couch and closed her eyes. Even though she didn't know her uncle Dave very well, Andrea felt bad to hear of the unexpected tragedy that had taken his life so suddenly. Life was full of ups and downs, and it could throw a curve when least expected. How thankful she was for her

Christian faith and the confidence that the Lord would be with her every day, guiding, directing, and offering encouragement through His written Word. Looking to the future and all of its uncertainties was much easier to do when a person had a personal relationship with Jesus Christ as their Lord and Savior. Andrea fully expected that if she and Brandon were blessed with children someday, they would bring them up in a home filled with love and the knowledge of the Lord. For now, though, she would concentrate on attending her uncle's funeral and being there to help Mom deal with the pain of losing her only brother.

Chapter 14

Walnut Creek

Orley guided his horse and buggy to the hitching rail at an Amish house on the other end of town. "I think when we're done looking at yard sales, we should grab a bite to eat before heading home."

"That sounds like a good idea." Lois dabbed her nose with a tissue. "I'm still hoping to find what I'm looking for at one of the sales."

Her husband set the brake and grabbed the thermos that sat in a box behind his seat. "Thank you for providing us with hot coffee to drink."

"No problem. With the temperature down the way it is, we need to keep warm."

Orley poured some coffee into his and Lois's mugs before putting the thermos back. "Most of the yard sales have been busy today. It's too bad we've come away from each of them without buying something."

"I agree, and I wish the weather was warmer. The older I get, the less my old bones like this chill." She sipped her hot beverage, feeling warm and toasty on the inside as she watched a woman carrying her purchase of a wooden chair over to her car. The lady opened the back door and tried to wrangle it into a spot, but from what Lois could see, it wasn't working too well.

"If that poor woman didn't already have so many other things piled up in the back, she would have more room," Orley commented.

"I'll get out and secure my horse and then see if I can help her." He handed Lois his mug, got out, and secured the horse.

Lois smiled. It wasn't unusual for her husband to do a good deed for people he knew or perfect strangers. She drank the rest of her coffee, put their mugs away, and climbed down from the carriage. As she followed Orley to the English woman's car, she heard him ask if he could be of assistance.

"No, thanks. I'll manage," the woman replied. "I'm used to doing things on my own."

"Do you think she'll get that chair into her car?" Lois asked, keeping her voice low.

Orley shrugged. "I'm not sure, but she seems determined enough. I'd say she'll win out and get it in there eventually."

The woman paused a few minutes, set the chair on the ground, and then climbed back into her vehicle, where she tried to rearrange the stuff already packed inside.

Lois continued to watch, wishing the bedraggled woman would have accepted Orley's help.

Finally, the woman pulled a table lamp from the back of the car and, with some effort, put it up front by the driver's seat. Then she closed the door and picked up the chair. With a little more work, it finally went in.

Orley looked at Lois and winked. "Are ya ready to see what this yard sale might have for us? It could be something exciting."

"Oh, I'm ready all right." Lois followed Orley, walking quickly to keep up with his strides.

"I hope we find something interesting here," Orley said as he and Lois entered the sale on this chilly Monday morning.

"It's too cold to be out here looking for vintage items, when we really should be at our store." Lois pulled her heavy sweater a little tighter around her neck and shivered. "I'm surprised there are so many yard sales going on this time of the year."

Orley nodded. "At least it's not raining."

"Or snowing," she added. "This frigid air makes me think it

won't be long before we see some heavy white flakes falling from the sky."

"That could be. Some years we have had *schnee* as early as October."

"I know, and I wasn't ready for it."

Orley chuckled. "Are we ever ready for things we don't like?"

"I suppose not."

They walked farther into the yard sale where several people milled around by two long tables full of kitchen utensils and some decorator items. Lois had spotted an old teacup she wanted to look at, but her attention was turned toward a loud voice coming from the aisle across from them. She turned to see who was shouting and was surprised to see a middle-aged English woman shaking her finger at the tall man who stood beside her.

"That tool you're holding is too expensive," the woman said, her voice rising higher with each word. "We can't afford to spend money foolishly, Ted."

The man's brows furrowed. "It's not foolish. I've been looking for a tool like this, and you can be sure that I'll put it to good use making some gifts to give out at Christmas."

The woman, who Lois assumed to be his wife, folded her arms and shook her head forcibly.

Lois glanced over at Orley to see his reaction. She wasn't surprised to see the wrinkles in his forehead deepen as the couple continued to argue.

Lois fought the urge to say something to the woman, who was doing most of the shouting, but she didn't feel it was her place to intervene—especially since these people were strangers. If they'd come into Memory Keepers and began quarreling, Lois was quite sure that Orley would have said something. And if he hadn't, she certainly would have.

The arguing couple made Lois think about Jeff and Rhonda Davis and the marital problems they'd had before they'd given their lives fully to the Lord. Both Orley and Lois had mentored the couple and prayed for them often. Although it was best to remain quiet right now, Lois would definitely remember to pray for the man and woman here at the sale. She felt relief when they stopped arguing and walked away—without the tool the man had wanted so badly.

Heavenly Father, Lois prayed, *please show that woman a better way of talking to her husband than yelling at him to make her point known. And if they are having serious marriage problems, please guide and direct them to the right person who can offer good counsel.*

<hr />

Apple Creek

"No, Mrs. Allen, it's not typically dangerous for your dog to eat grass. In fact, it's fairly common," Brandon patiently explained.

The elderly woman gestured to her cream-colored miniature poodle and frowned. "It's a nasty habit, in my opinion, just like digging holes in the yard."

"Most dogs do like to dig." Brandon stroked her dog's silky head. "Most of the time it's for play, to create a cool dirt bowl on a hot day or because they're bored."

Mrs. Allen blinked rapidly. "My Dixie's never bored. When she isn't sleeping, she keeps herself busy playing with her toys or following me around the house or yard."

Brandon smiled. "Dixie seems to be in good condition, and her weight is where it should be. I think you'll have her around for a good many years."

"I'm glad to hear it." The older woman picked up her dog and moved toward the door. "I hope she doesn't outlive me, though, because I have no one to leave her with after I'm gone."

"What about your daughter? Wouldn't she take Dixie in?"

"No, Karen's allergic to dogs—and cats too."

"I'm certain that your daughter will find Dixie a good home if it becomes necessary." Brandon hoped his words sounded reassuring.

He hated to send Mrs. Allen home from his clinic with a sense of hopelessness.

She nodded slowly. "Thank you, Dr. Prentice."

"You're welcome."

After the woman left the examining room, Brandon made a few notes on Dixie's chart and looked at his watch. *Andrea and her parents should be boarding the plane about now.* He closed his eyes to offer a prayer. *Please be with them, Lord, and keep the Wagners safe as they travel to Idaho. Offer comfort over the loss of Andrea's uncle to all of his family at the funeral tomorrow.*

Cleveland, Ohio

Andrea took her aisle seat in the second row of the first-class cabin, directly across from her parents. Andrea's father had accumulated quite a few air miles and used them to pay for their upgraded seats. Since there would be two stops along the way—one in Minneapolis and one in Seattle—the trip to Boise would take a little over ten hours, and they wouldn't arrive until nine forty-five tonight. The comfortable seats in first class would make the long trip a little more bearable.

Andrea stretched out, appreciative of the extra legroom, and put her neck pillow in place, hoping she might be able to get a good nap on the first leg of this flight. She hadn't slept well last night, worrying about Lady and how she would do at Colleen's place during her absence. Andrea had also thought about Brandon and wished he could have come with her on this trip. But his schedule at the clinic was full, and he had obligations to fulfill. She hoped he would be able to take at least a week off after their wedding for a honeymoon. Maybe by then he would have found another veterinarian to work with him in the clinic, which would ease the pressure he was under.

Andrea yawned and was on the verge of dozing off when an elderly woman with silver-gray hair stopped at her seat. "I'm sorry for the inconvenience, but would you mind stepping into the aisle so Serena and I can take our seat by the window?" The woman gestured to the carrier she held.

Andrea knew right away from the long, plaintive *meowww*, that Serena must be the cat in the carrier. She quickly stood up and stepped into the aisle, moving close to her mother's seat.

Mom looked up and gave Andrea a sweet smile, then she mouthed the word *Meow*.

Andrea nodded. One thing was for sure: if the cat's owner was the conversational type, Andrea, with her love of cats, would have plenty to talk about.

After she took her seat again, the older woman looked over at her and said, "My name is Darlene, and the noisy one in the carrier is Serena."

Andrea smiled. "It's nice to meet you. I'm Andrea."

"Where are you headed?" Darlene asked.

"Our first plane change will be in Minneapolis, and then it's on to Seattle. Our final destination is Boise, Idaho. Those are my parents sitting across the aisle from us. We'll be attending a funeral in the town of Caldwell."

"That's too bad. Funerals are always so sad. Was the deceased a friend or family member of yours?"

"The funeral is for my uncle. What's your destination?" Andrea asked, quickly changing the topic.

"I'll be getting off in Minneapolis. My daughter, Sandra, lives there with her husband and two teenage girls. Sandra's invited me to move in with them, so I thought it best to check things out before committing to anything permanent."

Andrea was about to comment when Darlene spoke again. "My husband passed away a year ago, and we only have one daughter. I do have a good many friends in Cleveland, and I'd miss seeing them if I moved away." With downturned facial features, she looked at her cat's carrier, where squeaky chirrups could be heard. "My other concern is that Serena might not be able to adjust to new surroundings. She's used to a quiet life in my home, with just the two of us now."

Andrea placed her hand gently on the woman's arm. "I understand. My fiancé is a veterinarian, and he's mentioned how everyone's pet is different. While some may adjust easily to new surroundings, others have a difficult time."

Darlene released a heavy sigh. "Guess I won't know till we get there and have spent a few weeks living in the basement apartment my son-in-law has fixed up for me and Serena."

"I have a cat too. Her name is Lady," Andrea said. "She has quite a unique personality."

Darlene tipped her head to one side. "In what way?"

"Somehow she managed to befriend my fiancé's dog, who up until recently was afraid of cats."

"That's remarkable. How did she accomplish it?"

Andrea explained the situation and ended it by saying, "Needless to say, Brandon and I are relieved that our pets are finally getting along. We'll be getting married in February, and we would have been faced with the decision of one of us needing to part with their pet if Lady and Duke couldn't even be in the same house with each other."

Darlene's eyes widened. "Oh my! I can't imagine being forced to give up my cat." She leaned over and put her hand against the carrier, which caused Serena's chirrups to turn to loud purrs.

Andrea smiled. It was nice to see the love this woman had for her pet. She hoped if Darlene decided to move in with her daughter and family that everything would work out well for both the sweet lady and her cat.

⁓

The plane had only been in the air thirty minutes when Evelyn glanced over and saw that her husband was engrossed in some movie. Flying had never bothered Ray as much as it did her. Unless food was being offered, he either slept or watched whatever movie caught his interest. Not Evelyn. She'd never cared for watching movies or much of anything at home on the TV. She enjoyed going out to lunch with her friend Fiona and managing their church library, and she felt thankful that Fiona had agreed to take care of Frisky while they were gone.

Evelyn thought about the things she did enjoy—she liked to knit, cross-stitch, spend time in her garden during warmer weather, and tend to her indoor plants year round. Some evenings she sat in the living room with Ray while he watched TV, but Evelyn's concentration was usually on whatever knitting or cross-stitch project she'd begun. It was difficult to sit here on the plane with nothing constructive to do.

Guess I should have brought a book along to read, she thought. *It would give me something to do that would help take my mind off the funeral service we'll be attending tomorrow morning.* Evelyn squeezed her eyes tightly shut. *I wish I could have talked to my brother one last time before he died. There's so much I would have said to him.* Tears seeped out from her lashes and trickled down her cheeks. Her brother had become a Christian in his late teens, so at least she had the confidence that Dave had gone to heaven when he died.

Evelyn opened her eyes and dabbed at her face with the tissue she'd put in her pocket before they boarded the plane. *I need to get a hold of myself so I can be strong for Dave's family when we get there. The last thing Karen or Vincent needs to deal with is me falling apart.*

She glanced across the aisle to where Andrea sat talking to the gray-haired woman beside her. With the noise of the plane, Evelyn couldn't make out every word they were saying, but she figured their conversation was most likely centered around the topic of cats.

She looked over at Ray again, clearly engrossed in what looked like an action/adventure movie. *I may as well join him. It's either that or try to sleep.* Evelyn slipped her earbuds in and touched the screen to see what her options were. Maybe one of the movies would be good enough to hold her attention. If not, she would watch the flight tracker on the monitor. At least that would keep her in the know about how far they were from Minneapolis, where they'd board their next flight. Evelyn hoped that when they arrived in Boise, someone from Dave's family would be there to pick them up.

Chapter 15

Apple Creek

Brandon had just finished eating supper when his cell phone rang. He picked it up quickly and was pleased to see that the caller was Andrea. "Hey, sweetie, it's sure good to hear from you. Are you in Boise?" Brandon stood and carried his dirty dishes to the sink.

"Yes, we just landed and will soon be pulling up to the Jetway."

"Glad to hear. Were all the flights good?"

"For the most part. We had some turbulence on the flight from Minneapolis to Seattle, but it wasn't too bad."

"I've been praying for you, and I'm glad you made it there okay. I will be praying for you and your family tomorrow too, when you attend your uncle's funeral service."

"Thanks. Prayers are always appreciated." There was a brief pause. "I'd better go, Brandon. We're pulling up to the Jetway now."

"Okay. Take care, and remember how much I love you."

"Love you too. Bye for now."

When Brandon ended the call, he sat quietly at the table, thanking God for giving Andrea and her parents a safe trip. He missed her already and looked forward to seeing his beautiful, sweet fiancée in a few days. He was glad to be marrying a good person who cared deeply for her family.

Woof! Woof! Woof!

Brandon opened his eyes and looked down at his dog, staring up at him with his head cocked to one side. "That's one way to cut short a person's prayer time."

The dog barked again, a little louder this time, and raced over to the back door.

"What are you after, Duke? Do ya want some attention, or do you need to go outside?"

Arf! Arf!

"All righty then. I know exactly what you want now." Brandon got up from his chair and opened the back door. Duke zipped right out and into the yard. Brandon stood on the porch and leaned against the railing as he watched the dog. Duke occasionally got what some people called the *zoomies*, when he would run around excitedly for no obvious reason. Brandon figured Duke's sudden burst of energy might be his way of expressing how happy he was. Sometimes Duke would exhibit his zoomie behavior at certain times of the day, like after he'd eaten or been given a bath. The last thing Brandon needed was for his dog to reinjure his leg, so he watched him closely.

Duke made two circles around the backyard, sniffing the ground. He finally went to the area where there was no grass, which Brandon had taught the dog to use as his personal bathroom. A short time later, Duke was back up on the porch.

"Ready to go inside now, boy?"

Duke wagged his tail and let out a few arfs!

"Okay, you can keep me company while I do the dishes." Brandon opened the door and waited for Duke to go inside, then entered behind him.

Brandon went to the sink to rinse the dishes before putting them in the dishwasher. He'd attempted to make himself spaghetti, which hadn't turned out so well. Now Brandon had some tough cleanup to do. Since he'd overheated the sauce and scorched it, cleaning the pan would be a chore.

Guess that's what I get for leaving the sauce simmering on the stove and looking in on that movie on the television. If Andrea had been here for supper this evening, she would've kept a closer eye on the things cooking, and I wouldn't be working so hard right now to clean up this pan.

Duke stood beside him, pressing up against the lower part of Brandon's leg. From his knowledge of dogs and their body language, Brandon knew this behavior was one of the signs that his dog loved him. There were other things too that Duke did to show love, such as curling up close to Brandon when he was resting on the couch, jumping up in excitement whenever he walked in the door, rolling around on his back to get his belly scratched, resting his head on Brandon's lap, and licking Brandon's face and hands.

Brandon looked down at Duke and smiled. "You're a good dog, and I'm glad that you've accepted Lady and will be able to adapt when Andrea and her cat move into this house after we're married." He left the partially cleaned pan in the sink to soak some more in the warm soapy water. Then Brandon rinsed off the suds that clung to him and dried his hands. "I could use a little break from putting dishes in the dishwasher."

Duke's response was a little grunt as he dropped to the floor and rolled over with all four feet in the air.

Brandon laughed and rubbed Duke's belly with the toe of his sneaker. *The only thing that could make this evening nicer would be if Andrea was here beside me right now.*

⁓

Caldwell, Idaho

Clutching her mother's arm, with Dad on the other side doing the same, Andrea entered the chapel inside the funeral home. If ever there was a time that Mom needed her support, it was now. The poor thing was taking her brother's death pretty hard. Last night when they'd arrived, Vincent had picked them up at the airport in Boise. He'd looked tired but seemed to be handling things well. It was another story for Vincent's mother, whom they hadn't seen until they got to the house. Aunt Karen had sobbed when she'd talked to them about her husband's untimely death. While the grieving widow sat in the front row of the chapel now, her shoulders shook.

It was hard to watch Aunt Karen bearing through the pain of her loss. Andrea wished there was something to ease all the suffering she felt and help with her mother's sadness too.

Before the service began, Andrea prayed for Aunt Karen, her mom, and the rest of the family gathered there. While praying, she heard weeping from her aunt nearby. Mom also started crying again. Andrea opened her eyes and saw Dad's arm come around her mother's waist as he gave a needed hug. She looked about the room. A mixture of fresh, neatly arranged flowers up front softened the area near the casket.

Andrea's heart went out to Vincent as he sat with both hands resting against his forehead. Although she hadn't known her uncle well, she felt the heavy loss her cousin obviously felt.

An usher had seated Andrea and her parents in the front row, reserved for family members of the deceased. Since Uncle Dave's parents were no longer living and his only sibling was Andrea's mother, it was just Vincent, Aunt Karen, Andrea, and her parents sitting in the first row.

Andrea glanced at her cousin again, sitting right beside her, and drew in a slow breath. She couldn't help noticing the spicy aroma of Vincent's aftershave. It reminded her of Brandon and how nice he always smelled when they were together. It had only been two days since Andrea had seen Brandon, and already she missed him. She wondered what her future husband was doing right now while she sat here waiting for the service to get started. Andrea figured he'd most likely be at work taking care of someone's dog or cat.

It wasn't long before Andrea heard someone speaking in a low, soothing tone. Her attention was drawn to the front of the room, where a man wearing a black suit, who she assumed was the pastor, stood at a podium not far from the closed casket.

Several minutes passed, and then Andrea glanced over her shoulder. Nearly every chair in the room had been filled. Apparently Uncle Dave had been well known and liked by several in the community and his circle of friends.

An unexpected thought popped into Andrea's head. *When I'm gone someday, I wonder how many people will attend my funeral. Since I have no brothers or sisters, no nieces or nephews, and just one cousin, if my parents are no longer living by the time I die, it may only be a few friends, some church people, maybe a few piano students, and of course the dear man I will soon marry.*

Then another thought overtook her, so emotionally gripping that she had to choke back a sob. *What if Brandon should go before me?* The idea of becoming a widow, whether in the prime of her life or as a senior citizen, caused a deep ache to penetrate Andrea's soul. She loved Brandon so much and couldn't imagine her life without him. Their bond was strong, and Andrea felt sure that nothing short of death could ever keep them apart.

~

As the eulogy was read, Evelyn reached over and clasped her sister-in-law's trembling hand. *Poor Karen.* It was a good thing her son, Vincent, still lived at home and would be available to help her get through the lonely days ahead. Of course, friends and people from church would be near, but Evelyn felt that having a family member close by would offer the most comfort for Dave's widow.

Ray sat on the other side of Evelyn, and she looked over at him briefly. His expression was stoic, and she wondered if he might be having the same thoughts. *How would I feel if it were me sitting here today, after having lost my spouse?*

Death held a certain finality, yet for a believer in Christ, when a person's soul left the body, it was not the end. It was a comfort to know that when a Christian died, they became absent from the body but present with the Lord.

As the minister preached a message on the very things she'd been thinking, Evelyn reminded herself to stay in touch with Karen through notes of encouragement and phone calls. It was the least she could do, since once they returned home, she couldn't be here in person to offer comfort.

In need of a breath of fresh air, Andrea stepped out of her aunt's home and into the yard. A meal provided by some of the women from Karen's church had been served at the house after the funeral and graveside service. Most of the people who had come to eat and visit with the bereaved had gone home, but a few people still lingered inside.

The chilly autumn air blew leaves from the trees, and Andrea buttoned her jacket all the way up. It was surprisingly much colder here in Idaho than it had been when they'd left home in Ohio, and she half expected to see snow falling from the sky any minute. She looked up but saw only a star-studded sky on this clear moonlit evening.

"Mind if I join you, or would you rather be alone?"

Andrea turned at the sound of Vincent's deep voice. "I don't mind your company. I just needed to get out of the house for a while and enjoy the quiet and breathe in some fresh air."

"I know what you mean. That's why I came outside too." He leaned against the trunk of a stately pine tree. "So catch me up with what's new in your life."

"You may have heard that I'll be getting married in February."

"Yeah, my mom mentioned that. Guess your mother told my dad the last time they talked, and she passed the information along to me." Vincent took a step closer. "Congratulations. It's great that you've found someone you want to spend the rest of your life with." He dropped his gaze to the ground. "Wish I could say the same."

"There's no special woman in your life?"

"Not right now, but that's okay. I keep busy with other things." He rubbed the bridge of his nose. "Besides, my mom's gonna need me more than ever now."

Slowly Andrea nodded. "Yes, she will, but you need your own life too."

"I have a job, my music, and a hobby of carving duck decoys that keeps me busy."

"You manage a hardware store, right?"

"Yeah."

"What kind of music do you like?"

"Mostly country. That's what I play with my guitar, but I also enjoy gospel music."

"I teach piano lessons to several students, and I also earn some money selling some of my paintings." She smiled. "Since we're both musical, it seems like we have a few things in common."

"You're right, and since we're both adopted, we have that in common too."

Her brows furrowed. "Adopted?"

"Yeah, both of us, when we were babies."

"Who told you that? Where'd you get such an idea?" Andrea felt sure that Vincent had made this up. But the question was—why?

"My folks told me I was adopted as soon as I was able to understand. Didn't your parents tell you too?"

A wave of heat cascaded over Andrea's body, driving away the cold. "No, they did not, and it can't be true." She pointed a shaky finger at him. "Why would you say such a thing to me? If my parents had adopted me, surely they would have said so."

He cleared his throat. "Well, uh. . .maybe. . ."

Andrea placed both hands behind her back, gripping one wrist tightly with the other hand. "Why would they have kept such a thing from me all these years?" She heard the tension in her own voice.

"I—I don't know. Maybe you should ask them since they're the ones who kept the truth from you for so long." Vincent shook his head. "Unbelievable. It is unbelievable."

Andrea bit the inside of her cheek. She had no choice but to confront them and find out the truth, but here, in the center of all this grief, might not be the best time. She would wait to talk to her parents until they were back in Ohio. If what her cousin had told her was the truth, then she would at least have the support of her fiancé to help her deal with this unexpected, shocking revelation.

Chapter 16

"Aren't you going to eat something for breakfast?" Evelyn asked her daughter after everyone had gathered around the table the following morning.

Avoiding eye contact, Andrea shook her head. "I'm not hungry, so I'll just have a cup of coffee."

Evelyn took a seat, wondering what was up with her daughter. *Did I or someone else in the house say something to make Andrea upset? Maybe she's not feeling well this morning and is keeping it to herself, but I will try again, because I'd like to know what's going on.*

"You really should have something to eat. Coffee alone might make you jittery, and a little protein or even some carbs will do the opposite." Evelyn gestured to the stack of toast she had put on the table along with some boiled eggs.

"I'll be fine with coffee, and I'll take it outside." Andrea kept her gaze on the table.

The sharp tone in Andrea's voice and her lack of eye contact were good indications that she was upset about something. She sat watching her daughter and thinking.

"But it's cold out there," Aunt Karen spoke up. "Wouldn't you rather stay in here and visit with us where it's nice and warm?"

Andrea's lips might be pursed, but at least she looked directly at her aunt, unlike her avoidance of me. Evelyn cringed. *Have I said or done something to irritate her? Could it be my comment about Andrea needing to eat something for breakfast?*

Before Evelyn had the chance to say anything more, Andrea pushed back her chair and got up from the table. "I appreciate everyone's concerns, but I only want coffee, and I'd prefer to drink it outside." She rushed out of the room before anyone could respond.

At the moment, Evelyn wished that she could also leave the room, but that would be impolite. She was embarrassed by her daughter's abrupt and strange behavior. *What caused Andrea to act that way?* Evelyn wondered. *I can't believe she would be so rude.*

Evelyn looked over at Karen and placed a hand on her arm. "I apologize for my daughter's abruptness. She's not normally like this, and I can't imagine what has come over Andrea this morning."

"It's okay," Karen responded. "Yesterday took a toll on all of us, and I think everyone's on edge."

"I'll talk to her." Vincent grabbed a piece of toast and quickly departed the room.

Evelyn hoped Andrea's cousin could help out in some way. Ray had stepped out to use the restroom, so he'd missed all the action. She wondered what his thoughts would be on this.

~

Andrea took a seat on the front porch, holding her steaming cup of coffee in both hands for the warmth. Aunt Karen had been right, it was a cold day. Even with her jacket on and buttoned all the way up, Andrea felt the frigid temperature seeping in. But worse than the cold air were the unanswered questions. *Am I really adopted? But why would my birth parents, if this is true, hand me off to complete strangers?*

She'd only been sitting there a few seconds when Vincent showed up. "Mind if I join you?" he asked in a muffled tone around the piece of toast as he ate.

Still upset, she looked over at him and mimicked his full mouth as she said: "What did you say?"

He blinked as though in surprise. "I'm sorry. Where are my manners? I said, 'Mind if I join you?'"

"No. Actually, I should be the one apologizing. I'm upset with my mom and took it out on you. I'm sorry, Vincent."

"It's okay. Yesterday was rough—especially for my mom, and my dad's funeral affected each of us in some way."

"I owe your mother an apology for dashing out of the house like I did."

"I'm sure she wasn't offended. Mom's emotions are so raw, she may not have even noticed what you said or did."

"Whether she noticed or not, I still need to tell her I'm sorry." Andrea shivered despite being bundled in a fleeced jacket. "It's pretty cold out here. You might want to put a jacket on."

He rubbed the arms of his red-and-black checked flannel shirt. "Naw, I'm fine. Truth is, I like this brisk kind of weather. It's a pleasant change from the dry hot days we often get during the summer months."

"Do you get much rain in this part of Idaho?" she asked.

"Some but not a lot. Nothing like they get on the west side of Oregon and Washington." He cleared his throat a couple of times. "Listen, about last night. . . I'm sorry for what I blurted out, but I really thought you knew that you'd been adopted."

The sound of the word *adopted* didn't sit well with Andrea. Not to mention that dealing with the shocking news had made her night miserable. While sleep had eluded her, she hadn't known what to think—one moment believing what Vincent had said and the next denying the words of her cousin and clinging to the hope that he was wrong.

Andrea gripped her mug a little tighter. "I had no idea, and I still can't believe it's true."

"Well, it must be. Like I said last night, I've heard my folks talk about it."

Andrea sat perfectly still, staring up at the gray-colored sky. Until she heard it from her parents' lips, she could not allow herself to believe what Vincent told her was factual. It just didn't seem possible.

"Have you talked yet to your mom or dad about what I said?"

She shook her head. "I thought it might be best to wait until we get back to Ohio, but maybe that's a mistake."

Vincent placed his hand on her shoulder and gave it a tender squeeze. "I agree. I think it would be best to get this out in the open once and for all. Otherwise, you'll probably be fretting about it all the way home tomorrow."

Andrea contemplated his words and stood. "You're right, Vincent. I'm going back in the kitchen right now and confront my parents about this matter. If I was adopted, they have some explaining to do."

~

When Andrea entered the warm kitchen, where the odor of coffee, toast, and eggs greeted her, she found Mom, Dad, and Aunt Karen still at the table. From the looks of the bowl of boiled eggs and plate full of toast, it didn't appear as if much had been eaten. Perhaps the grief they felt over losing Uncle Dave had diminished their appetites.

Andrea figured it wouldn't be good to blurt out the question she'd come here to ask in front of her aunt, so after she apologized to Aunt Karen for her abrupt departure, she looked at her father and asked, "Could I talk to you and Mom alone for a few minutes?"

He glanced at Andrea's mother, and when she nodded, Dad looked back at Andrea. "Certainly. Should we go to the living room?"

"That's fine." Andrea led the way but not before she gave a quick look in Aunt Karen's direction. The poor woman's eyes were red from crying so much the day before, and her lips were pressed firmly together as though she was trying to hold it together. The last thing the grieving woman needed was to witness their discussion, which could end up with some heated words.

In the living room, Andrea took a seat in the rocking chair, and her parents sat next to each other on the couch.

"There's no easy way to ask this question," she said, leaning slightly forward. "So I may as well spit it right out."

Mom sat up a little straighter. "What do you want to ask?"

"Was I adopted?"

With jerky motions, Andrea's father rubbed the back of his neck, and her mother drew in a series of short breaths as though she needed more oxygen.

"Was I adopted or not?" Her voice had risen, but it was too late to lower it now.

"Yes, you were." Dad's face turned as red as a springtime radish.

Andrea bit her lip until she tasted blood. "Then Vincent was right when he told me last night that something we had in common was the fact that we both had been adopted."

Mom's cheeks had become flushed too, and the skin around her eyes had tightened. "You were just a day old when we got you."

Andrea got up from her chair and moved over to stand in front of them. "Why did you keep this from me? Didn't you think I had the right to know?" It became increasingly difficult for her not to shout.

"Of course we did," Mom said tearfully. "We just could never find the right time or the right words to tell you about it." She lifted her hands and then let them fall into her lap.

"That's right." Dad's eyes darkened. "The longer we waited, the harder it became."

"So you allowed me to believe your deceptions because there was never a good time to tell me the truth?" Andrea's jaw clenched as she folded her arms firmly across her chest in an attempt to control the anger she felt bubbling in her soul. In all her thirty-two years, she'd never felt this frustrated with the parents who had raised her. *But they aren't my biological parents*, she thought with regret. Andrea lowered her gaze. *How could they have done this to me?*

"Please hear us out." Her mother's chin quivered as she laid a hand across her breastbone. "We'd like the opportunity to explain the situation more fully."

"I believe I've heard enough for now." Andrea turned and started for the front door.

"Where are you going?" Dad called out.

"I need to make a phone call, and then I'm going to pack. It's time for me to go home."

"Right now?" Mom's question was barely a squeak.

"Yes, if I can get a flight." Andrea turned and raced out the front door.

On the porch, she took a seat and pulled her cell phone from her jacket pocket. Although it was a weekday and Brandon would no doubt be at the clinic, she took a chance and called his number anyway. When he didn't pick up, Andrea left a message. "Hi, Brandon, it's me. If I can get a flight, I'll be coming home later today. If none are available, then it will be the day after tomorrow, as I'd told you before. Something's happened that has me pretty upset, and I need to be with you as soon as possible. I'll call you again and let you know if I was able to get an earlier flight. Otherwise, I'll see you two days from now as planned." Andrea's voice cracked. "I—I love you, Brandon. That's the only thing I'm sure of right now."

~

Apple Creek

At noon, when Brandon took his lunch break, he checked phone messages and found one from Andrea. After listening to what she'd said, Brandon put down his cell phone and leaned forward, resting both arms on his desk. *I hope she's okay. She sounded upset. I wish Andrea had explained why she wants to come home two days sooner than planned. I should give her a call right now.*

Brandon glanced at his phone and noticed that he'd received a text from Andrea, which had come in half an hour ago. He clicked on it and read her message: Couldn't get a flight today. No need to call. I'll see you at the airport when you pick us up the day after tomorrow.

That's odd. Why wouldn't she want me to call her back? And what happened that made Andrea want to come home today? I hope it's nothing serious.

Tap! Tap! Tap! A knock sounded on Brandon's office door.

"Come in," he called.

"I'm sorry to interrupt your lunch, Dr. Prentice, but a man just came in with a dog that needs immediate attention." Fran, his assistant, frowned. "Apparently, the poor animal got in a fight with another dog, and it looks like he's lost a lot of blood. The dog and his owner are in the first examining room."

Brandon snapped his lunch box shut and stood. "I'll be right there." For the time being, he needed to set his concerns for Andrea aside and concentrate on the emergency at hand. When he picked Andrea and her parents up at the airport at the expected time, he would find out what was going on.

Caldwell

Evelyn had watched their daughter walk straight out the door, and she could do nothing to stop her. "Oh, Ray, we've made a big mistake by not telling Andrea that she was adopted. She was really upset, and I'm afraid she might never forgive us for withholding the truth about her adoption." Evelyn grasped her husband's arm.

"I've often wondered when or if this might all come out. To tell you the truth, I'm glad the matter of Andrea's adoption is no longer hidden."

"Seriously? Even with the way she's acting toward us?"

He reached over and took hold of her hand. "She won't stay mad, Evelyn. Our daughter has a forgiving spirit, and once she's had time to deal with the information, she'll calm down and realize how much we love her. She's bound to know that we did what we felt was best and certainly didn't mean to hurt her."

"I hope you're right. To be honest, it is good to have the burden of the secret we've kept far too long finally lifted." Evelyn sniffed deeply. "I hope you are right, Ray, because if you're not, I fear the wonderful relationship we've established with Andrea might be over."

He shook his head. "I think you're worried about nothing, dear.

Our daughter loves us, and she'd never turn her back on the parents who raised her."

A lump formed in Evelyn's throat, making it difficult to swallow. "I'm not so sure about that. Didn't you see the look of betrayal on our daughter's face when we admitted that she was adopted?"

"I saw her expression, but I think it revealed more confusion and hurt than betrayal." Ray gave her fingers a gentle squeeze. "Everything will be fine. You'll see. We just need to pray and ask God to work this all out."

Evelyn felt helpless and was unsure of how to fix the mess they'd created by putting off being honest with their daughter. She tried to put herself in Andrea's shoes. *If my folks had done something like this to me, I'd be pretty upset—especially when you count on your parents to be honest and trustworthy.* Evelyn dabbed at her eyes. *I will pray, but it won't stop me from being concerned. If we lose our daughter over this, I'll never forgive myself.*

Chapter 17

Boise

After a tearful goodbye with Aunt Karen and Vincent, Andrea followed her parents through the TSA line and placed her carry-on items on the conveyor belt. She was exhausted, and her throat hurt from crying so much. It still didn't seem possible that she'd been adopted. Andrea had felt disoriented ever since her parents had admitted the truth. It was as though she didn't know who she was anymore.

It had been difficult to engage in conversation with Mom and Dad since learning that she'd been adopted. Even now, as Andrea sat across from her parents waiting to board their plane for Seattle, Andrea chose to remain quiet. She needed time to think it all through before asking them more questions that had been floating through her mind. What city and state was she born in? Did they know who her biological parents were or where they lived?

Do I even want to know the answers to those questions? Andrea asked herself. *If I learn who the woman who gave birth to me is, should I try to contact her?* Andrea massaged her throbbing forehead. *I wonder if Vincent has tried to contact his biological parents. I should have thought to ask.*

She pulled out her cell phone, and sent her cousin a text message. A few minutes later, he responded. No, I've never felt the need to seek out my biological mother or father. I've always felt that the parents who raised me were my real mom and dad, and that's been enough for me.

Andrea wasn't sure how to respond to that, so she texted him back with a few simple words: TAKE CARE, VINCENT. WE'LL LET YOU KNOW WHEN WE GET HOME. She paused and added one more thing: I'LL KEEP YOU AND YOUR MOTHER IN MY PRAYERS AS YOU DEAL WITH THE LOSS OF YOUR DAD.

Vincent's text was a thank-you, followed by: I'M PRAYING FOR YOU AND YOUR FOLKS TOO. I FEEL BAD THAT I GAVE YOU THE NEWS OF YOUR ADOPTION. PLEASE GIVE YOURSELF SOME TIME BEFORE DECIDING ON WHETHER TO SEARCH FOR YOUR BIOLOGICAL PARENTS OR NOT.

She swallowed around the thickness in her throat. Part of Andrea wanted to know who had given birth to her, but the thought of finding out was frightening too. Besides, at this point she didn't even know where to begin.

"We will begin boarding at this time, starting with those passengers who need a little extra time getting down the Jetway, followed by first class." The voice behind the loudspeaker drove Andrea's thoughts aside.

She told Vincent goodbye, and after all the preboarders had shown their boarding passes and started down the Jetway, Andrea boarded the plane behind her parents. They were in the bulkhead seats on the right side of the plane this time, but Andrea's seat was two rows back, on the left side. She would be sitting next to a stranger again, but that didn't matter. She would watch a movie and, with any luck, drown out all thoughts about her adoption.

Walnut Creek

"Today was a good day, *jah*?" Orley asked after he'd joined Lois on the back seat of their driver's van.

She smiled and nodded in response.

"Weren't you surprised at how many people came into our store?"

"We did have more than usual, but that's probably because of all the activities going on in our area right now. Fall is always a busy time of the year." Lois shifted on the seat and reached around to rub a sore spot on her back.

"Are you hurting?" Orley reached over to touch her arm.

"It's nothing serious. As you know, my back always tightens up if I'm on my feet too long."

"Jah, mine too," Orley responded. "But I can't complain. We sold a lot of merchandise today, and I was able to talk to that one English man who'd been struggling with his faith in God since his wife died."

"It was good he came in during a time when there were no other customers. Otherwise, you wouldn't have been able to talk privately with him."

"True."

"I'm sure a lot of business at our store will be for gift giving, since Christmas is on its way," Lois responded.

"You're right about that," their driver, Todd, spoke up. "Seems like this year Christmas decorations were up in other stores before Halloween was even over. What's up with that?"

"I have no idea," Orley said. "It's funny, though, how some folks want to move on so fast instead of enjoying the time that is right before them."

"I suppose it might be that some people are just too impatient," Lois interjected.

"It's true," Orley agreed. "A lot of people are in a hurry and are quite unhappy, especially when they have to wait for anything. For example: driving behind our buggies seems to bring out some impatient drivers, and some end up doing something foolhardy as they hurry down the road. In my opinion, our slow mode of transportation is nice and can help a person to unwind, refocus, and enjoy living more simply."

"I have to agree." Todd glanced over his shoulder briefly, then looked back toward the road. A few minutes later, he drove the van up Orley and Lois's driveway and shut off the engine.

"I'll go in the house and get supper started while you're paying for our ride," Lois said when she and Orley stepped out of the vehicle.

"Okay. Since we're both tired, let's keep things simple and have leftover soup and sandwiches."

"Good idea. *Danki* for the suggestion."

Lois made her way toward the house but stopped short when she reached the front lawn, where several letters and magazines had been scattered. "For goodness' sakes!" Although her back hurt more than it had on the ride home, she bent down and picked up each of the items. *I wonder why this stuff was not put in our mailbox, and how did it end up in the yard? We must have had some strong winds here today to blow it all over like that.*

Lois stepped onto the front porch and was surprised to see a few more pieces of mail along with a package. She entered the house and placed the mail that she had picked up on the entry table, then went back out to get the package and rest of the mail on the porch.

When she reentered the house, Lois gathered up the package and all of the mail and placed everything on the kitchen table. Preparing to open the package first, she looked at the return address and realized it was from her sister Rebekah. Curious as to what could be inside, Lois quickly opened the package. Inside, she discovered several handmade dish towels, two jars of apple butter that had been protected with bubble wrap, and a business-sized white envelope with a sticky note attached to the outside. It read: *I found this envelope inside our daed's Biewel, and since it had your name on it, I figured I should send it to you right away.*

I wonder why Dad would write my name on an envelope and put it inside his Bible. Lois took a seat at the table and tore the envelope open. Tears welled in her eyes as she read out loud what her father had written:

> *Dear Lois,*
> *Someday when I'm gone, I hope you will find this*

letter inside my Bible and have a better understanding of my actions toward you during the time you lived under my roof. After your mamm *died, I put more responsibility on you as the oldest daughter. In addition to needing your help, I expected you to behave a certain way, but you were often rebellious. I spoke to you harshly sometimes, which I'm sure put a distance between us that has remained to this day. I want you to know that I'm sorry for not being the kind of father you needed, and I hope you will find it in your heart to forgive me for every poor decision I made in regard to you. Please know that I have always loved you, even though I didn't show it in the best way.*

With all sincerity,
Daed

Lois blinked as tears escaped her lashes and rolled down her hot cheeks. *Oh, Daed, I wish you were still alive so I could say to your face that I have forgiven you. The past is in the past, and it can't be changed, and even though I didn't agree with some of the decisions you made, I have always loved you. Oh, how I wish that I could tell you that. If only I'd had the chance to be with you prior to your heart attack, but unfortunately, I waited too long. You may not have even heard the words I spoke to you before your death.*

She sat several minutes, holding her father's letter, until the tears finally stopped. It was time to dry her eyes and take yesterday's soup from the refrigerator so it would be heated by the time Orley came inside.

Cleveland

Brandon stood in the baggage claim area, waiting for Andrea and her parents to arrive. He knew their plane had landed because she'd texted him a few minutes ago. He was excited to see her and still curious as to why she'd wanted to fly home the day after her uncle's funeral. *I wonder if her folks had also wanted to leave Idaho a day early. Guess I'll know soon enough.*

Brandon kept watch for passengers beginning to enter the baggage claim. No luggage had shown up on the conveyer belt yet, but it usually took anywhere from fifteen to twenty minutes for the luggage to arrive. Some travelers who'd been waiting near a different conveyor belt nearby hustled to grab their bags from a previous flight. Brandon glanced at them as his anticipation mounted for his future family to appear.

He was on the verge of pacing when several people pulling their carry-on bags entered the area. With heart pounding, he stood watching until Andrea and her parents came into view. Andrea walked ahead, while Ray and Evelyn, moving slowly, lagged behind. No doubt they were tired from the long day of travel, not to mention the stress and sorrow of attending Andrea's uncle's funeral, and the two days afterward.

As Andrea drew closer, Brandon smiled and waved.

Releasing what sounded like an uncontrolled sob, she ran and practically threw herself into his arms. As her sobs increased, he rubbed the small of her back. "What's wrong, Andrea? Surely you're not crying because you missed me so much after only being gone a few days."

"I—I did miss you, but my tears are for a different reason, which I can't talk about right now," Andrea whispered as she glanced over her shoulder in the direction of her parents.

"All right then, we can talk on the way to your house after I drop your mom and dad off at their place."

Andrea nodded, and as her parents approached, she moved over to the conveyor belt where the luggage had started to come down.

Brandon greeted Evelyn and Ray and said he would get their luggage.

"We just have one suitcase between us," Ray responded. "I can get that while you fetch Andrea's."

"Okay." Brandon looked at Evelyn and saw that her eyes were red.

No doubt, she too had been crying. Was it because of her brother's death, or had something else caused Evelyn and Andrea's tears?

～

Apple Creek

After Brandon dropped Andrea's parents off at their home, Andrea pushed hard against the back of her seat and released a heavy sigh. It would be a relief to get home to her own place, where she wouldn't feel obligated to make idle conversation with her parents or fight the need to ask for more information about her adoption. She still hadn't decided what the best approach to this whole situation should be and needed more time to think about it.

As he pulled out of her parents' driveway and onto the road, Brandon reached across the seat and placed his hand on Andrea's arm. "Are you going to tell me what's going on now? Have you and your parents had some sort of falling out?"

"I guess you could call it that." Andrea clutched her purse straps so tight that it caused her fingers to ache. "The evening of my uncle's funeral, my cousin, Vincent, informed me that I had been adopted."

"Seriously? And you had no prior knowledge of that?"

"None whatsoever. I grew up believing the people I have called Mom and Dad were my biological parents." Andrea released her purse straps and locked her hands into fists. "You can imagine how shocked I was to learn that all these years my parents have been lying to me."

"Did you tell them that your cousin told you about it?" he asked.

"Yes, but I waited until the next morning to confront them, and I believe they were equally shocked to learn that I knew the truth about their deception." She paused and drew a few short breaths in through her mouth. "Not only was it a shock to learn that I was adopted, but my parents' deception has caused me not to trust them now. I mean, if they would withhold the truth about my adoption, what else haven't they told me?"

"Did they offer an explanation as to why they had kept your adoption a secret?"

"Mom said they couldn't find the right time or words to tell me. My dad said the longer they waited, the harder it became." Andrea groaned. "What lame excuses. They had plenty of time and opportunities."

"Maybe when you were a child they felt like you weren't ready to hear that you'd been adopted."

"Are you defending them now?"

"No, of course not. I'm just thinking maybe you should try to understand."

"I understand all right. Two people I have loved and trusted since I was a baby didn't care enough about me to tell the truth. My cousin said he's known that he was adopted since he was a child."

"It would probably have been better if they'd told you sooner, but—"

"Can we not talk about this anymore? I just want to go home and get a good night's sleep so I can get up early tomorrow and go over to Colleen's to pick up Lady. I'm sure she's missed me while I've been gone."

"Okay, I understand. I'll drop you off, and we can talk again tomorrow." He touched her arm again. "Andrea?"

"Yeah?"

"Please remember that I love you very much, and I'm here for you when you're ready to talk more about this."

Andrea sagged against her seat. "Thanks, I appreciate that." It was good to know that she had her future husband's support, and tomorrow, when she told Colleen about her adoption, she felt sure that she would have her support as well.

She closed her eyes tightly, trying to keep tears from falling. *Now I just need to decide what my next step regarding all of this should be.*

Chapter 18

The following day, Andrea was up bright and early, eager to head for Colleen's to pick up Lady. Andrea hoped that getting back into her routine of painting, teaching piano lessons, and taking care of her house and cat would help get her mind off the fact that she had been adopted and was never told about it by her adoptive parents. If it weren't for Vincent, she would still be living in total unawareness of the truth. She had to wonder whether Dad and Mom would have waited indefinitely to confess the matter if the truth hadn't come out unexpectedly. Most likely, her folks would've said nothing and continued to live as though Andrea's adoption had never taken place.

She picked up her coffee cup and took a couple sips. *When I put myself in my mother's shoes, I feel certain that I would have told my child the truth. It's not fair to be my age and find out that I'm not really their biological daughter.* The whole thing hung over Andrea like a dark cloud about to burst open. If she had been informed of this when she was a child, she would have come to grips with it by now and might even have contacted her biological parents.

Andrea stared at her unappealing, mushy bowl of cereal and plucked a few frozen blueberries out of the bowl. *Maybe Colleen will have an idea about what I should do. She's not close to the situation, so her thinking will be much clearer than mine is right now. I'm sure that Colleen will be understanding and give me total support concerning my frustrating situation.* Andrea drank a few more swallows of coffee. *I'll need to do more praying, asking the Lord to give me wisdom in mending my relationship with my parents—especially since I'm hardly speaking to them at this point.*

Andrea's cell phone vibrated, and she picked it up to see who had called or sent her a text. Seeing that it was a text from Vincent, asking if she and her parents had gotten home okay, she slapped a hand against her forehead. *Oh great. I can't believe I forgot to let him know last night. It may have been late here, but Idaho is two hours behind Ohio, so I wouldn't have disturbed him by calling or sending a text.* The fact was Andrea's fatigue, coupled with the stress she felt, was the reason she'd forgotten to let him know. Hopefully, her mother had contacted Aunt Karen. *But if she did, then why is Vincent texting me now?*

Andrea responded to him: WE MADE IT BACK SAFELY, BUT IT WAS LATE WHEN WE GOT HOME. SORRY, I SHOULD HAVE LET YOU KNOW SOONER.

Another message came back: GLAD TO HEAR IT. TAKE CARE, AND LET'S STAY IN TOUCH.

YES, DEFINITELY. PLEASE LET AUNT KAREN KNOW WE MADE IT HOME TOO.

WILL DO.

After Vincent's last message, Andrea slipped the phone into her purse and cleared her dishes. She flushed the cereal down the disposal, but she managed to drink the rest of her lukewarm coffee before heading out the door.

⁓

"How was your trip?" Colleen asked after Andrea had entered her house and given her friend a hug.

"Sad, tiresome, and emotionally draining." Andrea poked her tongue against the inside of her cheek while exhaling.

"That makes sense. The death of a loved one is always difficult, not to mention the fatigue of traveling that far with a two-hour time change. You must be exhausted."

"Yeah."

Colleen gestured to the living room. "Let's go in there and take a seat. Hopefully, we'll have a few minutes to visit before my rambunctious two-year-old gets up."

Andrea followed her friend into the other room and collapsed on the couch. "Where's Lady? Is she hiding out somewhere?"

Colleen shook her head. "The last time I looked, she was asleep on Tyler's bed."

Andrea rolled her eyes. "That figures. I leave my cat for just a few days and already she's forgotten about me and has become your son's best friend."

"Oh, she missed you all right. The first twenty-four hours you were gone, Lady hid under Tyler's bed. I tried coaxing her out with food, and so did Shawn, but all we got out of her was a fierce-sounding *meow*. It took our little boy crawling under the bed with Lady to get her out." Colleen laughed. "They've been best buddies ever since."

Andrea smiled. "When I take Lady home, you may have to get a cat of your own so Tyler won't miss her so much."

"Maybe when he's a bit older and can help take care of a pet." Colleen brushed an unruly strand of hair away from her face. "I pretty much took care of all your cat's needs."

"Thank you for that." Andrea looked down at her hands, clasped tightly in her lap. "I need to tell you something." She lifted her gaze. "Needless to say, I was totally shocked when I found out this news."

"You look so serious. Is anything wrong?"

Andrea nodded. "The night of my uncle's funeral, I found out that I'd been adopted. My cousin, Vincent, let the cat out of the bag."

Colleen's eyes widened. "Are you serious?"

"Couldn't be more. I confronted my parents about it the next morning, and they admitted that they'd adopted me when I was a baby."

A little gasp came out of Colleen's mouth. "And this was the first time you knew anything about it?"

"That's right. They've been lying to me all these years." With both arms held firmly across her stomach, Andrea leaned forward. "You can only imagine how shocked I was—and still am, for that matter."

"I'm sorry, Andrea." Colleen patted her back and then spoke in a much-needed sympathetic tone. "Did your folks explain why they'd never told you about the adoption?"

"Their excuse was that they'd never found the right time or words to say it, and the longer they waited, the harder it became." Andrea looked upward, despairingly shaking her head. "I feel as though my identity has been taken from me, and I don't really know who I am anymore." Her eyes stung with unshed tears. "I can't help feeling betrayed by the parents who raised me. I'm upset by the fact that they kept something so important from me."

"I'm so sorry you've had to deal with this." Colleen's words were spoken in a gentle, soothing tone.

A few tears rolled down Andrea's cheeks. "How could so-called loving parents keep such a secret for so long from someone they claimed to love? Isn't love supposed to be based on respect, honesty, and trust?"

"Yes, but sometimes well-meaning people do things without thinking it through properly. Your parents may have thought they were doing you a favor by keeping your adoption from you."

Andrea's toes curled inside of her shoes. "Humph! It was no favor to me. How could it be, Colleen? In addition to feeling betrayed, I don't know who I am anymore."

"What are you going to do now? Will you try to find your biological parents?"

"I—I don't know. I haven't had time to think it through."

Colleen opened her mouth as if to say something more, when Tyler plodded into the room with Lady in his arms. When the cat spotted Andrea, it jumped down and leaped onto her lap. After a thorough licking of Andrea's hands, arms, and chin, Lady pushed against her and began to purr.

"You missed me, didn't you, girl?" Andrea stroked the cat's silky head. "I missed you too."

The fluffy animal finally settled down in her lap while continuing to purr. Andrea felt loved by her cat's affection, and it made her situation feel a bit more bearable.

Tyler plodded over to the couch and climbed up beside Andrea. Then he reached over and ran his hand down Lady's back. "Kitty cat."

She smiled and nodded. "It's nice to see you, little man. I hear that you liked having my cat around."

Tyler grinned before leaning his head against Andrea's arm and continuing to pet Lady.

"Let me get Tyler some breakfast, and then I'll be back so we can talk some more," Colleen said as she fussed with the barrette in her curly blond hair. "I have some coffee made. Would you like a cup?"

"That would be nice, but I really need to get home. I have a piano lesson to teach at noon and a few other things to get done before Brandon comes by this evening."

"I understand. Maybe we can have lunch together someday soon. You choose the place, and I'll buy."

"That'd be nice. I'll call you tomorrow, and we can set up a day." Andrea picked Lady up and stood. "I'll follow you to the kitchen to get Lady's carrier and food, and then I'll be on my way."

They all headed for the kitchen. After Andrea put Lady in her carrier, Colleen snapped her fingers and said, "Say, I have an idea."

Andrea tipped her head. "What's that?"

"Since you're struggling with this whole adoption thing, why don't you write a letter to the Dear Caroline newspaper column? Whoever the author is, she seems to have some pretty good advice."

Andrea gave a small laugh. "You really think I want to talk to some stranger about this?"

"You wouldn't be talking to her. It's just a letter, signed anonymously."

"Yeah, maybe. I'll think about it." Andrea moved toward the

door. "Again, thanks for watching Lady. Whenever you need a sitter for Tyler, I'll return the favor."

Colleen's eyes brightened. "I might take you up on that offer."

Andrea grinned and headed out the door. At least some things in her life hadn't changed, such as the moral support and encouragement she'd received from her good friend.

~

Evelyn picked up the phone and dialed her sister-in-law's number. Karen answered on the second ring.

"Good morning, Karen. I hope I didn't wake you."

"No, I've been up for hours, looking for things to keep me busy. If my hands are occupied, then my brain doesn't have to work so hard."

"I understand." Evelyn paused and drank some of her mint-flavored herbal tea. "The reason I called is two-fold. One, to let you know that we made it home okay, and two—to find out how you are doing."

"Yes, I heard from Vincent that you made it safely home. I guess he and Andrea had texted each other earlier this morning. And to respond to your second reason for calling—I'm doing as well as can be expected under the circumstances."

"I can't pretend to know what you're going through because I haven't lost my husband. However, I can relate to your pain in that I'm grieving the loss of my brother."

"Yes, I understand you two were quite close when you were children."

"We were, but we kind of grew apart after he left home and moved to Idaho."

"It's difficult to be away from family when you are miles apart, but I'm glad we can keep in touch via phone calls and visits in person whenever possible."

"True." Evelyn toyed with the idea of bringing up the situation with Andrea finding out about her adoption but figured Karen had enough to deal with right now and didn't need to hear her frustrations over the way Andrea had responded to her and Ray since she had learned the truth. This, in addition to the sadness Evelyn felt over losing Dave, was almost too much to bear. But with God's help and Ray's support, she would somehow get through it. All Evelyn could do at this point was pray for Andrea and hope that she would forgive them. Her desire was that their relationship could be restored and ultimately become stronger. If not, Evelyn didn't know what she would do, because she loved Andrea so much and couldn't imagine being estranged from her indefinitely.

Brandon glanced over at Duke sitting on the seat next to him and smiled. They were on their way to Andrea's place, and Brandon had picked up some burgers and fries for supper. Although it wasn't the healthiest meal, he looked forward to spending the evening with his future wife and hoped that his dog would get along with her cat. Since the animals hadn't been together for several days, it was possible that Duke might revert to being skittish around the cat.

"We'll know soon enough, buddy." Brandon reached across the seat and gave his dog's head a pat. Duke responded with a loud *Woof!*

A short time later, Brandon pulled his rig onto Andrea's driveway, turned off the engine, got out, and reached in the back seat for the takeout bag. Duke bounded out after him and made a dash for the front porch, barking all the way. Brandon took it as a good sign that the dog was eager to be here. The question was, had the excitement been about seeing Andrea or was it regarding her cat?

Brandon was about to knock when Andrea opened the door. "Ah, so that's the barking I heard." She pointed to his dog. "I see you brought Duke along."

"Yeah. Besides the fact that he started carrying on as soon as he saw me getting ready to leave the house, I figured it would be good to see if Duke and Lady will still get along."

"Good idea."

He stepped inside the house and handed her the sack. "Should we eat these burgers while they're still warm?"

"Of course."

Brandon noticed Andrea's quieter-than-normal demeanor. She hadn't even given him her usual welcoming smile. Was she still upset over her uncle's passing, or did it have more to do with the news she had received about having been adopted?

As Andrea and Brandon ate the burgers, fries, and cut-up veggies she'd contributed to the meal, she watched Duke and Lady lying side by side across the room. What a difference from the days when the poor dog trembled and hid at the mere sight of her cat. It seemed like a miracle that the cat and dog had not only been getting along but seemed like good friends.

"How did your day go?" Brandon asked. "Did you have any piano lessons to teach?"

"Just one, and it went okay." Andrea drank some of her cold apple cider.

"That's good. Did you talk to either of your parents?"

"No, and frankly, I dread seeing them at church this Sunday because I don't even know what to say."

Brandon reached for a few more fries and a couple of sliced cucumbers and carrots. "I assume you're still upset because they kept your adoption a secret from you."

"Of course I'm upset. If you were in my place, wouldn't you be?"

"I suppose, but—"

"When I went over to pick up Lady at Colleen's today, she gave me some food for thought."

"What was that?"

"Since I can't make up my mind what to do about all of this, Colleen suggested that I write a letter to Dear Caroline."

Brandon's forehead wrinkled. "Who's that? Don't think you've ever mentioned anyone by that name before."

"I doubt that it's her real name, but she uses it for the newspaper column she writes."

"Newspaper column?"

"Yes, people write to her with their problems, and she offers them advice."

He lifted his gaze to the ceiling. "I hope you're not actually considering that."

She shrugged. "I don't see how it could hurt. Maybe Dear Caroline will have some words of wisdom for me."

Brandon's neck bent forward, then stiffened back up. "You can do whatever you want, Andrea, but I think it's a dumb idea."

Andrea made no comment, but she wasn't about to admit to Brandon that tomorrow morning she planned to pen a letter to Dear Caroline regardless of what he thought.

Chapter 19

Walnut Creek

Lois stepped into the living room, where Orley sat reading the newspaper. "Sorry to interrupt, but I forgot to remind you about the errands we need to run tomorrow before heading to Memory Keepers, so we'll need to get an earlier start."

He looked up from the paper and smiled. "No problem. I remembered, and I'll make sure to set the alarm by my side of the bed so we can be up early, eat breakfast, and be ready in plenty of time before our driver gets here."

She pursed her lips. "I wish we had a place for the horse behind our store so we could take the horse and buggy instead of paying a driver to take us to work when it's too cold to ride our bikes."

"That would be nice, but there's no room for a barn there, and we can't leave the poor animal tied to a hitching post all day."

"True." Sometimes Lois wished their place of business was closer to home or even on the same property so that getting to and from work wasn't an issue.

"Do you think you'll have time on our day off this week to fix that leaking gutter near our front door?" Lois asked, changing the subject. It frustrated her when it rained and she sometimes got soaked by the stream of water that poured from that spot.

"Yep, but I think I'm going to need a part from the hardware store, unless I've got what I need in the barn to fix it. I'll check in the morning."

"Danki." Lois smiled. "I need to answer a couple of letters for my column now, so I'll let you get back to reading the paper."

"All righty then."

Lois returned to the kitchen and sat down at the table to read the letters she'd recently received for her Dear Caroline column. Some were about problems encountered with friends, relatives, or neighbors. One in particular had caught Lois's attention because, as she read the letter out loud, she could almost feel the frustration of the person from the words they had used:

> *Dear Caroline:*
>
> *I just discovered as an adult that I was adopted when I was a baby, and it's quite overwhelming. How do I cope with this unsettling news, and how can I ever trust my adoptive parents again, who should have told me this when I was a child?*
>
> *—Late Discovery*

Lois's lips pressed together as she tapped her pen against the tabletop, contemplating the best way to respond to this letter. When nothing came to her, she closed her eyes and prayed about it, asking God to give her the right words. At times like this, she felt inadequate to be offering advice, especially to people she had never met and didn't know personally. It made it even harder when they asked her questions about serious topics, like this one from someone who'd been adopted. What if she gave the wrong answer? What if the person who wrote the letter took her advice and things got worse?

After more contemplation and prayer, Lois opened her eyes and spoke the words as she wrote on a separate piece of paper:

> *Dear Late Discovery:*
>
> *No two people are the same. What's best for you will depend on your needs and circumstances. You may want to reach out to friends or family members for*

understanding and support. Since you are having trouble trusting your folks, hopefully you can find someone to speak to about this who would be objective. It's important that you decide what is comfortable and best for you.

Lois held the pen above the paper. *Is that enough, or should I say anything more? This one seems harder than normal for me because I don't want to give a wrong answer about something so important.*

Orley entered the room, and Lois's thoughts came to a halt. "Are you still working on those letters?" he asked.

She nodded.

"I thought you'd be ready for *bett* by now." He pointed to the clock on the kitchen wall.

"I just have a few more to do," she responded. "Why don't you go on ahead to bed?"

"I'd rather wait for you." He pulled out a chair on the opposite side of the table and took a seat. "Is there anything I can help you with?"

"No, not really." She patted the two envelopes she'd placed on her left side. "As soon as I answer these, I'll be done for the night."

"Do you enjoy writing the Dear Caroline column?"

"Most of the time, but there are moments when I wonder if the advice I give is what people need to hear." She sighed deeply. "I feel inadequate to be telling others what I think they should do."

"You pray about it, don't you—asking God to give you the right words?"

Lois bobbed her head.

"If you write what you believe God has directed you to say, then your words are not inadequate."

She smiled. "Danki for reminding me of that."

"You're welcome." Orley pushed away from the table and stood. "I'll go brush my teeth and get ready for bed while you finish up here. Hopefully, you won't be too long. Tomorrow's a big day at the store since it'll be the first of November and we're having our 25 percent off everything sale."

"I haven't forgotten, and I'll join you shortly."

Orley came around to her side of the table, bent down, and gave Lois a kiss on the cheek. "See you soon."

Lois felt blessed to have such a loving, caring husband as Orley. After he left the room, she picked up her pen again to reply to the next letter addressed to Dear Caroline.

Apple Creek

The shrill, desperate-sounding cry of a baby woke Andrea. She sat straight up in bed and looked around, realizing that she was in her own room and must have been dreaming.

But it seemed so real. Andrea rubbed the corners of her eyes. *I saw a baby crying for its mother, but no one would pick it up.* She had never dreamed about a baby before. *Why now?* she wondered. *Could it have something to do with me having been adopted?*

Andrea's head jerked back when Lady jumped up on the bed and began meowing while licking her face.

"Okay, girl, I get the hint. You want to be fed, don't you?" She gently pushed the cat aside and climbed out of bed.

Lady jumped down too and continued meowing as she moved back and forth, rubbing Andrea's legs.

"You're sure persistent, aren't you? Well, just give me a few minutes." Andrea slipped her robe on and stepped into the slippers near her bed. She went over to the window to look out. Pulling back the curtain, she was surprised to see white flakes falling from the sky. "An early snowfall," Andrea murmured. "I wonder if that's an indication of a cold, snowy winter ahead."

She rubbed her arms briskly. "I hope not, and this snow had better not keep me from meeting Colleen for lunch later today."

Andrea thought about her and Brandon's wedding, which was now just three and a half months away. No doubt the weather would be cold and the ground white on Valentine's Day. The plan was for them to go to sunny Florida for their honeymoon, which would be nice. Andrea looked forward to being someplace where the weather was much warmer than Ohio.

The cat meowed and bumped against her leg while Andrea wondered how Brandon would do driving to work if the snow kept falling. The winter weather didn't seem to make a difference to him since he had a four-wheel-drive vehicle. Andrea wished she could look at the snow with no reservations, but it made her nervous at times—especially thinking of how bad the upcoming winter conditions could get.

She glanced down at Lady, who was now making circles around her legs. "Okay, you persistent little thing. Let's go to the kitchen."

⁓

A short time later, Lady lapped up her food while Andrea sat at the table, eating a piece of toast spread with chunky peanut butter and perusing the newspaper.

She sought out the Dear Caroline column, hoping there might be an answer to the letter she'd written. It had only been a little over a week since she'd mailed it, so Andrea wasn't surprised that there had been no reply. Besides, if Dear Caroline received a lot of letters, she might not have time or space in the paper to respond to all of them. Andrea figured some may even get tossed.

"Oh well," she said aloud, "I'll keep looking, and if I don't hear something within the next few weeks, I'll give up on Dear Caroline and go with plan B." She gave a quick shake of her head. "Whatever that is." Truth was, Andrea had no plan B. For the last two Sundays, she'd made excuses not to get together with her parents and hadn't even sat on the same pew with them during church. She needed to ask some important questions but wasn't ready to ask them just yet. Andrea wanted a little more time to think of everything she needed to know, and she'd been so stressed out that she'd barely begun to make a list.

Brandon had no more than pulled up to the veterinary clinic when his cell phone rang. He turned off the ignition and answered the call.

"Good morning, Son. I hope I didn't interrupt anything."

"No, Mom. I just got to work and haven't gone inside yet." He glanced at his watch and then at the snow as it stuck to the front windshield. "I have a few minutes now, or I can call you back during my lunch break if you want to talk longer."

"I don't want to bother you while you're eating. I just called to tell you that I ran into Andrea's mother at the store yesterday. She was pretty upset because Andrea has barely said more than a few words to her and Ray since they got home after attending the funeral of Evelyn's brother." There was a brief pause. "I felt so bad seeing the sadness in her eyes, and when I asked her what was wrong, she quickly changed the subject."

"I guess she didn't want to talk about whatever was bothering her." Brandon suspected Evelyn's sadness might be because of Andrea's recent and unexpected adoption discovery, but he didn't think it was his place to reveal this information to his mother.

He looked to his left when a car pulled in with its wipers going at fast speed. *Because of the weather, I wonder if the clinic won't be as busy today.* The snowflakes that had begun falling earlier this morning had thickened, and a couple of inches of snow covered the ground already.

"Sorry, Mom, but I need to cut this conversation short and get inside. Someone just pulled up to the building, and they're getting out of their vehicle."

"Oh, okay. I'll call you sometime this evening. Goodbye for now, Son."

"Bye, Mom." Brandon felt relieved when his mother hung up. He was fairly certain that she'd called hoping he would try to persuade Andrea to make amends with her parents. *But that's not my place, and Mom needs to let the Lord work things out,* he told himself. *If I start pressuring her to talk to her folks when she's not ready, she might pull away from me.* Brandon pushed his shoulders straight back as he opened the door and stepped out of his SUV. *If there's one thing I know for certain, I need to stay neutral in the situation with Andrea and her parents and, above all else, make sure that my future wife knows she has my love and support.*

~

Walnut Creek

"I'm sure glad the snow has let up," Andrea commented as she and Colleen sat at a table inside Rebecca's Bistro, where they had met for lunch. "This is one of my favorite restaurants, and I didn't relish the idea of canceling our plans."

Her friend nodded. "Me neither. The white stuff is pretty, but it can cause an awful mess on the roads and make driving hazardous."

"I know. If it had kept up the way it was when I first got up this morning, I probably would have called you and canceled our lunch date."

"I understand how nervous you get this time of year when the roads start to get slick." Colleen smiled and gestured to her apple, pecan, blue cheese salad with poppy-seed dressing. "I'm glad we didn't have to cancel, because this is so good. You should have ordered one too."

Andrea twirled her spoon around in the bowl of tomato basil soup setting on her place mat. "Your salad looks good, but I'm fine with a bowl of warm soup." She gazed out the window, then looked back at Colleen. "I haven't had much of an appetite lately."

"Because you're still fretting about the fact that you're adopted?"

"Yes. If I'd been told straight up when I was a child that my parents had adopted me, I could have accepted the idea. It's the fact that they kept it a secret that bothers me so much. My cousin was told when he was a child, which was why he assumed that I already knew about being adopted. He seemed surprised that I had no idea I'd been adopted all those years ago." Andrea blew on her soup and tasted it. The sweet and savory flavors balanced perfectly. "I've never felt so emotionally crushed—especially by the two people I love so dearly. I don't understand how parents who go to church every Sunday and call themselves Christians could lie to their only child."

Colleen leaned forward, resting one arm on the table. "They didn't really lie, my friend. Your parents simply chose not to mention that you'd been adopted."

Andrea's face tightened. "Which was wrong."

"Yes, it was," Colleen agreed, "but they apologized for that, right?"

Andrea nodded before releasing a sigh. "Even so, I'm still having trouble dealing with all of this, and I have so many unanswered questions."

"Have you met with your parents to ask those questions?"

"Not yet." Andrea paused for another bite of soup. "I have started a list, and I also took your advice and wrote a letter to the Dear Caroline newspaper column."

Colleen looked at Andrea and blinked several times. "Really? Did she respond?"

"Not yet, but I hope she will soon and that her words might give me a sense of direction." Andrea heaved another sigh. "Right now, I don't know which way to turn. I keep asking myself if I should try to find my biological parents or if that would be a mistake."

"What would keep you from searching for them? Is it because you don't want to hurt the parents who raised you?"

Andrea squeezed her eyes shut as she rubbed the bridge of her nose. "That's part of it, but there's something else to consider."

"Such as?"

"What if I did find the woman who brought me into this world, and she wanted nothing to do with me?" Andrea's chin quivered. "I don't think I could deal with the rejection."

"Try not to worry about that, and remember to keep praying about your situation."

"That's all I can do for now, but in the meantime, I'm struggling with the fact that I don't know who I really am, where I came from, or who my biological parents are."

Colleen offered her a playful smile. "You're my good friend, Andrea Wagner, who will soon be Mrs. Brandon Prentice."

"You don't understand. Since I found out I was adopted, part of me feels homesick for a place I've been but don't remember." Andrea took a drink and blotted her lips on the napkin. "When I look in the mirror, I don't recognize myself anymore."

Colleen lifted her gaze to the ceiling. "You're still the same person you always were."

"I guess so, but I can't help wondering why my birth mother gave me up. How could she have turned me over to complete strangers? If I had a child, I wouldn't give her up for anything in the world."

"There may have been extenuating circumstances. She may not have had any choice."

Andrea's gaze dropped to the table. "I have to know the reason, and I need to pursue this, no matter what."

Chapter 20

Apple Creek

A week later, as Andrea sat down to eat a cold sandwich for supper, she picked up the newspaper to read the Dear Caroline column. To her surprise, her question had been answered.

> *Dear Late Discovery:*
>
> *No two people are the same. What's best for you will depend on your needs and circumstances. You may want to reach out to friends or family members for understanding and support. Since you are having trouble trusting your folks, hopefully you can find someone to speak to about this who would be objective. It's important that you decide what is comfortable and best for you.*

Andrea sat quietly, mulling over Dear Caroline's response and trying to decide what she should do.

It's probably time for me to talk to my folks. I need to have some questions answered. Yesterday Andrea had finished her handwritten list. It was filled with what she thought was important to ask them about her birth mother. *I hope my parents will freely give me all the information that I am desperate to know. I'm also hoping they'll be honest with me now, because I truly want things to be better between us.* It was harder to trust them now, but Andrea wanted to give her folks a second chance.

She finished eating her meal and went to get the phone. If her mom and dad were home, she would go over there now.

Andrea's heart pounded as she made her way up the porch steps of her parents' house. She had called earlier to see if she could come by this evening. Mom had sounded pleased until Andrea mentioned that she wanted to talk about her adoption. Then her mother had cooled off a bit and seemed hesitant until Andrea pushed the issue. Now that she was here, she hoped it would go well, because she had considered the risks and weighed all the pros and cons and had come to the place that she felt almost desperate to know the circumstances of her adoption. It was time to get started on this new and important venture.

Andrea's father answered the door after she knocked. He stood tall and welcomed her with a hug. "Come on in. Your mother will join us in the living room in a few minutes. She's getting some brownies ready to serve that she baked when she heard you were coming over."

"Okay." Andrea followed him into the other room and seated herself on the couch. Her mother knew she loved brownies, and Andrea wondered if she'd made them as some sort of peace offering to show how sorry she was for keeping the truth from her all these years.

As Dad took a seat in his favorite chair, Andrea opened her purse and got out the list she'd created. *I really want to learn something about my birth mother today and have a better understanding of why she gave me up for adoption.*

Mom entered the room, carrying a plate of perfectly shaped brownies. Her parents' home was warm and cozy, which felt inviting, but tonight that feeling was reinforced by the fragrance of freshly brewed coffee and just-baked chocolate permeating the air.

"Hello, Andrea. It's so nice to see you." Mom smiled and placed the plate on the coffee table in front of Andrea, along with three napkins. "Please, help yourself."

I hope you're not going to try and butter me up with something sweet to eat. "Maybe later, after we've talked awhile," she mumbled.

"Oh, okay." Her mother took a seat in the rocking chair and folded her hands. She glanced briefly at Andrea's father and then back at her. "I see you have a piece of paper. Would that be a list of questions you want to ask us?"

Andrea nodded.

"Well, fire away," Dad spoke up. "We'll answer all your questions to the best of our knowledge." He looked at Mom. "Right, Evelyn?"

She gave an affirming nod. "Of course."

Andrea lifted the paper she held and cleared her throat. "I'd like to start by asking if you know or have at least met my biological mother and father."

"I'm sorry, but we never met either of your birth parents." Andrea's father shifted in his chair as though trying to find a more comfortable position. "It was a closed adoption, so we don't even know the name of the woman who gave birth to you."

Andrea's shoulders drooped as she lowered her head. "I just thought. . ." Her voice trailed off. If it was a closed adoption, and they didn't know the woman's name, how was she ever going to find out who had put her up for adoption?

Andrea looked down at her paper, realizing that most of her other questions would not get an answer. *This isn't going so well—not at all like I had hoped it would.*

Lifting her head, Andrea posed the next question. "Where were you living when you adopted me?"

"Right here in Ohio," her mother replied. "We went to Pennsylvania to pick you up at the hospital."

"Wasn't my birth mother there too?"

"If she was, we were never introduced to her," Dad responded. "A woman from the adoption agency was there, and once we signed the official paperwork, we took you home with us."

I wonder if my biological mother is from Pennsylvania. If so, maybe she's still living there. "So my biological mother could have still been at the hospital when they gave me over to you?" Andrea pressed a hand against her abdomen.

"Well, I. . .umm. . .suppose, but if she was, no one said so."
A pink flush appeared on Mom's face and neck. Was she hiding something or just flustered from talking about this?

"So you have no other information to give me?" Andrea's ribs grew tight, restricting her breath.

"No, not really," Dad spoke up. "It was pretty much cut and dried."

She blinked several times, trying to process this. *Why wouldn't they have asked my birth mother's name—maybe even asked to meet her? I would think they would have wanted to know as much about her as possible. What if she was a criminal, a drug addict, or both?* Andrea's scattered thoughts danced in her head as she stared at her list. *My parents make it seem as though they want to help me, but I'm not feeling helped at all.*

Andrea's frustration mounted as she looked at her mother again. "Surely you must know something about the woman who brought me into this world but chose not to raise me. I can't believe you would have adopted a child without knowing anything about the infant's background or parents."

"We only know that it was a young, unwed mother who was not in a position to raise a child." This answer came from Andrea's father.

"Seriously? That's all you can tell me?" Andrea heard the tension in her own voice. *I'm not gaining anything at all.*

"Please stop pushing, Andrea. We've told you all that we know." Tears gathered in Andrea's mother's eyes and dribbled down her crimson cheeks.

At least you know who your real parents are. Andrea shoved the piece of paper back in her purse and stood. "Fine then. I'll find out what I need to know on my own." *I can't believe I let myself get my hopes up for this.*

"Where are you going? Don't you want to have a brownie and talk with us some more?" Although Mom's pleading voice would have normally prevented Andrea from leaving, she headed for the front door, calling over her shoulder: "I can't talk about this right now."

When Andrea got into her car a few minutes later, she let her head fall forward and sobbed. This meeting with her parents hadn't gone well, and not one thing had been resolved. Andrea knew as little about her biological mother now as she had when she'd walked through her parents' front door. She didn't know how or where to begin, but Andrea made up her mind that no matter how long it took, she would find out who her birth parents were.

———

"Andrea doesn't believe us," Evelyn sobbed from where she still sat in her rocking chair with Frisky in her lap. "If we'd only prayed about this and trusted the Lord to help us to tell our daughter the truth years ago. We made a horrible mistake by not telling Andrea when she was a child, and now we've lost her and may never get her back."

"I must admit there have been times through the years when my faith hasn't been the strongest. And I should've been a better spiritual leader in our home. I think it's time for both of us to draw closer to the Lord. There are times when I feel like we're basically warming a pew on Sundays and giving a small tithe. That isn't enough." Ray got up from his chair and walked across the room. Then he picked up the dog, set him on the floor, and pulled Evelyn to her feet. "We haven't lost her. She's just upset and frustrated because we did not have the answers she sought."

"But you saw her reaction. She walked out of the house without saying goodbye or even eating one of my brownies."

He gently patted her back and spoke to her like one would to a distraught child. "Eating a brownie would not have changed anything, dear."

Evelyn sniffed. "Yes, it would. It would have given me the reassurance that she's not mad at me."

"I don't believe she's angry—just disappointed and hurt. We need to give her more time and be supportive."

Evelyn pulled back and swallowed hard as she looked up at Ray.

"How much time?"

"As long as it takes."

"How can we be supportive if she won't talk to us? Our daughter would barely look at us while she was here."

"I'm aware of that."

"So what are we supposed to do—sit here and twiddle our thumbs while we wait for her to forgive us?"

Ray shook his head. "We can pray and help Andrea search for her birth mother."

Evelyn's eyes opened wide, and her mouth dropped open. "Are you kidding?"

"No, I'm not. It's our duty to try and help her." He paused. "We need to trust the Lord that this will all work out."

"I'll try." Evelyn's voice trembled as she sank into her chair. "If she connects with the woman who bore her, we might lose Andrea for good."

"That's negative thinking. We raised Andrea. She can't erase all the years we've spent together and all of the things we've done with and for her." Ray spoke in such a tone of assurance that Evelyn almost believed him. Even so, her heart was filled with doubts. If they lost their only child because they hadn't told the truth in the first place, Evelyn would never forgive herself.

I'm glad my husband was honest about his lack of faith, and I need to be too. Another thought popped into her head. *If Ray and I could find Andrea's biological parents, would she be grateful and forgive us then?*

Brandon was on the verge of dozing off in his recliner when Duke started barking and ran for the front door. He sat up and rubbed his gritty eyes, wondering what all the commotion was about.

"What's the matter, boy? You need to go out?"

Arf! Arf! Arf!

"Okay, okay. . .I'm coming." Brandon got up, yawning, shuffled toward the front door, and turned on the porch light. He had put in a long day at the clinic and more tired than usual this evening. And he couldn't help being irritated, because he'd let Duke out half an hour ago, yet here the dog was asking to go outside again. *Maybe he drank more water than he should have.*

When Brandon opened the door, nearly tripping over Duke, he was surprised to see Andrea standing on the porch. Her face looked puffy, and the whites of her eyes were red.

"What's wrong, sweetie? Have you been in an accident? Are you hurt?"

She shook her head and gulped on a sob.

"Come in. Get out of the cold." Brandon took Andrea's hand and guided her into the house. Once inside, he led her to the living room, and they sat together on the couch. Duke, who obviously had no need to go outside, sat in front of the couch with his tail wagging.

Brandon gave Andrea a few minutes to compose herself before he asked her again what was wrong.

"I. . .I just came from seeing my folks. I went there to ask if they knew who my biological parents were, and they said no." She paused and drew a shaky breath. "They said it was a closed adoption and that they'd never met my birth mother and don't know her name."

"I'm sorry, Andrea." He reached over and clasped her cold hand.

"I'd really hoped that when I went over there today, they'd be able to answer most of the questions I'd brought with me." She looked over at him and squinted her eyes. "I think they might have lied to me about that."

"For what reason?"

"They're afraid if I know who she is I will make contact with her."

"Would that be so bad?"

"They might think I'd like her better than them. I don't know." Andrea shrugged. "Maybe. I suppose knowing who she is could turn out bad for me."

"How so?"

"My birth mother no doubt has made a life for herself. She

could be married and have children that she didn't choose to adopt out." Tears rolled down Andrea's puffy cheeks. "She obviously didn't love me, or she wouldn't have given me to strangers."

"It's hard to say." Brandon spoke softly and chose his next words carefully. "There are many reasons why a mother might give up her baby—one being that she may have been young and single, unable to care financially or physically for a child."

Andrea lowered her head. "It's too late for me to go back to my mom and dad's place tonight, but I do need to talk to them again soon and apologize for leaving in a huff and not even bothering to say goodbye." She looked at Brandon again. "When I left their house, I made a decision."

"Oh? What was it?" he asked.

"Even if the parents who raised me don't want me to, I'm going to search for my birth mother." Andrea swiped a hand across her face. "If I'm able to locate her and she doesn't want to see me or make me a part of her life, at least I won't spend the rest of my life wondering who she is and what she's like. The truth is, I have a lot of questions for her that I'd like to ask."

Chapter 21

Walnut Creek

"I think it's time for me to buy a new coin purse. This is no good anymore." Lois held hers up.

Orley glanced over at her from the driver's seat of their carriage. "What's wrong with it?"

"The clasp is broken, and I lost some of my money."

"When did that happen?"

She shrugged her shoulders. "I'm not sure. I first noticed it after supper when I was going to leave a tip for our waitress at the restaurant in Berlin. It was after you left the table to use the restroom."

"I'm confused. Why would you feel the need to leave a tip when I had already left one?"

A warm flush crept across Lois's cheeks as her chin dipped down. "I didn't think it was enough."

"Oh, so now you think your husband is a cheapskate, huh?"

"Not at all. The young woman waiting on our table was so attentive to our needs, and I thought she deserved a little extra."

"I see. Did you have enough in your coin purse?"

"There was a five dollar bill, which I gave her, but that's all I had. Apparently, the rest of my bills, plus the coins, must have fallen out sometime today; maybe when I went to the post office for stamps."

"It was nice of you to give the extra tip to our waitress." Orley reached over and patted her arm. "I'll give you some money tomorrow so you can buy a new coin purse."

She smiled. "Danki. You're such a kind, thoughtful man. I did well when I married you."

"I'm the one who did well. I couldn't ask for a better fraa." Orley spoke in such a sincere tone it caused Lois to tear up. There were times when she didn't feel deserving of his love.

<hr />

Apple Creek

After Brandon brought Duke in from his nightly walk, he took a seat in his recliner and picked up his cell phone to make a few calls. The first would be to his mother in response to the message she'd left him earlier today when he'd been at the clinic. If it had been an emergency, he would have called sooner, but the message she'd left had been about the rehearsal dinner, which was still nearly three months away.

"But that's my mom." Brandon chuckled. "She's a stickler for details and always ahead of the game."

Duke's ears perked up, and he gave out an *Arf!*

Brandon rolled his eyes. "I wasn't talking to you, buddy, but that's all right."

The dog cocked his head to one side before leaping onto his owner's lap.

"You always want my attention, don't ya, boy?" Brandon scratched behind Duke's ears and smiled when the dog burrowed against his hand.

"If you were a cat, I bet you'd be purring real nice right now." Brandon continued to scratch Duke's ears, alternating with a few pats on the animal's head. It wasn't long before Duke's eyes closed, and he conked out on Brandon's lap.

Brandon reached into his shirt pocket and pulled out his cell phone. It was time to call Mom. He wasn't surprised when she answered on the first ring. Apparently, she'd been waiting for him to return her call.

"Hey, Mom. How's it going?"

"It's going fine here. I've been working on my list for the rehearsal dinner and needed to ask you a few questions. But before we get into that, I wanted to tell you something."

"Sure, Mom. What's up?"

"I ran into Andrea's mother today at the styling salon. I was totally surprised by what she told me."

"Oh? What did Evelyn have to say?"

"She said that she and Ray adopted Andrea when she was a baby and that Andrea found out about it while attending her uncle's funeral. Did you know about this, Son?"

"Andrea told me after she and her folks got home from Idaho."

"How come you didn't mention it to me or your dad? Why the big secret since the news was out?"

Brandon cringed. He felt like a young boy getting a reprimand from one of his parents.

"It wasn't my place to tell. I figured if Andrea or her parents wanted others to know, they would do the telling."

"I suppose that makes sense." His mother's tone was a little softer now. "Evelyn said Andrea is quite upset and doesn't understand the way her parents feel about this."

"Andrea's hurting too, Mom. Learning that she'd been adopted was a real shock. She's trying to work through it and deal with her emotion, but it's difficult."

"I understand that, but I would think that Andrea could be more understanding of Evelyn and Ray's feelings."

"I would think her parents could be more understanding as well, since they should've been honest with her from the beginning."

"Of course, you're right, but still. . ."

Brandon yawned. "I put in a long today, Mom. Can we drop this topic and talk about the rehearsal dinner some other time?"

"All right, but let's not put it off too long. It's important to get all the details ironed out before the big day arrives."

"I know. I'll call you in a few days."

"All right then. Good night, Son."

"Night, Mom. Tell Dad I said hello."

"I will."

After Brandon ended the conversation with his mother, he wanted to see how Andrea was doing, so he punched in her number.

"Hi, sweetie," he said after she picked up. "Just wondered how your day went and if you're doing okay."

"No lessons to give today, and I didn't do any painting either, but I did call my mom and apologized for last night," she replied.

"That's good. I'm sure it must have made you both feel better about things."

"I felt better for clearing the air with her but not better about learning that I was adopted." Andrea paused, and he heard her draw in a deep breath. "I think I'm having an identity crisis. It's like I don't know who I am anymore."

"I know exactly who you are, Andrea. You're the woman I love and am planning to marry in a few short months. That hasn't changed, and neither have you. You're the same person now as you were when we first met."

"I know, but. . ." Her voice trailed off. "It's hard to explain, and unless you had also been adopted, I wouldn't expect you to understand. It's hard not to focus on the differences between me and my adoptive parents."

"There aren't that many differences, Andrea. All three of you are Christians who enjoy many of the same things."

"True, but I'm musical, and neither of my parents plays any kind of an instrument."

Brandon was about to comment when Andrea spoke again. "And think about it. . . I don't look anything like either of them. My hair is auburn, and Mom's is light brown. Dad's hair is blond with a little gray mixed in. Our eye color doesn't match either. Mine are brown, and theirs are both blue. I never thought much about it till I discovered that I was adopted, but the evidence has been right there in front of me the whole time."

"Lots of children don't have the same hair or eye color as their parents. Those characteristics can be passed down from grandparents, aunts, uncles, or—"

"Not in my case, though. I don't look like my parents because I have none of their blood flowing through my veins."

Brandon wanted to tell Andrea that she had been fixating on all of the unimportant details, but he thought better of it. No point in giving her something more to be upset about. Instead, he said, "Despite the differences between you and your adoptive parents, the one thing that has always rung true to me is their undying love for their daughter. You know that, right?"

"Yes, but they didn't love me enough to tell me the truth."

"I can't begin to understand all their reasons for that, but we all make mistakes that we wish we could undo. I'm sure keeping your adoption from you was one of the things they deeply regret."

"I believe you're right." She released a yawn. "Sorry about that. I didn't get much sleep last night, and I spent most of today cleaning and organizing some things around here, so I'm pretty tired."

"That's understandable, and on that note, I think I will say goodnight and let you go. We'll talk again soon, though."

"Okay. Thanks for calling and for your support. I love you, Brandon."

"Love you too. Sleep well."

"You also. Bye for now."

When Brandon clicked off his phone, he closed his eyes and said a prayer for his bride-to-be. *Dear Lord, please give Andrea a sense of calm, and help her to remember to focus on the people in her life who love her so much.*

"You seem much calmer this evening than you were last night after Andrea left in a huff," Ray commented when he carried his supper dishes over to the sink where Evelyn stood, rinsing her own dishes.

"I've felt a little better since Andrea called me this morning to apologize for her abruptness last night."

Ray handed Evelyn his dishes and placed both hands on her shoulders. His gentle touch made her relax. "I believe Andrea still loves us, Ray."

"Of course she does. From the time we brought her home from the hospital, we've nurtured our daughter and showered her with our love and attention." He began massaging her shoulders. "Remember how excited we got when Andrea took her first few baby steps?"

"Our daughter was unwavering, even when she fell." Evelyn smiled. "I can still picture Andrea pulling herself up in front of the couch and taking a few more steps with a determined look on her pretty little face."

"Yeah." Ray took a few dishes from the sink and placed them in the dishwasher. "Whenever Andrea has wanted something, she's always gone after it until she accomplished her goal."

"And now she has a new goal—to find her birth parents." Evelyn's shoulders sagged. "Truthfully, I can't say that I'm excited about her newest goal."

"Are you afraid we're going to lose her?"

She shrugged. "I hope not. Our bond has always been strong. My biggest concern is that if she's not able to locate her biological parents, she'll feel a sense of emptiness and defeat." Evelyn sidestepped Frisky and added a few more dishes to the dishwasher. "My other concern is that Andrea may find her birth parents and discover that they want nothing to do with her. I believe that would upset her as much, or more, as learning that she was adopted."

Ray waited until Evelyn had filled the dispenser with the dishwasher liquid, then shut the dishwasher door and turned on the machine. "It will be a risk for Andrea to take, but we'll be here to help her deal with whatever the outcome will be."

Evelyn nodded. "Yes, and I intend to assist our daughter in her endeavors to locate the woman who chose to give her away nearly thirty-three years ago."

He looked at her pointedly. "How exactly do you plan to go

about that?"

"I'm not sure yet, but the first thing I plan to do is tell Andrea the name of the adoption agency we used."

"Let's hope the place is still in business. Remember, it's been almost thirty-three years."

Evelyn blinked. "Oh dear. . . I hadn't even thought of that possibility. I'll do some investigating in the morning."

It was well past her usual bedtime, and Andrea had been lying under the covers for over an hour, listening to her cat's gentle purring from the foot of her bed, while trying to relax. She'd muted her cell phone so she wouldn't be interrupted, but the quiet of the evening had not evaporated Andrea's scattered thoughts. She'd felt a bit better after talking to Brandon earlier, but now the doubts she'd felt before had crept back in.

Another twenty minutes went by, and when sleep still wouldn't come, Andrea got up and plodded out to the kitchen to fix a cup of calming herbal tea. Once it was brewed, she took her cup and went to her art studio, which she also used as a home office. Taking a seat in front of her desk, Andrea booted up her computer.

A short time later, she was online, looking at a website on how to find a person's birth parents. Since Andrea had called her mother this morning and apologized for leaving so abruptly and being curt with them last night, she now felt ready to start a new chapter in her life as she began the search for her biological parents.

The first article Andrea found described how to find birth parents involved in either an open or closed adoption. An open adoption would obviously make it easier, but Andrea was not without hope—not yet, anyway. *Leave no stone unturned*, she reminded herself. *I won't quit until I've done everything I can to find my biological parents.*

Andrea scrolled until she came to the closed adoption information. Right off the bat was a reminder that a person looking for his or her birth parents needed to be prepared for both a good or a disappointing outcome.

Andrea paused to ponder that fact. *If I located my biological mother, how would I respond? Would I have the courage to contact her, and if so, what if she didn't want to meet me?*

She pivoted her chair and reached for the cup of lavender-mint tea she'd brewed thirty minutes ago. One sip and she frowned. It was barely lukewarm.

Andrea got up and went to the kitchen to heat the tea in the microwave. While it heated, she grabbed two peanut butter cookies and a napkin. Once the tea was the desired temperature, Andrea returned to the desk in her art studio. Continuing to read from the website she'd found, she focused once again on the information about closed adoptions.

"Step one," Andrea said aloud. "Collect information." She scratched her head. "How am I supposed to do that? I don't have any information."

She scrolled a little farther and read some questions to answer. "What is the year, month, and date of your birth?" That was easy enough since Andrea knew she'd been born on March 21 and would be turning thirty-three in a few months. She also knew, according to what her parents had said the other night, that the adoption had taken place in Pennsylvania. *But what city and which adoption agency?* Those were questions she had forgotten to ask. Andrea wrote them down on the notepad next to her computer. "Okay, what's next?"

"Step two: Use a mutual consent adoption registry." After reading that the site mentioned was a common format for adoptees, birth parents, and siblings to register their information in the hope that it would match with another searcher, Andrea jotted down the name of the website.

She paused for a drink of tea and went on to read the third step, which was DNA matching. To go this route would mean that Andrea would need to order a DNA kit from one of the major

DNA services like MyHeritage, AncestryDNA, FamilyTreeDNA, or 23andMe. She wrote the names of those sites down as well.

Step four: Hire an adoption detective.

"I'll bet a detective would be expensive." Andrea frowned, but she wrote it down anyway, marking it as a last resort.

She leaned back in her chair and breathed a lingering sigh. *I can see that searching for my biological parents could take a lot of my time and energy. How am I going to do all those things listed and continue with my plans for a wedding?*

Chapter 22

As Thanksgiving Day approached, Andrea found herself wondering what her biological parents might be doing to celebrate the holiday. *Do they live in Pennsylvania, where I was born? Are they married? Do they have other children?*

To take her mind off things, Andrea decided to work on making up the dessert for tomorrow's holiday meal. The recipe she enjoyed using was foolproof, always tasted good, and was not that difficult to make.

She pulled out the apples from the refrigerator and noticed Lady coming into the kitchen. "Hello, pretty kitty."

The cat swished her tail as she strolled over to her water dish and began to drink.

Andrea got out the rest of the items needed to prepare the apple pie. It wasn't long before Lady was underfoot and meowing up at her. "What's up, pretty kitty? Are you hungry?" Andrea looked at the time and realized that it had been a while since the cat's last feeding. "Okay, okay, I'll take care of you first."

Andrea picked up the cat's empty dish and filled it with the proper amount of dry cat food. Lady stayed right by Andrea's feet. "You act as though you haven't eaten all day, but we both know that you ate this morning." She set the bowl next to Lady's water dish. "Now I need to get back to making the pie."

Andrea peeled and sliced all the apples she had bought the other day. The fruit looked so good, she ate a couple slices before mixing in the rest of the pie-filling ingredients. When that was finished, she went to the refrigerator and got the chilled pie dough to roll out. Once the pastry, filling, and the last shell were in place, Andrea's creative side kicked in, and she enjoyed fluting the edges of the crust to look fancy.

Living at home as a child, Andrea had been intrigued with the pictures in her mother's cookbooks and had learned to cook well by the time she was a teenager.

Andrea put the chilled ball of dough on the floured surface and used the rolling pin to smooth out the crust and make it the correct thickness. She wanted this pie to be just right for Thanksgiving.

Andrea's mom and dad had also been invited to join her and Brandon at his parents' house for Thanksgiving. It would be the first time they'd all been together for a meal since their dinner out, when she and Brandon had announced their engagement.

Andrea wondered if the topic of her adoption would come up and if Brandon's parents even knew about it. Most likely he had told them, or maybe Mom had said something since she and Jennifer were friends.

She placed the evenly rolled dough inside the pie pan and poured the sliced apples that had been mixed with cinnamon, sugar, and butter on top. *Perhaps Brandon hasn't mentioned my adoption to his folks. He may think it's my place to do the telling if I choose to.* Her lips compressed. *I hope he hasn't said anything, because I'd like to get through Thanksgiving without any additional stress.* Thinking about the need to find her biological parents was one thing, but talking about it brought Andrea's feelings to the surface. The last thing she wanted to do was break down and cry in front of her future in-laws. If that should occur, Andrea's mother would probably do some crying of her own, which would make it even more embarrassing.

I'd better take my lavender-scented roller bottle with me tomorrow, Andrea reminded herself. *I may need it in order to stay calm if any stressful topic is brought up.*

Forcing herself to focus on the task at hand, Andrea covered the apple filling with a second neatly rolled crust, fluted the edges, and placed it in the oven, closed the door, and set the timer. Soon the kitchen would be filled with a wonderful aroma, which would make it difficult not to try a piece once the pie was done and had cooled sufficiently. But Andrea would restrain herself and satisfy her sweet tooth with a pumpkin-flavored protein snack bar and a cup of apple-cinnamon tea. Following that, she had some more adoption research to do.

Walnut Creek

"Business has been rather *langsam* today," Orley commented as he and Lois worked together, opening four boxes they'd taken from the storage room. Each one was filled with some newly found items they hoped to sell. Now that yard sales were few and far between because cold weather had set in, there wasn't a lot left in the storage area to pull out and add to their displays in the store.

"Things may be slow right now, but it'll be a different story on Friday when many people will be out doing their Christmas shopping," Lois responded.

"Good point." Orley held an antique washboard in his hands. "I wonder if this might be of interest to somebody."

Lois tilted her head from side to side as she studied the object. "I suppose it could lend a nostalgic touch to someone's washroom, but I doubt anyone would be inclined to use it." She smiled. "I'm certainly grateful for my diesel-generated ringer washing machine. It gets our clothes much cleaner and is easier on a person's back than bending over a galvanized tub, scrubbing clothes against a washboard like our ancestors used in the past."

"Do you wish you had a machine that would dry our clothes, like most English people use?" he questioned.

"I don't mind hanging things out to dry—especially during nice weather. When I bring them back inside after they're dry, everything smells so nice and fresh."

"That it does, and I always appreciate climbing into bed with clean-smelling sheets."

The bell above the front door jingled. Lois glanced toward the front and was surprised to see Jeff Davis enter the store.

Orley must have seen him too, for he stood up and hurried forward to greet him.

Lois clambered to her feet as well and joined them.

"It's sure good to see you, Jeff." Orley shook the young man's hand.

"It's great seeing you two as well." Jeff gave Lois a hug. "How have you both been?"

"Getting along just fine," Orley replied, and Lois nodded.

"Glad to hear it. Your names come up in Rhonda's and my conversations quite often."

"We talk about you as well." Orley gave Jeff's back a couple of thumps. "So how are things with you, Rhonda, and your little girl these days?"

"Good." Jeff's eyes brightened. "Our daughter is getting quite spoiled, what with all the attention Emily gets from the people who stay at our inn."

"We'll have to drop by and see her again one of these days," Lois interjected.

"How about tomorrow?" Jeff gave a broad smile. "I know it's a last-minute invitation, but if you don't have other plans, Rhonda and I would like to have you join us for Thanksgiving dinner."

"Orley and I were going to have a quiet dinner, just the two of us, but being part of your celebration would be lovely," Lois was quick to say. "We wouldn't want to intrude on your family gathering, however. I'm sure you'll have a full house."

Jeff shook his head. "Not really. My dad and Rhonda's mom will be there, but her siblings and mine all have other plans."

"What about guests at the inn?" The question came from Orley.

Jeff turned his palms upward. "Only two couples are staying

with us right now, and they both have plans to spend tomorrow with family members in the area." He looked steadily at Orley and Lois. "Please say yes. We'd really enjoy having you as our guests."

Orley looked at Lois, and when she nodded, he smiled and said, "Name the time, and we'll be there."

"We'll eat at two, but feel free to come anytime after noon."

"We shall definitely come a bit early," Lois said. "That way I can help Rhonda with whatever needs to be done in preparation for the meal. I'd also like to bring something. Perhaps a green bean casserole or a pumpkin pie?"

"Either one, or both, is fine." Jeff winked at Lois. "You're such a good cook, and I'm certain we'll enjoy whatever you bring."

Her face warmed at the compliment. "Please tell your dear wife that I shall bring the casserole as well as a pie."

"Sounds great. Rhonda will be glad to know that you're coming." Jeff turned toward the door. "I'd better get going. I promised to pick up a few things at the store before going home."

"We'll see you tomorrow." Orley shook Jeff's hand again, and Lois gave another hug. The thought of spending Thanksgiving with the Davises had put a spark of joy into her day and wiped away the fatigue she'd felt earlier. Lois looked forward to visiting with the adults tomorrow, but more than that, she could hardly wait to see sweet little Emily again.

When Orley guided their horse and buggy up to the hitching rail outside the Davises' beautiful country inn, a sense of joy swelled in Lois's soul. Jeff and Rhonda had come a long way since she and Orley had first met the couple, who'd been struggling in their marriage. So much had happened since then—the Davises had committed their lives to the Lord, their marriage had been restored, they'd purchased this inn, and Rhonda had given birth to a sweet baby girl. It almost seemed like the couple now lived the perfect life. *But that can't be true*, Lois reminded herself. *No one's life while living on this earth is perfect. There will always be some sort of trouble to face.* Lois wondered how those who did not have a personal relationship with Christ dealt with the unpleasant and sometimes tragic situations they had to face. At least those who were Christians could go to God in prayer during difficult times and seek spiritual and emotional counsel through others who were like-minded and had put their trust in Jesus. Lois didn't know what she would have done while going through various trials and disappointments over the years without her faith in God and the ability to give her troubles to Him through prayer and Bible reading.

"Sure is nice that Jeff had a hitching rail put on their property soon after they purchased this place." Orley's comment drove Lois's thoughts aside.

"Jah," she agreed. "It's helpful for people like us who come here to visit and also for Amish folks in the area who want to stay at the inn for a night or two to experience a kind of mini-vacation."

Orley nodded and handed Lois the reins. Then he stepped down from the buggy and secured Biscuit to the rail. While he was doing that, Lois got out and reached into the buggy to retrieve the container that held the pumpkin pie and green bean casserole she was contributing to the Thanksgiving meal.

When Lois and Orley stepped onto the porch that encompassed almost the entire front of the inn, Orley rang the bell. Within a few seconds, the door opened, and Jeff greeted them with a wide smile and welcoming hug. "Welcome, friends, and Happy Thanksgiving!"

"*Hallich Dankfescht*," Orley responded.

Jeff grinned. "You said, 'Happy Thanksgiving' in Pennsylvania Dutch. Jah?"

"That's right." Orley nodded. "Have you been studying our language?"

"I've picked up a few words here and there." Jeff took the container Lois held. "I'm guessing this goes in the kitchen?"

Lois smiled. "That's right. The green bean casserole is my contribution to dinner, and the pie's for dessert."

"I'll take it to the kitchen and let Rhonda know you're here. Her mom and my dad haven't arrived yet, but they should be here soon, I expect." Jeff gestured to the coatrack in the entryway. "You can hang your jackets there, and feel free to take a seat in our living room down the hall." Jeff looked at them. "You know the way to our living quarters here at the inn, right?"

"Jah, but if we get lost and can't find it, I'll give a holler so you can send out a search party for us." Orley winked at Jeff before the young man headed off toward the kitchen, shaking his head.

After they took off their outer garments and hung them up, Lois bumped Orley's arm with her elbow. "You were just teasing about getting lost, I hope. This isn't the first time we've been here, you know."

Orley wiggled his brows as he looked at her with a smug expression. "Of course I was only kidding."

With a quick roll of her eyes, Lois followed him down the hall. When they entered the living room, Lois stopped short. Sweet little Emily sat on the floor, surrounded by several toys. The child looked so angelic, it was all Lois could do to keep from swooping the little girl up and giving her a big hug. She held herself in check, though, because Emily didn't know them that well, and she didn't want to frighten the child. To avoid doing anything that might cause Emily to cry, Lois quietly took a seat in the rocking chair across from where Orley had seated himself in one of the two recliners.

When the little girl looked their way, Lois gave a little wave and watched Emily pick up the baby doll lying beside her and give it a hug. The tender scene brought tears to Lois's eyes. She glanced at Orley and noticed that he seemed to be watching Emily too. *Is my husband thinking the same thoughts I am?* she wondered. *Does Orley wish we could have had a child of our own? If we had, we could likely be grandparents by now.*

Lois was glad when Rhonda entered the room with Jeff, ending her musings. It wasn't good for a person to dwell on things that were not meant to be or feel sorry for oneself.

Lois and Orley stood, and each gave Rhonda a hug.

"Thank you for inviting us to join you today," Lois said. "Is there something I can do in the kitchen to help you right now?"

Rhonda shook her head. "Everything is pretty much ready. As soon as our newlywed parents get here, you can help me put things on the table."

Jeff slipped his arm around his wife's waist. "They've been married to each other for almost two years now, honey, so they've gone beyond being called newlyweds."

"Compared to us, they are." Rhonda smiled. "Who would ever have thought that my mother and Jeff's father would end up getting married?"

"That's right," Jeff agreed. "And it just goes to show that with God all things are possible." He gestured toward his daughter. "What do you think of our Emily? Hasn't she grown since the last time you saw her?"

"For sure," Orley responded. "And she's a beautiful little girl, just like her mother." He gestured to Rhonda, who smiled in return.

"Oh, I don't know about that," Jeff interjected. "I kinda think our little girl looks a bit like her father. Even if she doesn't," he added, "I bet our son will take after me."

"Your son?" Lois turned to look at Rhonda, whose cheeks had turned rosy. "Are you expecting another baby?"

Rhonda nodded. "The last ultrasound I had let us know that we are having a boy this time."

Happy tears sprang to Lois's eyes. "Congratulations. I am so pleased for you."

"I am as well." Orley looked at Jeff and gave him a big grin. "Maybe you'll be right, and your son will look like you, but no matter who he resembles, one thing I'm sure of is that, just like Emily, your boy will be loved."

The doorbell rang, and Jeff said, "That must be my father and mother-in-law. I'll go let them in, and shortly after we can all eat until we're too full to get up from the table."

"You sure outdid yourself with this tasty meal," Andrea's father said to their hostess as he took another slice of succulent turkey and put it on his plate.

Jennifer smiled while gesturing to Andrea and her mother. "I can't take all the credit. Your wife and daughter contributed with the two different salads they brought. They also helped me serve everything up after you all arrived."

"And don't forget about the pies both women brought," Andrea's dad put in. "My heartfelt thanks goes out to each of you dear ladies, but I may not be as thankful when I'm so full of food that I can't push away from the table." He chuckled and patted his stomach. "When it's time for dessert, I'm sure I'll find room for that too."

Andrea fought the urge to roll her eyes or say something about his ability to exaggerate when he thought it was humorous, but she kept silent. So far the day had been going well, and she wasn't about to say something that might disrupt that pattern.

"You know, Ray, you could just learn to say no to second helpings," Brandon's dad, Larry, put in.

"Good point." Andrea's father held up his thumb. "But it's hard to say no when there's so much good food available."

"Too bad Joe and his family had other plans and couldn't join us today," Brandon interjected. "I'm sure my brother would have eaten enough for two people." He looked over at Andrea's father and grinned. "That would have saved you from feeling the need to eat so much, because with him at the table, there might not have been enough food for seconds."

Everyone laughed, including Andrea. It felt good to laugh and relax around the dinner table with Brandon's parents and hers. Being here today had helped to take her mind off the need to find her biological parents and focus instead on how thankful she felt for the parents who had raised her. Andrea had been fairly calm since she and Brandon had arrived at his folks' house, and she hadn't needed to use the lavender rollerball she'd put in her purse.

She looked across the table at Brandon's mother and father, now chatting with her folks about the light dusting of snow still on the ground. *I'm thankful for Larry and Jennifer too*, she thought. *I could not ask for a nicer couple to have as my future in-laws.* She glanced at Brandon sitting beside her. *And I'm ever so thankful for my soon-to-be groom.*

Brandon reached for her free hand and gave it a gentle squeeze. She wondered if he was having similar thoughts about being thankful.

Walnut Creek

"You're awfully quiet," Orley said as they headed home from Jeff and Rhonda's place that evening. "Did you eat too much food and end up with a *bauchweh*?"

Lois reached across the buggy seat and bumped his arm. "I did eat more than my share, but I don't have a stomachache. I am just tired and pleasantly full."

"Same here."

Lois had no intention of admitting to her husband that she felt a bit sorry for herself because they had no children or grandchildren. She didn't want to hurt Orley's feelings or remind him that he was unable to give them children. After they'd first learned of his condition, they had decided not to adopt. Lois had been fine with it at first and never complained. But as time went on and she observed other people with their children, Lois fought moments of envy and had to pray about it. Keeping busy helped, but at times like today, after enjoying the Davis family, deep regrets set in.

I need to stop this negative thinking before self-pity takes over, Lois told herself. *I can't let Orley know what I've been feeling. It would hurt him deeply.*

"It was a full day for us." Orley's statement pushed Lois's thoughts aside. "I can understand why you'd be tired."

She yawned as he snapped the reins, which got his horse moving a bit faster. "It was a *gut* day, though, jah?"

"Yes, the food was good, and so was the time we spent visiting with the Davises and their parents."

"That little girl of theirs sure took a shine to you," Lois said.

"That's probably because I gave her so much attention."

"Emily's a sweet child. Jeff and Rhonda are blessed to have her—especially after they waited so many years for Rhonda to conceive. The good Lord gave them a miracle with the birth of that child."

"He certainly did."

Lois held both hands firmly in her lap as she closed her eyes and offered a prayer. *Heavenly Father, please help me to learn to be content and appreciative for all that I have. Continue to use me and Orley whenever You open the doors for us to minister to others who are hurting and in need of spiritual guidance. Help me to be the kind of wife Orley needs, for he certainly has been a good husband to me.*

Chapter 23

By the first week of December, enough snow had fallen that children had begun to bring out their sleds. Lois chuckled, watching from the window as her husband pulled his well-used sled up the hill out behind their house. He'd invited her to join him, but Lois had declined. She had received more letters sent to her Dear Caroline column and needed to answer them this morning, on their day off from the store. Christmas cookies waited to be baked, and she'd already rolled out four cookie sheets full of them. She'd added crushed peppermint candies to half of the dough. These cookies were some of Orley's favorites and went well with hot chocolate. She'd slid in sheets of vanilla-flavored sugar cookies. Like a child, she couldn't wait to sample the first of this year's delights.

The timer sat ticking as Lois paused to stir hot cocoa in a kettle on the stove. The warmth from the copper-bottomed pan and the heat from the oven made the room feel cozy. As the fragrance of the peppermint began to fill the room, her mouth watered in expectation of having her hot beverage with a soft, warm sugar cookie.

When the buzzer sounded, Lois grabbed two pot holders, retrieved the baking sheets from the oven, and placed them on cooling racks. *When Orley comes in from outside, he'll surely want one.*

Lois had put two more sheets of cookies in the oven, when the kitchen door swung open and in walked her husband. A chill of air followed him, and she watched as he shook some snow off his pant legs.

"It feels good here in the house." His eyes seemed to brighten as he sniffed the air. "And somethin' sure smells mighty nice."

Lois set the timer again. "I have hot chocolate on the stove and some fresh-baked sugar cookies to enjoy."

"I came in for a drink of water, but what you've suggested sounds much better." He stepped over to the sink and washed his hands.

She got out a mug, poured his hot cocoa, and set two cookies on a napkin. "Did you want to sit down at the table?"

"No, I'll just stand while I eat these." He took a sip of his drink and ate a cookie.

"How does it taste?"

"Very good. Your *kichlin* are always tasty."

"Danki." Lois took a freezer container from the cupboard. "I'll put the cookies in this when they've cooled and then pop them into the freezer. When it gets closer to Christmas, I can add some frosting to them."

He held the second cookie in his hand. "This tastes fine just the way it is."

"Thank you, and eating them with less sugar is probably better for us."

He nodded. "When I'm done here, I'm going back outside to do more sledding. It's nice out there, and it feels like we could get more snow. Are you sure you don't want to join me?"

"I need to get some of those letters answered and a few Christmas cards made out as well." Lois pointed to the mail on the table. "It would be nice if I could answer all of them today, but it does take time to come up with what I hope will be the right answers."

"I'm sure the people needing advice from Dear Caroline would appreciate an answer pretty soon," Orley commented.

"Yes, and some of the letters aren't too difficult to answer, but other times I'm not sure if I have an answer."

"If you need my help, let me know." Orley popped the last bite of cookie into his mouth and carried his cup to the back door.

"Are you leaving already?"

"Yep. I'll take what's left in my mug and head outside."

"Okay, have fun out there." Lois watched him go out the door. She grabbed the container and put the cooled cookies inside.

Not long after, the timer went off, and she removed another batch of cookies from the oven. She wanted to keep baking, but those letters needed to be answered. Lois turned the oven off and placed the dirty dishes in the sink. She wrapped the remaining cookie dough up tight in waxed paper and placed it in the refrigerator.

Lois glanced toward the window and saw that snow was coming down again. It looked mesmerizing as it drifted in sparkly flakes to the ground. She imagined how a decorated snowman would look out in the yard, greeting people passing by on foot or riding in their vehicles. *If it weren't so cold outside, I wouldn't mind making a snowman, and I'm sure I've got some notions in my sewing room to give it a face.* Lois heaved a sigh. *But I'm afraid that will have to wait for another time when I'm not so busy and it's not quite so cold.*

Lois poured herself a cup of hot cocoa and picked out one plain and one peppermint cookie from the baking sheet. She then brought her treats over to the kitchen table and took a seat. Her first bite of the soft, warm sugar cookie tasted so good as it melted in her mouth. After a sip of cocoa, she set the mug down and read the Christmas card they'd received from her stepmother. Sarah had included a letter, wishing them a Merry Christmas and stating that she planned to visit her son in Colorado for the holidays. Lois had hoped that her father's widow might decide to move there to be close to her family, but Sarah kept insisting that she was happy living in Kentucky.

Lois sighed. *It's Sarah's choice, so all I can do is pray that she continues to do well and reaches out to others in her community for help and companionship if she needs it.*

Setting the Christmas card aside, Lois picked up one of the letters that had been sent to her Dear Caroline column. After reading it, a smile covered her face.

> *Dear Caroline,*
>
> *I'm having a problem with my neighbor who doesn't*

like the color of my house. Apparently, the elderly lady doesn't like yellow. She says it's too bright and informed me that she wears sunglasses when she walks past, even if the sun is not shining. I want to be a good neighbor, but I like the color of my house and don't want to change it. Is there an answer to this problem?

—Yellow Makes Me Happy

Lois took another sip of hot chocolate and shook her head. *Now how am I supposed to answer that one? Should I ignore this letter? Tell the person to change the color of their home?*

She set her mug down and reached up to massage her forehead. *Maybe I should put all this away and go sledding with Orley.* Lois rubbed her arms. *Dealing with the cold weather and climbing back up the hill might be easier than trying to come up with answers to people's problems.*

Lois left her chair and got out a bag of mini-marshmallows. After putting several in her cup of hot chocolate, she picked up the mug and left the room.

Maybe I ought to quit the Dear Caroline column, Lois told herself as she wandered into the living room. *When Orley and I mentor people, we talk face-to-face and have a better chance of knowing whether they took our advice.* The problem with the Dear Caroline column, aside from it taking up a lot of time, was that she never found out whether the things she'd suggested helped anyone.

Lois took a seat in her rocking chair and set the mug on the small table beside her. *Pray, Lois. You need to pray,* her inner voice commanded.

Without hesitation, she bowed her head. *Dear Lord, please give me a sense of direction concerning the Dear Caroline column. If I'm supposed to continue writing it, please give me a sign—something that will let me know if my responses are helpful or not.* Lois continued with her prayer by thanking God for the many blessings He had bestowed upon her and Orley, including the antique business and their marriage.

Lois ended her prayer with a heartfelt request: *Lord, please keep my husband safe while he's out there in the cold, taking chances on that old sled of his.*

—————

Orley's boots crunched as he tromped through the snow. Being outside with white flakes coming down was exhilarating and made him feel like a kid again. But of course it would be more fun if he had someone to share it with. *Too bad my fraa doesn't like being out in cold weather. She'd probably like it if we lived in one of the southern states where it's warm most of the year.*

Orley trudged up the hill, pulling his sled by the rope attached to the handles. His feet almost went out from under him once, but he regained his balance in time and kept on going.

"Next time I go sledding, I'm gonna invite one of our neighbor kids to join me," he mumbled. "It'd be a lot more fun than trompin' up the hill and sledding down by myself. At least there would be someone for me to laugh with when we both took tumbles or did something really stupid."

When Orley reached the top, he positioned himself face-down on the sled and pushed off. The ride down the hill was exhilarating, and when he reached the bottom, he didn't even mind when a little snow went up his nose.

He thought about Lois again, wishing she'd come out here to cheer him on and watch. Although it could just be his imagination, Orley thought his wife had seemed a little down lately. Could it be that she'd been thinking about her father's death? The Christmas holiday fast approaching could be a harsh reminder that loved ones who had passed on would not be here to celebrate what should be a cheery, festive season.

Of course, Orley reasoned, as he made another trip back up the hill, *Lois and her father hadn't been close, and he'd never come here for Christmas. Even so, it was quite possible that she was still grieving.*

Maybe I should do something special for my fraa for Christmas, Orley told himself. *I just need to think of what she might like.*

Apple Creek

Brandon stepped out of the first examining room and glanced at his watch. Things had been busy at the clinic all morning, and he was more than ready to eat lunch. He'd dealt with everything from a dog that had eaten its flea collar to a finicky cat that wouldn't eat anything except a certain kind of expensive cat food. Both pet owners had been concerned about their animal's eating habits—especially the one who had a German shorthaired pointer that preferred his own flea collar to a rawhide chew stick or a beef-flavored doggie treat. Fortunately, the flea collar hadn't appeared to make the dog sick, but if the dog ate enough of them, eventually there might be a serious problem.

Brandon's advice to the finicky cat owner was to keep trying some other foods in the hope that Snowball would eventually find one she liked. To the collar-eating dog owner, he suggested that he quit buying flea collars and protect the dog by other means, such as a flea bath, powder, or special pill.

Brandon entered his office and took a seat at his desk. He had a few phone calls to make before he ate lunch—the first one would be to Andrea.

He picked up his phone and brought up her number. A few seconds later, she answered.

"Hello." Andrea's voice sounded groggy, like she'd just woken up.

"Hi, sweetie. You weren't sleeping, I hope."

"Uh, no." He heard a noisy yawn. "I am tired, though. I was up late last night trying to finish a painting that someone ordered for Christmas. I have two more to complete for someone else, and then I'm done," she added after a second yawn.

"That's cutting it pretty close to Christmas," he commented.

"I suppose so, but I have fallen behind because I've been spending a lot of time on some of the internet sites for people who are searching for their biological parents."

Brandon stiffened. He was tempted to ask Andrea if that's all she cared about anymore. It sure seemed like it, which caused him some concern. Their wedding was only two months away, and they still had some details to work out. At the rate things were going, they'd never be ready on time.

"Umm, listen, the reason I called is to invite you for supper this evening." The phone was quiet on Andrea's end as he sat waiting for her response. "Andrea, did you hear what I said?"

"Yes, I did, but I got distracted by a text message that just came in."

"Was it important?"

"I'd say so. It was one of my adult piano students, letting me know that she won't be at the piano recital I have scheduled for next week because she broke her arm in a sledding accident, which means she can't play."

"That's too bad. Hopefully, all your other students can be there."

"Yes, because I've gone to a lot of trouble planning this recital, and I'm hoping for a good turnout."

Brandon paused a few seconds and took a drink from his bottle of water. It wasn't cold, the way he liked it, but his thirst was quenched, and that was all that mattered. "Now back to the reason I called. Will you be free to go out to supper with me this evening?"

"Not tonight, Brandon. I have more work to do on the paintings, and after that, I want to spend some time on the computer."

"More adoption stuff?" Brandon tried not to let his irritation show, but he was pretty sure she could hear it in his voice. This was not the first time Andrea had turned down an invitation to spend the evening with him. She'd passed up the opportunity for them to spend time together twice last week.

"I'm planning to do a DNA test soon," she said. "And I want to make sure of all the details and that I'm doing it right."

Is it really that important for you to locate your birth mother? Brandon thought, but he didn't voice the words that he felt sure Andrea would take offense to. "I hope it goes well." The words nearly stuck in his throat. It would have been right to say something encouraging, but those words wouldn't come out of his mouth.

"Sorry, Brandon, but I'm getting another call. I'll talk to you soon, okay?"

"Yeah, sure. Have a good rest of your day."

After they'd ended the conversation, Brandon sat with his lips pressed together and his arms folded. He wanted to talk to someone unbiased about this situation. The question was, who?

He scratched his head and gave it some thought. *Maybe I'll give my dad a call tonight and see what he has to say.*

———

Brandon didn't seem very understanding, Andrea thought after she'd set her cell phone aside. *Doesn't he realize how important it is for me to find my birth mother and learn about my heritage? I've always been accepting whenever he's been busy with work and can't spend time with me. Why is this any different?*

Releasing a sigh of frustration, she got up from the couch and headed for her art studio. As desperately as Andrea wanted to be on the computer right now, she was determined to finish the paintings so she could get paid. Normally, by this time in December, Andrea had all her Christmas shopping done. But that wasn't the case this year because in addition to earning a living, her top priority was finding her birth mother.

"But what if I never locate her?" Andrea spoke out loud. "Can I go through the rest of my life not knowing who she is or why she gave me up for adoption?" She shook her head. "I don't think so. I need to keep digging until I find answers, and I won't let anything or anyone get in the way."

Chapter 24

"Do you have a minute, Dad?" Brandon asked the following evening when his father answered the phone.

"Sure, Son. I always have time for you."

"Is that Brandon?"

Brandon heard the excited tone in his mother's voice. It sounded as though she was close to Dad's phone.

Brandon's fingers clenched around his phone. *Oh great. Dad obviously has his speaker mode on.*

"Yes, Jennifer. It's our son. He called to talk to me."

"Oh, I see." Mom's tone had changed to what Brandon recognized as one of disappointment.

It wasn't that Brandon didn't want to talk to his mother—just not now. He needed a private talk with Dad. Mom was the emotional one in the family and would no doubt offer advice that could end up getting him in trouble with Andrea, which would only make things worse. It had gotten harder for him to deal with his fiancée's seemingly fanatical mindset to find her real parents. Andrea's preoccupation had caused her to neglect their wedding plans and any quality time for them to spend together, which didn't set well with Brandon. His forehead creased. *My sweet Andrea seems to have morphed into someone I don't know. I need some advice before things get any worse.*

"Listen, Dad," Brandon said, "would it be possible for us to meet someplace for lunch tomorrow? I need to discuss a few things with you that could affect my future." He grimaced and nearly bit his tongue. If

Mom was still listening, which no doubt she was, she might assume that he and Andrea were having some kind of problem and try to fix it. While his mother was good at fixing little things that had broken around their house and was helpful in many ways, she often made things worse when she tried to meddle in affairs of the heart. Brandon remembered when he was dating a girl named Nadine in high school. They had disagreed about something, and when Mom got into the act, giving her thoughts on the topic to Nadine, the girl broke up with Brandon. Although their relationship probably wouldn't have lasted, Brandon blamed his mother for the split and wished she had kept out of it. He'd seen her interfere in a few other people's lives over the years, and her actions usually spelled disaster. He felt sure that his mom always meant well, but he would not give her the chance to mess things up between him and the woman he planned to marry.

"Brandon, did you hear what I said?"

"Umm. . .no, Dad, sorry. I was thinking."

"About where we should go to eat?"

"No, something else." Brandon moistened his dry, chapped lips. "Are you free to meet for lunch tomorrow?"

"Yes, I am. Should we eat at Lem's Pizza at noon?"

"Sounds good, Dad. I'll see you then. Say hi to Mom for me too, okay?"

"She's standing right here. Why don't you tell her yourself?"

Brandon shifted in his chair to look at Duke, standing by the front door. "Hi, Mom. Say, I have to cut this short because my dog needs to go out. I'll see you at church, Sunday, okay?"

"Sure, Son. Have a good rest of your evening."

"Bye, Dad. Bye, Mom." Brandon clicked off, slipped on a jacket, and went to take care of Duke. This was one time when he was glad for the inconvenience of going out into the cold.

⁓

Jennifer stepped away from Larry and folded her arms. "I can't believe our son did not want to talk to me."

"Didn't you hear what Brandon said? He had to let his dog out."

She took a seat on the couch. "That may be true, but he didn't include me in your lunch plans."

"I guess Brandon wants a little father-son time. Is there anything wrong with that?"

"Well no, but he said that he wanted to talk about his future, which involves Andrea, no doubt."

Larry picked up the remote and pointed it at the TV from his recliner.

"Please don't turn that on right now. We are in the middle of a discussion."

Larry looked at her pointedly. "There isn't much to discuss, and I don't believe there's any need for you to be concerned. Brandon probably wants to discuss some financial matters with me, and since I'm a bank manager. . ."

She fiddled with the gold bracelet on her right wrist. "What makes you think it's a financial issue? He might be having a problem that involves Andrea. She hasn't been acting like herself since she found out she was adopted, and maybe it's affecting their relationship."

He waved the remote in her direction. "You worry too much when you should be praying."

Jennifer shook her head vigorously. "That is not true, and you know it. I do plenty of praying. When our son shuts me out, I feel like he doesn't want me to be part of his life."

"Brandon is his own person, Jen, and if you pray like I keep reminding you to do and give it to the Lord, you won't worry so much—especially when we aren't even sure what it's about." His forehead creased. "And even if you did know what's going on in Brandon's life right now, it would be out of your control."

"I'm not trying to control anything. It would just be helpful if I knew what to pray about."

"For now, you can pray that my lunch with our son goes well tomorrow, and if it's anything you need to know, I'll say so." Larry pointed the remote at the TV again. "Can we please not talk about this anymore? I'd like to catch the news before it's time for bed."

"Okay, but I'm not interested in watching the news. It reminds me of all the horrible things going on in our world right now." She rose from the couch. "I'm going to our room and get ready for bed." Jennifer moved across the room. "Oh, and I will definitely pray for our son and his bride-to-be after I get into bed." She rushed out of the room before he could say anything more. Jennifer felt incredibly frustrated when she was left out of things.

She turned on the hall light so Larry could see when he came to bed. *I wish Brandon had invited me to join them for lunch too, but hopefully Larry will tell me whatever our son says when he gets home from work tomorrow evening.*

~

Andrea squinted as she rubbed the bridge of her nose. She'd been sitting in front of her computer for nearly three hours, looking at various sites for people who had been adopted and taking notes. There was so much information out there, it made her head swim.

"If I had my original birth certificate, it would make things easier," she muttered. "At least then I would know my biological parents' names." The birth certificate Andrea's parents had gotten when they adopted her was legal and included their names, as well as the one they had chosen for her, but it did not give Andrea the information she needed to locate her biological parents.

"Why did they agree to a closed adoption?" Her jaw ached as she clenched her top and bottom teeth, and she reached for her rollerball filled with lavender essential oil. "Apparently, they didn't want me to know who had given birth to me."

Andrea paused to roll some of the essential oil on her wrists, neck, and forehead before leaving the website where she'd been reading about the difference between closed and open adoptions and clicked on AncestryDNA. She'd looked at similar sites, but this one had very large databases, so she decided to open an account and purchase a DNA kit online. She'd receive a prepaid envelope and a test tube, which she'd need to fill with a saliva sample and return to the company through the mail.

Andrea's heartbeat quickened as she read that Ancestry relied on a large online database that might include relatives who had done similar testing in the past. If this had occurred, she would not only discover her ethnic background but also any relatives who had tested as well.

Without hesitation, Andrea purchased the DNA kit. "There, that's done. Now all I have to do is wait for it to arrive, and the rest will be up to me."

Lady stirred from where she lay curled in Andrea's lap and let out a quiet *meow*.

"Sorry, girl, I didn't mean to wake you." Andrea glanced at the computer clock at the bottom of her screen. "Twelve thirty already? Where did the time go, my sweet little Lady? I need to shut this computer down so we can go to bed."

Andrea turned it off, picked up Lady, and headed down the hall to her room. Tomorrow would be another long day, filled with teaching piano lessons and putting the final touches on some paintings she'd been hired to do. Even so, she would squeeze in some time to look at more adoption sites because, to her, that was most important.

Walnut Creek

"Are you ready for bett?" Orley called from the living room where he'd been reading a magazine article about identifying certain kinds of old bottles.

"I'll be there soon," Lois responded. "I have a few more letters to answer."

He grimaced. *Again? Is there no end to those letters that keep pouring in?* As much as Orley didn't want to admit it, he figured a lot of people must enjoy Lois's Dear Caroline column.

Feeling a bit put out, Orley told Lois goodnight and left the room. *Am I envious of her?* Orley asked himself as he plodded down the hall. *Lois is reaching a lot more people through that column than I ever could in our store.*

He paused to scratch an itch behind his left ear. *It's been a long time since anyone's come in with a problem and asked my advice. Maybe I should start a column of my own and offer it to the newspaper. I could call it Dear Amos, and it could be a column for men.* He clunked the side of his head. *No, that's a* dumm *idea. I'm good with words when talking to someone one-on-one but not with the written word. My grammar would be off, and I'd be so rattled trying to think of the right answers, I would be a nervous wreck.* Orley shook his head. *No, I don't think I could express myself right unless I was talking directly to a person. So I'd better scratch that idea and stick to what I do best.*

Orley reached the bedroom and got a drink of water from their bathroom sink. That way his wife could keep working undisturbed at the kitchen table.

He smiled to himself, thinking about yesterday when he and Lois had made a snowman together in their front yard with the sun shining against the glistening snow. Although his wife had a lot on her plate these days, it was good when she took time out to do something fun.

Apple Creek

"Coming here to Lem's Pizza was a good idea, but I think I'm gonna opt for a sub sandwich," Brandon said. "They make some pretty good ones."

"Agreed," his dad said. "Think I might have one of those too."

The place was busy, but that wasn't unusual. Brandon studied the menu before ordering a turkey and provolone full-size sub with lettuce, tomatoes, green peppers, pickles, and onion, along with a cup of coffee. His father placed an order for the same sandwich, only he asked for swiss cheese, mushrooms, and green olives to be added to his.

"It's interesting that this place was opened by a man named Mark Lemon, whose nickname was Lem," Dad commented as he sat across the table from Brandon.

Staring into his cup of coffee, Brandon nodded.

"This restaurant sure has some neat local memorabilia on the walls, both historical and current."

"Uh-huh."

"Son, you're not really listening to me, are you?"

When Dad snapped his fingers, Brandon blinked and looked up. "Umm. . .no, guess I wasn't. I have other things on my mind."

"That's the reason you wanted to meet with me, correct? It was something about your future you needed to discuss."

"Yeah, Dad. I'm worried about my relationship with Andrea."

Dad's brow furrowed a bit. "What about it? Things are okay between you two, aren't they? You're still planning to be married in February, right?"

Brandon shrugged. "I'm not sure."

"She hasn't called off your engagement, I hope." Dad's gaze flitted around the room, and he looked back at Brandon with furrowed brows. "Your mother has made a lot of plans regarding the rehearsal dinner, and she'd be pretty upset if—"

Brandon held up his hand. "As far as I know, the wedding is still on, but the thing is. . .she's so caught up in trying to find her biological parents that she doesn't have time for me anymore."

"Seriously? Did Andrea tell you that?"

"No, but she's turned me down several times when I've wanted to get together for a meal."

"Did she state the reason?"

Brandon's neck bent forward, and his shoulders slumped. "She's either too busy teaching piano, painting pictures, or researching on the internet for ways to locate her birth parents."

"Haven't there been times when you've been too busy to get together with her?"

"Yeah, of course, but it's not just her busyness that bothers me. When we are together, which isn't as often as before, all she talks about is her need to locate her birth mother. We don't discuss much else."

"Have you been supportive of Andrea's desire to know about and possibly meet her biological family?"

"I've tried to be, but it seems like it's becoming an obsession with her, and I don't want that to be all we talk about."

"It's understandable."

"What if Andrea hasn't found her birth mother by the time we get married?" Brandon rubbed a twitching eyelid. "I want my future wife's full attention when I talk to her about something, and after we're married, it'll be even more important."

"Have you discussed this with Andrea—told her how you feel?"

Brandon shook his head before taking a sip from his cup. "If I say too much, she might think I'm not being supportive enough, and that would only make things worse." He looked directly at his father. "What do you think I should do?"

Dad rubbed his clean-shaven chin. "If I were you, I'd take a chance and discuss your feelings with her. Andrea may be so caught up in her quest to find the woman who gave birth to her that she's unaware of the fact that she is shutting you out."

Brandon gave a brief nod. "Could be."

Just then their sandwiches arrived, and they paused to pray. When Brandon opened his eyes, he bit into the sub, and his dad did the same.

"I'll give what you said some serious thought." Brandon drank some more coffee. "Thanks for taking the time to meet with me today. I really appreciate it."

"No problem. That's what dads are for."

Brandon ate more of his sandwich, then paused to ask another question. "Would you mind keeping our conversation to yourself? I'd rather not let Mom know what's going on between me and Andrea. She would only fret about it and maybe try to intervene on my behalf." His brows furrowed. "I'm sure that wouldn't go over well with Andrea, because then she would know that I've been talking about it to someone other than her."

"No problem," Dad said. "I won't say anything to your mother or anyone else."

Brandon felt relieved about that much at least. Now if he could only decide how and when to tell Andrea the way he'd been feeling. Maybe it would go better than he thought. Andrea might understand and make more time to spend with him while spending less time on a quest that could end up at a dead end with no other place to go.

Chapter 25

Saturday afternoon when Andrea entered the church she and her parents had attended since she was a child, she was greeted by the custodian, Arnie Smith.

"The building is plenty warm, and lights are on in the sanctuary as well as the fellowship hall. Everything's ready for you and your students." The elderly but still active man gave Andrea a pleasant smile.

"Thank you, Arnie. I appreciate being able to use the church for my students' piano recital." She returned his smile with one of her own. "And I am grateful for all that you've done in preparation for my event."

"It's part of my job. But I enjoy what I do here at the church, and I'm thankful to be employed." He gestured toward the sanctuary. "Is there anything else you need me to do at this time?"

"No, I think we're all set. I'll take the refreshments I brought to the fellowship hall, and then all that's left is waiting for my students and their families to arrive."

Arnie gave a nod. "All right then. I'll be back in a couple hours to clean and close up the church."

"Thanks. Have a good afternoon."

"And you as well. I hope everything goes real good here today."

Andrea smiled. She hoped it would too.

~

Andrea sat on the front pew, watching and prompting her piano students when necessary as they took turns playing their pieces. So far, everyone had done well, and it was nice to hear the appreciative applause from those in the audience. Andrea's parents had come to cheer her on, but she was a bit disappointed that Brandon hadn't made it, although she understood why. He had called her shortly before the recital started to let her know that he was needed at a farm to deliver a calf whose mother was having a difficult labor.

And so goes the life of a veterinarian, she thought. *I'd better get used to it if I'm going to marry him, just like he needs to realize that I lead a busy life too. Even so, I do wish Brandon could be a little more understanding when it comes to my decision to search for my biological parents. I've been supportive of him and have tried to be understanding when he can't always attend events that are important to me, such as this one recital.*

Andrea refocused when her last and only adult piano student finished playing her piece and everyone applauded. She felt pleased with how well the recital had gone and was proud of her students. Even Peggy, who had previously said she wanted her parents to find a different teacher, had done a good job, although she still hadn't trimmed her fingernails adequately. Since Peggy's parents had insisted on keeping Andrea as their daughter's teacher, the teenager had become easier to teach and, for the most part, did as she was told.

Andrea left her seat and stood on the platform, holding a microphone. "Thank you all for coming here today. I am pleased with how well all of my students did, and I have every hope that they will continue to learn and improve in the weeks and months ahead. Now, before you return to your homes, I hope you will all join me in the fellowship hall, where refreshments are waiting."

Everyone clapped again and rose from their seats. As they began filing out of the sanctuary, Andrea's mother came up and gave her a hug. "Your students are progressing nicely, and your father and I are so proud of your accomplishments as both a pianist and an artist."

"Thank you, Mom. I enjoy what I do, and it's a good feeling when my students do well at their recital."

Andrea's father joined them and gave Andrea a hug too. "That was a great recital. Your mom and I enjoyed it very much, and now

I'm ready to go see what you brought for refreshments."

Andrea laughed. Dad was a man of few words, unless it came to food.

～

Berlin

After Brandon left the farm call in Mt. Hope, where he had helped a struggling cow give birth, he'd decided to visit some of the stores in Berlin. He wanted to give Andrea a special gift for Christmas and hoped he would find something in one of the shops. He had tried talking to her last night about their relationship, but he'd made no progress whatsoever. She had made light of his concerns and said it was just a busy time for her right now and that once she found her birth mother, things would be better all the way around. As they'd continued to talk, their conversation had turned into a near-argument, so Brandon had dropped the subject.

"Yeah, right," Brandon mumbled after he left one of the gift stores and got into his vehicle. He could feel Andrea pulling away from him a little more each day and couldn't help worrying. What if she never found the woman who'd given birth to her? Would Andrea push him further away until they had no relationship at all?

Maybe if I give her something really nice for Christmas, it'll smooth things over with her for not being able to attend her students' recital today and for the heated words we had last night. Brandon put the key in the ignition. *She likes vintage items. I wonder if I should pay a visit to that antique store in Walnut Creek she told me about. I bet they might have something she would like.*

～

Walnut Creek

Earlier today, Lois and her husband had gone through several boxes of antiques in the back room that they'd received from an English woman whose mother had passed away. The woman said she didn't have time to sort through all the old things or run an ad to try and sell them, so Orley had paid her what he felt was a fair price. He'd told Lois that he figured some or all of the items might have value. Yesterday and again this morning, Lois had helped Orley clean and price an old table lamp, some jewelry, a variety of books, several pieces of clothing, and a few other vintage items.

"I'll be able to put some of these items out now." Orley ran his thumb up and down one of his black suspenders as he looked at Lois.

"I was surprised that we received so many items from her, and it's all a little different from what we have in our shop." Lois held up an old washboard. "This one is bigger than the one we have out front on display."

"I agree, and this old oil brand sign is in nice shape for its age too." Orley gestured to it. "Not to mention there are some old tools, gardening reaping hooks, oil cans, and other vintage items."

"We will definitely have more things to put out on the floor before Christmas." Lois smiled as she picked up a small box with a few indistinguishable items inside. "I'll find places to put these, but I'd like to get your opinion first."

Orley followed her from the back of the store, carrying the sign that needed to be displayed on the wall for prospective buyers. They'd no more than approached the register when the phone rang. Lois placed the box on the counter and answered their business line, which they'd recently received permission from their church leaders to have in the store. "Hello, Memory Keepers."

The person on the other end asked about their hours and wondered if they had any antique jewelry. Lois said they did have some and told the man that he was welcome to come by for a look. Then she hung up with the customer and waited, wanting to show her husband what was inside the box she held.

Meanwhile, Orley had leaned the sign against the wall he'd chosen for its display. "I think it will go well right here. What do you think, Lois?" he asked.

"It's a good spot and blends well with the others that are hanging there already." Lois gestured to the small box on the counter. "Would you care to see what I have here?"

"Sure thing." He came up by the register. "Whatcha got?"

"I picked these up a while back and forgot about them." She unwrapped each one from the tissue paper. "I'd like your thoughts on these."

He leaned closer as she placed three small Amish dolls on the counter.

"What do you think?" Lois asked.

He pushed his glasses up to the bridge of his nose and picked up the first doll. "This boy doll is made of plastic, so it's probably not worth much," he stated. "But the girl doll made of wood and the other one made from cast iron would probably go for more."

Lois nodded. "That's what I was thinking. I'll set them out next to the other vintage dolls we have on display. Since it's so close to Christmas, someone might come into Memory Keepers and buy one or more of the dolls we have for sale."

Orley pointed to the doll made of wood. "Do you think someone would buy an old doll like this for their little *maedel*?"

Lois shrugged. "Could be. I had one when I was a girl. In fact, this *bopp* looks quite similar to mine." Her brows knitted together as she stared intently at the doll. "But, of course, it's not the same."

"What'd you do with your wooden doll?" Orley asked.

"My sister Elizabeth ended up with it." Lois had a faraway look in her eyes as she stared across the room. "I had other dolls too."

"What happened to all your dolls? Do you have them tucked away somewhere and never bothered to show them to me? Were you worried I might want to sell them?"

She shook her head. "I gave most of them away when I grew too old to play with dolls anymore." Ending their conversation, Lois picked up the dolls and made her way across the room, where she placed them on the shelf with the other dolls that hadn't yet sold.

Orley gave his head a quick shake. He seriously doubted that any young girl, English or Amish, would want a rigid-looking doll that they couldn't cuddle. More than likely, if any of the dolls here sold, it would be to a doll collector.

He looked back at the wall where he'd left the metal sign. *I'll try to get that hung at some point today if it doesn't get too busy in here.* Orley grabbed a piece of candy from the small plastic bowl sitting by the register for their customers to enjoy. Lois usually filled it with peppermint candy, but for Christmas she'd added some cinnamon candies too, which made the red and green colors look festive.

"I'm returning to the storage room to see what else we might have to put out on display," Lois called to him before she headed off in that direction.

"Okay, but don't get too involved looking. Anyway, the oil lamp and that washboard can be brought out to sell."

"I'll get them first."

"If things start to get busy, like they were earlier this morning, I may need your help out here," he reminded her.

"If that should happen, please come and get me," Lois responded before she disappeared into the storage room.

My wife sure seemed to be in a hurry to leave this room, Orley thought. *I wonder if she has more of those Dear Caroline letters to write and is afraid I might say something about it.*

Lois came back a short time later with the items he'd spoken of and rearranged the places where she'd chosen to set them. Orley couldn't help but smile. His wife had always liked things a certain way both at home and here in the store.

After Lois returned to the storage room, Orley's thoughts shifted gear. *I hope my dear wife will like the gift I got her for Christmas.* He bent down to tie a loose shoelace. He'd almost finished tying it when he heard the bell above the front door jingle. *Oh good—sounds like a prospective customer.*

When Brandon entered the antique store, a combination of odors wafted up to his nose. This small building smelled like wood, leather, and musty cloth with a few other scents he couldn't identify mixed in.

He glanced around the building but saw no one in sight. Brandon cupped his hands around his mouth. "Hello! Anyone here?" Surely the shop owners wouldn't leave their business unattended—especially with so many valuable vintage items displayed. And this place was full of old things. In every direction, he saw things like antique furniture pieces, old dishes, iconic business signs, vintage clocks, a shelf full of books, and many other items that looked and smelled old.

Brandon was getting ready to take a stroll around the room when a middle-aged Amish man with a full beard popped up from behind the front counter where an antiquated cash register was located.

"Good afternoon," the man said. "My name is Orley Troyer, and I don't believe we've met before. Are you new around here?"

"Not new to the area, but this is my first time in your store. My name is Brandon Prentice, and I live in Apple Creek. My veterinarian clinic is there too."

"Oh, so you're an animal doctor?"

"Yes, I am. And since I was in Walnut Creek today, I decided to stop here to see if I could find a nice Christmas gift for my fiancée."

"Are you looking for anything in particular?"

Brandon shrugged. "I'm not sure. She likes antiques, so I'm hoping if I can find something to her liking, she might pay more attention to me and spend less time doing research on her computer." A knot formed in Brandon's stomach. *Now what made me say something like that to a man I've never met before? I can only imagine what he must think of me.* "Sorry, I shouldn't have blurted that out. I'm feeling a little stressed right now and not thinking as clearly as I should be."

Orley stepped forward and placed a hand on Brandon's shoulder.

"Are you and your future wife having some problems right now?"

"Truthfully, yes. She recently found out that she was adopted as a baby, and now she's so busy trying to find her biological parents that she doesn't have time to spend with me or even finalize the plans we've been making for our upcoming wedding." Brandon didn't know why, but strangely enough, he felt comfortable talking about this with the Amish man. Maybe it was the look of concern on Orley's face, or perhaps it was being able to speak with someone who was completely removed from the situation.

"I'm a pretty good listener," Orley said. "I've also been known to hand out a little advice to people who choose to share their problems with me."

"I see." Brandon thought over the man's statement for a few seconds, and then, throwing caution to the wind, he said, "What would you do if the woman you were engaged to marry became so involved with the quest to find her birth mother that she had no time for you anymore?"

Orley's lips pressed together, and he tipped his head to one side as though contemplating the question. A few seconds passed, and then he looked directly at Brandon and said matter-of-factly, "I would sit down and have a talk with her about it. I'd mention that I feel left out of her life and miss spending time with her."

Brandon nodded. "I did that the other night, but I think my comments fell on deaf ears."

"She didn't say anything in response?"

"Oh, a response came from her all right, but it was one I didn't like." Brandon shifted his stance. "She said I should be more understanding and stated quite firmly that after she finds out who gave birth to her, she'll have more time to spend with me."

"That could be a difficult, time-consuming process. What if she never finds out?"

"Exactly." Brandon frowned. "I don't like the way things are headed, but at least she's agreed to spend Christmas with me. Of course, we'll spend part of it with her folks and mine, but I'm sure there will be some time when we're alone and can hopefully discuss our wedding plans." Brandon glanced across the room, then back at Orley. "Speaking of Christmas. . . Is there anything here you think my fiancée might like?"

"Let's see now. . ." Orley started across the room, and Brandon followed him over to a large bookcase. "Does she like to read old novels?"

Brandon shook his head. "She keeps busy teaching piano lessons and is also an artist, so she doesn't have much time for reading."

"Here's something interesting she might like." Orley moved over to another shelf where some old dishes had been placed and picked up an ornate dome-shaped item. "This is a very old butter dish that was made in England a good many years ago."

Brandon leaned forward and studied the piece. It appeared to be quite fragile and would no doubt break easily if bumped or knocked over. He could see the disaster that would follow if Andrea's cat, who sometimes hopped up on things, brushed against the vintage butter dish and it toppled to the floor. *Goodbye Christmas present, and hello upset wife-to-be. No, not a good gift for Andrea.*

"Think I'd better find something that's not so easy to break." Brandon moved to the area where some furniture had been displayed and leaned down to place his hand on top of an antique coffee table that was in good shape. "This might be nice. Yeah, I think my bride-to-be would like this, and it won't clash with any of my furniture when she moves into my home after we're married." He looked at the price tag attached to the table and smiled at the bearded Amish man. "I'll take it." *And if I know Andrea as well as I think I do, I believe she'll like this vintage coffee table.*

"Let's go up to the checkout counter, and you can pay for it there," Orley said. "Then I'll help you take it out to your vehicle."

"I appreciate the offer, but I should be able to manage it on my own." Brandon followed Orley to the front of the store. "Thanks for allowing me to share my problems and also for taking the time to offer your advice."

Orley nodded. "It was my privilege to do so. If you're ever in the area again, feel free to stop by, even if it's just to talk."

Brandon smiled. "I might take you up on that offer. I can tell that you're a man who cares about people."

"Yes, I do, but God cares about folks even more."

"That's true. I've been a believer since I was a young boy, and I don't know what I'd do without the Lord in my life."

"Me either." Orley spoke with a certainty in his voice. "On that note, I'll just say that God knows about whatever problems we may have to face in this life, so the best thing to do when dealing with any kind of situation beyond our control is to pray about it and let the Lord work things out."

"Good advice," Brandon agreed. "And thanks for the reminder, because I'm the kind of guy who often tries to figure things out on his own. When it doesn't work out and nothing gets resolved, that's when I remember that I should have taken it to the Lord in prayer right away and let Him help me with the problem."

Orley nodded. "I'm guilty of that too, so the words I just spoke were to myself as well as to you."

Brandon reached into his pocket for his wallet to pay for the coffee table. He was glad he'd come by here today. Meeting Orley Troyer and talking about his troubles had been good for him and brought things into a better perspective. Quite likely in the days ahead he would find an excuse to drop by Memory Keepers Antique Store again.

Chapter 26

"*En hallicher Grischtdaag!*" Orley said when he entered the kitchen where Lois was busy getting their breakfast ready to put on the table.

"A Merry Christmas to you too." She smiled and went to give him a hug.

"Have you been to your sewing room this morning?" he asked.

She gestured to the pancake batter she was about to pour on the griddle. "The only place I've been is right here, preparing our Christmas breakfast, and I certainly don't have any time to sew."

Orley chuckled. "I wasn't asking you to. I just wanted to know if you had been to that room."

She shook her head. "No, and I probably won't go there until sometime next week when I do some much-needed mending."

"Well, please turn off the burner and let's go there right now."

Lois looked puzzled. "What's gotten into you, Orley? Aren't you *hungerich* this morning?"

"Jah, I'm hungry, but eating breakfast can wait till you've opened your Christmas present from me."

Lois figured that if her gift was in the sewing room, Orley must have gotten her a new sewing machine. She didn't really need one—hers was fine—but if that was what he'd bought, she would be appreciative.

Lois turned off the stove and removed the griddle from the burner. "All right, my dear husband, please lead the way."

When they entered the sewing room, Lois was surprised to see what looked like it could be a piece of furniture covered with one of Orley's tarps. From the size of it, she was sure the item was not a sewing machine.

"Go ahead and open your present." Orley pointed to the large object.

Lois stepped up to it and pulled one corner of the drop cloth aside, and as she continued pulling, her mouth opened wide. "*Ach*, my! This oak desk is *brechdich*!"

Orley grinned. "I think it's pretty magnificent too." He moved closer to her. "I'm glad you like it."

"I do—very much so in fact. Danki." She gave him a hug.

"You're welcome. I thought this would be better for you to sit at while you answer your Dear Caroline letters than being seated at the kitchen table. And I think there's enough room for it to be kept right here in your sewing room, which is why I asked our neighbor, Harvey Miller, to help me bring it into the house last night after you'd gone to bed."

"You're a sneaky one." She poked his arm playfully. "And I agree about keeping the desk here—just not in the middle of the room."

"Course not. You choose where you want the desk, and I'll move it there."

"How about up against the wall by my sewing machine? With two windows on that wall, I'll have plenty of light when I'm sitting at the desk during daylight hours."

"Good point. I'll move it there right now."

"Here, let me help you."

"No, that's okay. I can do it." Orley positioned himself near the center of the desk and pushed. He'd barely gotten it against the wall, when he put both hands against the small of his back and let out a yelp.

"What's wrong?" Lois's pulse quickened as she rushed to his side.

"My back spasmed. It really hurts. Think I'd better sit down."

Bent over at the waist, he made his way slowly over to the chair in front of Lois's sewing table. Orley winced as he lowered himself into it.

"I think you should lie down before the pain gets worse," Lois said. "I'll help you to the couch and get an ice pack to put against your back."

"No, I'll be all right. Just help me to the kitchen so I can eat."

She placed her arm gently around his waist and guided him in that direction. When they reached the table, Orley gritted his teeth and lowered himself into a chair. Lois hoped he'd be able to get out of it after he finished eating breakfast—all because her stubborn husband wouldn't accept her help when it came to moving the desk.

Lois felt bad that she hadn't been able to give Orley the gift she'd bought for him before his back went into spasm, but that could wait until they'd eaten breakfast and he'd made it to the couch to rest with an ice pack on his back.

Lois didn't voice her thoughts to Orley, but if his back pain didn't improve by noon, they wouldn't be going to his brother's house for dinner. She pulled her fingers into the palms of her hands. *What a way to begin our Christmas. I hope it gets better as the day goes along.*

Orley lay face-up on the couch with a cold ice pack under his back. Lois had talked him out of going to Samuel and Esther's, which meant his sweet wife had to come up with something to fix for their afternoon meal. Orley wished he hadn't been too stubborn to let Lois help him move that desk. Now he was paying the price for not swallowing his pride and trying to prove how strong he was. He'd asked his neighbor for help getting the desk into the house. He should have let Lois help him move it.

"I have something that might cheer you up." Lois came over to the couch with a green gift bag in her hand. "Merry Christmas, Orley." She placed the bag on his belly.

"You didn't have to get me anything."

"Of course I did." She smiled. "Now reach inside and see what it is."

Orley tipped the bag over, put his hand in, and pulled out a nice-sized Mississippi harmonica. Tears welled in his eyes. "Danki, Lois. This looks like the harmonica my grandpa Troyer used to play for me and my brothers when we were boys." He looked up at Lois and smiled. "Where did you find this mouth harp?"

"At the thrift store near Berlin. Do you like it?"

"Jah, I sure do. It was a thoughtful gift."

Lois took a seat in the rocking chair near the couch. "Do you feel up to playing something—maybe a Christmas song?"

"I can try, but it's been a good many years since I've had a harmonica between my lips."

"I bet it's just like riding a bike," she said. "Once you learn how, you never forget."

Orley rolled over onto his side and pulled himself to a sitting position. Placing the ice pack behind his back, he held the harmonica up to his mouth and blew a couple of notes. Then, like it was yesterday, Orley played "Silent Night" followed by "Away in a Manger." He looked at Lois and grinned, despite the continued throbbing in his back. "This gift has made my Christmas a little brighter, and I thank you for that."

She left her seat and came over to give him a kiss on the cheek. "Your Christmas present made me happy as well." Lois patted his knee. "If it doesn't hurt too bad to keep sitting up, why don't you continue to play while I go to the kitchen to fix our Christmas dinner."

"I believe I can do that."

As soon as Lois left the room, Orley began playing the mouth harp again. Being able to fill the room, and maybe the whole house, with music helped to take Orley's mind off his sore back. His thoughts were on Jesus and how thankful he felt for God's precious gift to the world.

Apple Creek

Andrea had spent Christmas morning on the computer while she nibbled on a piece of toast with peanut butter. It wasn't much of a breakfast, but she'd have plenty to eat when she and Brandon went to his parents' house for Christmas dinner. Brandon would be by to pick her up around twelve thirty, but that was an hour from now, so she could continue browsing the internet for a while yet.

Andrea had clicked on a page about adoption that she hadn't been to before, when her cell phone rang. She recognized Colleen's number and answered right away.

"Merry Christmas, my good friend." Colleen's voice had an upbeat tone.

"Merry Christmas to you too. Have you opened your presents yet?"

"We just finished, and now there's wrapping paper and bows scattered around the living room." Colleen chuckled. "You should have seen Tyler tear into his gifts. He was one excited little two-year-old."

"I can imagine."

"Shawn and I waited till Tyler had opened all his gifts and was busy playing with his new toys until we opened our presents. And that leads me to one of the reasons I called. I wanted to thank you for the beautiful painting you gave me of an Amish home with a horse and buggy going by."

"Do you like it?"

"It's beautiful. Sure wish I had your ability to paint. You are one talented lady."

"Thank you, and I'm glad you like the painting. When I dropped the gift by your house two days ago, I figured you might open it then."

"I admit I was tempted, but it's so much fun to wait and open presents on Christmas Day, I decided to wait."

"I understand." Andrea shifted on her chair when Lady leaped into her lap. She rubbed the cat's ears as she continued her conversation with Colleen.

"I haven't opened your gift yet either. It's still under the little tree I set up in the living room."

"Why don't you open it now? I'd like to know whether you like it or not."

"Sure, I can do that. Hang on while I get to the tree." Andrea lifted Lady off her lap and put her on the floor. Then she headed for the living room and picked up Colleen's gift. Although her friend had chosen to wait until Christmas Day to open her gift, Andrea had not committed to doing the same. She'd planned to open it last night, after Brandon brought her home from Christmas caroling with a group of single adults from their church, but she'd been too tired. Andrea had stayed up late nearly every night since she'd learned of her adoption and pushed herself each day to get all the necessary things done. Now she was on the brink of exhaustion.

Andrea put the phone in speaker mode and placed it on the couch beside her so she could keep talking while opening the gift.

"Okay, I have the gift, and I'm going to open it now." Andrea spoke loudly with her head turned in the direction of the phone.

"Great. Let me know what you think."

Andrea tore the wrapping paper off, lifted the lid on the box, and withdrew a square glass container with a beautiful red cardinal painted on it. "Oh, Colleen, it's beautiful!"

"You like it?"

"Of course I do. You know how excited I get whenever I see a cardinal."

"Yes, I do, and I gave it to you for another reason as well."

Andrea set the container on the end table near the couch and picked up the phone. "What's the other reason?"

"Since you love to paint and are such a talented artist, I thought you might want to consider painting some things on glass jars, bottles, or..."

"Oh, I don't know, Colleen. I'm really too busy right now to start any new projects."

"Of course, because of your wedding plans, right?"

"Umm...yeah...that and trying to locate my birth mother."

"Have you found anything out so far?"

"No, and I'm pretty discouraged. I ordered my DNA kit a few weeks ago and still have not received it." Andrea sighed. "I figured the kit would have been here by now."

"With the holiday season, the mail's probably slow. I'm sure it will arrive soon—maybe after the first of the year."

"I hope so. I'll take the test as soon as it gets here and send it back right away."

"Have you considered waiting until after you and Brandon are married to pursue your quest to find your biological parents?"

"No way! This is too important to me, and I can't wait that long."

"Okay. Like I've said to you before, let me know if I can be of any help."

"I will. Thanks, Colleen—for the painted cardinal and your friendship."

"You're welcome. I appreciate your friendship too."

The doorbell rang, and Andrea got up from the couch. "I'd better go. I think Brandon's here to pick me up to go to his parents' house for dinner. I'll talk to you again soon, okay?"

"For sure, and please let me know if there's anything I can do to help with either your wedding plans or the search for your birth mother."

"I will. Have a good rest of your day, and please tell your hubby I said, 'Merry Christmas.'"

"Will do, my friend."

After Andrea clicked off, she headed for the front door, nearly tripping over Lady, who'd found the wrapping paper from the box Colleen's gift had been in and was joyfully batting at it with her front paws.

When Andrea opened the front door, Brandon stepped inside, out of the cold, blustery day. "Merry Christmas, my beautiful wife-to-be."

"Merry Christmas, Brandon."

He enveloped her in a hug. "I have your gift in my vehicle. Should I bring it in?"

Andrea couldn't miss the gleam in his eyes. Whatever the gift was, she knew he was excited to present it to her. "That would be fine," she responded. "Unless you'd rather give it to me at your parents' house."

He shook his head. "The gift belongs here in your house—for now at least. Once we're married, I'm sure you'll want to bring it to my place when you move in with me."

She tipped her head then glanced at his SUV parked in the driveway. "Yes, please bring it in. You've aroused my curiosity."

"Okay. Take a seat in the living room, and I'll bring it right in."

After scooping Lady into her arms, Andrea did as he asked and seated herself on the couch. Brandon had left the front door open, and the last thing she needed was for her cat to make the great escape into the snowy front yard.

Several minutes went by before she heard the front door close, and then Brandon entered the room, carrying a beautiful vintage coffee table. "I hope you like it," he said, placing the table in front of the couch.

She let go of Lady, who promptly resumed playing with the wrapping paper, and placed both hands against her cheeks. "Oh my . . . It's so beautiful! Where did you get this old piece of furniture that's in such good condition?"

"I bought it at the same place you went to have that old quilt you bought this summer appraised."

"Memory Keepers in Walnut Creek?"

"Yes. The man who co-owns the shop was sure friendly and talkative."

"His wife was too. Did you meet her as well?"

Brandon shook his head. "Just Orley." He gestured to the table. "Do you like it?"

"Yes, very much. Thank you, Brandon. It's a thoughtful gift."

He offered her a wide smile and sat down beside her to give her a tender kiss. "I can't wait to make you my wife. February can't come soon enough."

Andrea swallowed hard and pulled her tongue across her lips. "About that. . . I'm wondering if it would be best to postpone the wedding."

Deep wrinkles formed across Brandon's forehead, making him look older than his thirty-five years. "Are you saying that you don't want to marry me?"

She shook her head vigorously. "No, no, I'm not saying that at all. I just think Valentine's Day is too soon."

His eyes narrowed as though in confusion. "Too soon for what? That's the day we both chose, and we'll be sending out wedding invitations next month, so we can't change the date." His voice had risen, and a sheen of sweat covered his forehead. Brandon was clearly shaken by her suggestion, but she needed to explain.

"The invitations haven't been sent to the printer yet, so there's still time to change the date."

"I don't want to change the date, and I can't believe that you apparently do." He stared at her. "What's the problem, Andrea? Do you not love me anymore?"

She clasped his arm. "Of course I love you. It's just that I'm so busy right now trying to find my biological parents, and it's taking longer than I'd hoped."

"I get that, but it's a concern to me that you would want to set our marriage plans aside in order to keep searching for someone who may not even want to be found."

Andrea's jaw tightened as she folded her arms across her chest. "I don't need that reminder, and I wish you'd be more understanding of the way I feel about finding my birth mother and knowing my true heritage."

Her words had apparently cut like a knife, and Brandon was quick to retaliate. "I've tried to be understanding, but you're so caught up in your search that you're not making time for us anymore."

She drew in a sharp intake of breath. "That's not true. We were together last evening, and I'm with you right now."

"Yes, but last night was the first time in a couple of weeks." A vein on the side of Brandon's neck bulged, the way it always did when he was upset.

Andrea was upset too. *He should be more understanding*, she thought. *And this is Christmas, so we should not be arguing.* She wished now that she hadn't brought up the topic of postponing the wedding. If they kept up with this conversation, they might end up canceling it altogether.

Chapter 27

"Let's table this discussion until later, okay?" Andrea left the couch and went over to stand by the Christmas tree. Did she know how upset he was, and was that why she felt the need to put some distance between them?

Brandon sat silently, unable to respond. The way he saw it, she cared more about finding her biological parents than becoming his wife. The fact that she'd even suggested postponing their wedding was like a punch in the gut.

Andrea has the right to look for her blood family but not at the expense of her relationship with me. Brandon closed his eyes and leaned his head against the back of the couch. *If Andrea had known about her adoption when she was a child and had found her birth parents by now, this would not be happening to us.*

"Brandon, did you hear what I said?"

His eyes snapped open.

"I have something for you." She handed him a silver-colored gift bag. "It's not nearly as nice as the gift you gave me, but I got you something that you'd said you needed."

Brandon took the gift and reached inside. The black wallet he took out was made of leather and provided plenty of space for credit cards, driver's license, and even a few business cards. "Thanks, Andrea. The wallet is great, and I appreciate your thoughtfulness."

"I'm glad you like it." She offered him a pleasant smile, then glanced at her watch. "It's about time we headed to your folks' house, don't you think?"

"Without finishing our conversation that involves you wanting to cancel our wedding plans?" With forced restraint, Brandon spoke through his teeth.

She shook her head. "I said postpone, not cancel. After things settle down in my life, we can sit down together and set a new date for our wedding."

I believe she's already made up her mind to do what she wants, no matter how this hurts me. "What if I don't want to postpone the wedding? Shouldn't I have some say in this?"

"Well, of course, but. . ." Andrea looked at her watch again. "We're gonna be late if we don't leave now, and I would prefer to discuss this some other time."

This bad news has spoiled my holiday cheer. And next we'll be going to my parents' place to ruin theirs and Andrea's parents' too. Brandon's spirits sank like a stone that had been tossed into a well. Unable to look at Andrea, he folded his arms and stared straight ahead. "I'd like to resolve it now. You either want to marry me or you don't."

"I do want to marry you, Brandon. Just not in February. As I stated before, I think it's too soon."

"No, it's not. We've been planning this for months already. My parents have made plans for the rehearsal dinner, and your folks have secured a venue for the reception."

"I'm sure they could get their money back or have it applied to a different date once we've decided when that will be."

"Maybe, but places like that are difficult to secure, and since you haven't suggested an alternate date for our wedding, there might not be time to get the nice venue for our reception that your parents want."

"I can't give you a specific date because I have no way of knowing when I might find my biological parents."

Brandon pulled his fingers through the back of his hair. "So let me get this straight. . . . You're not planning to marry me until you locate the woman who gave birth to you. Is that what you're saying?"

She fingered the hem of her dark green velveteen dress. "Not exactly."

"What are you saying?"

"I'm in the early stages of all this and don't even know the name of my birth mother. There's plenty more I still need to do, and it's going to take some time."

"I get that, but you can continue your search after we're married."

"I'd rather resolve this first so that after we're married, we can concentrate fully on each other."

Brandon's chin jutted out as he tapped one foot against the carpeted floor. This conversation was going nowhere, but he had one more thing to say, and he'd better say it quick, before he lost his nerve. "I love you, Andrea, but I am not going to take a back seat to your determination to find someone who may not even want to be found."

She pulled back as though she'd been slapped. "Are you saying that if I don't marry you in February, there will be no wedding at all?"

Is that what I'm saying? Brandon asked himself. *Am I willing to give up the woman I love because I don't want to wait indefinitely?*

Brandon cleared his throat a couple of times as he tried to make sense of everything. Endless moments passed. He turned to Andrea and said, "Okay, for now we can postpone the wedding. I'll give it a few months and see how it goes." Brandon leaned in, hand on one knee. "And while we're at my folks, eating our so-called merry Christmas dinner, you can be the one to tell both sets of our parents."

Andrea sat stiffly in the passenger's seat of Brandon's SUV as they headed for his parents' house. It had begun to snow again, and she kept her gaze on the road rather than looking at or conversing with Brandon.

Brandon remained quiet too. No doubt he was unhappy with her.

Andrea couldn't believe that he expected her to make the announcement to both sets of parents that they'd decided to postpone their wedding. *Maybe he's hoping they'll be upset over my decision and try to talk me out of pursuing my search.* She rolled her shoulders. *Or maybe they'll understand my situation. I guess Brandon wants them to know it was my idea and not his.* She fiddled with her purse straps. *In all honesty, it is, but I had hoped he might help me tell them. Maybe Brandon will back me up when I give the news. That's the least he should do since he agreed to my suggestion about postponing the wedding, although his disappointment was evident.*

She had hoped Brandon would be more understanding about the urgent need she felt to locate her biological parents and learn her true heritage. Apparently, that wasn't important to him. It bothered Andrea to realize that the man she planned to marry had so little understanding of what was driving her. If Brandon were in her place, wouldn't he want to know who had given him up for adoption and why they had done it?

Brandon turned right and drove up his parents' circular driveway, bringing Andrea's contemplations to a halt. Her father's car was parked near the garage, and Brandon pulled his vehicle next to it and turned off the ignition. She thought he might say something to her, but he just got out, opened the back door, and took out the box with the gifts they had brought along for their parents.

Andrea glanced at her reflection in the visor mirror and got out. She reached inside to get the plastic container holding the two desserts she'd brought along. She would need to force a smile on her face before going into the house and pray that everyone would understand when she told them about the wedding being postponed.

Walnut Creek

"I sure enjoyed your tasty egg drop soup." Orley tipped his mug and drank the last bit before setting it down. Even though they hadn't eaten a big Christmas meal today, he'd gotten stuffed with cheeseballs, crackers, and his wife's delicious soup.

"I'm glad you liked it." From across the table, Lois smiled at him. "I'm also happy that your back is feeling a bit better."

"Me too. The way it was hurting earlier, I wasn't sure I'd be able to leave the couch at all today." He grinned back at her. "I'm sure it was the cold ice packs and liniment you rubbed on my back that made it feel better."

"I'm glad it helped, but you should probably go lie down again while I clear the table and do the dishes." Lois gazed at him with sympathy in her eyes. "When you hurt, I do as well, and I want to make sure you take it easy for the rest of the day."

"I appreciate your concern, and I will heed your advice." He pushed slowly away from the table and stood. "When you're ready for dessert, can we eat it in the living room?"

"Of course. I'll bring it in after I finish the dishes. In the meantime, why don't you get comfortable on the couch and play some more Christmas songs on your harmonica? Or maybe you'd rather take a nap."

"No, I dozed long enough this morning, and if I keep napping, I won't sleep tonight when we're in bed."

Lois took an ice pack from the freezer section in their refrigerator and handed it to him. "You might want to take this with you."

"Danki. You're such a thoughtful fraa."

She waved his compliment aside. "Go on with you, now, and take it slow and easy."

"I will." Orley made his way out of the kitchen and ambled into the living room. Although his back didn't throb like it had earlier, he could still feel a strain, so it would feel good to sit or lie down on the comfortable couch again.

After he'd taken a seat and positioned the ice pack behind him, he picked up the mouth harp and played "The First Noel."

What a nice gift my wife gave me, he thought. *I'll always be thankful for the day I met her and even more thankful that she agreed to become my fraa.*

Apple Creek

When Andrea and Brandon entered the house, they were greeted by his parents. After they exchanged hugs, Jennifer took the container Andrea had brought and excused herself to return to the kitchen, while Larry said he was going back to the living room. Andrea's parents came from the back of the house just then.

"You look lovely in that velveteen dress," Andrea's mother commented after she gave Andrea a hug.

Andrea forced a smile. "Thanks. You look nice too."

"You do look pretty," her father agreed, "but your droopy eyelids make me think you may not have been getting enough sleep lately."

Andrea stiffened. *Since when is Dad worried about how much sleep I get?*

"Honey, don't you know it's rude to tell someone they look tired?" Mom nudged Dad's arm.

"Sorry. I was just stating a fact, and as a father, it's my right to worry about my daughter." He turned to Brandon, gave him a hearty handshake, and said, "You'll find that out someday, when you and Andrea have children."

"Yeah, I suppose." Brandon threw Andrea a glance, and then he looked back at her father. "Shall we join my dad in the living room to visit and watch TV till dinner is ready?"

"Sounds like a plan. That's what Larry and I were doing before you and Andrea arrived."

Brandon bent down and picked up the box with the gifts he and Andrea had brought. After giving Andrea one more quick glance, he followed her dad to the living room.

"Jennifer and I have things pretty well under control in the kitchen." Andrea's mother gave Andrea's arm a pat. "If you'd like to relax in the living room with the men, that's fine with me."

Andrea shook her head. "I'm sure there must be something in

the kitchen for me to do."

"Yes, dear, I suppose there is, but as your dad pointed out, you do look a bit tired, so I thought maybe. . ."

"I'm fine, Mom, and I'm going to the kitchen with you." Andrea couldn't believe that her mother had brought up the topic of her looking tired, when a few moments ago she'd told Andrea's dad that it had been rude of him to comment on her tired appearance.

Mom gave Andrea's arm another pat. "Okay, dear, if you don't want to rest, we'll find something for you to do."

$\sim$

"You've outdone yourself this year," Brandon said, looking at his mother as he held up a piece of turkey. "This is a really tender piece of meat, and it's not a bit dry either."

His mother smiled. "Thanks, Son. I'm glad you like it. I bought an organic turkey this year and cooked it in one of those baking bags."

"It's very good," Andrea spoke up. It was the first thing she'd said since they had all taken their seats around the dining room table. Brandon wondered if his parents and hers felt the tension growing stronger between them with each passing minute.

Is she ever going to bring up the topic of our wedding? he asked himself. *I hope Andrea's not waiting for me to do it—especially since I made it clear that since the change of plans was her idea, she'd need to be the one to make the announcement.*

"Every bit of food on the table is delicious," Evelyn spoke up. "Even the green bean casserole I brought." Her cheeks colored. "I don't mean that in a bragging sort of way. I just followed the recipe I found in a magazine not long ago."

"It's okay," Andrea's dad said, leaning close to her. "The casserole, like all the food you ladies served, is real tasty. You and Jennifer have every right to brag. And I'm eager to try some of the pumpkin bread and apple pie Andrea brought for dessert," he added. "She takes after her mother when it comes to her baking skills."

Andrea dropped her gaze to the table.

The conversation moved from raving over the food to discussing the weather.

"I'm glad it has finally stopped snowing," Jennifer commented. "A white Christmas is beautiful and really sets the mood, but I'm already looking forward to when spring comes and brings warmer weather."

Everyone nodded except Andrea. She stared at her half-eaten meal while pushing a green bean slowly around on her plate.

Talk about the weather continued, and then it changed a few more times when someone brought up a new topic. Still Andrea had not said anything about their wedding plans.

Finally, when Brandon thought he couldn't stand it anymore, he gave Andrea's foot a little nudge under the table. She looked over at him with furrowed brows but made no comment.

Several more minutes passed, and after clearing her throat a few times, Andrea finally said, "There's something Brandon and I need you all to know."

"What would that be?" her father asked.

She looked at Brandon as though hoping he might say something, but he didn't budge.

Without looking at anyone in particular, she proclaimed, "We've decided to postpone our wedding."

"Wh–what?" Andrea's mother gasped. "You're not getting married?"

Andrea shook her head vigorously. "Oh no, I didn't say that. It just won't be in February."

"Why not?" The question came from Brandon's mother, who spoke in a disbelieving voice. "So many plans have already been made. I can't imagine why you'd need to change them—especially at this late date."

"That's right," his dad put in. "It makes no sense to cancel when you're this far along with your plans."

The only parent who had not spoken up was Andrea's dad. He

just sat there, slowly shaking his head. Finally, he looked over at Brandon and said, "Have you and my daughter had a falling out? Is that the reason you want to postpone the wedding?"

"No, no, Dad. . .that's not it." Andrea's chin trembled, and Brandon knew it was time for him to speak up on his own behalf.

"I still love Andrea very much, and it wasn't my idea to delay our wedding."

"Why then?" her mother asked, looking at Andrea again.

"As all of you know, I have been in the process of searching for my biological parents." Andrea paused and sucked in a quick breath. "The process is taking some time and could take even longer. If I were to marry Brandon in February, as we had originally planned, I may still be looking for my birth parents." She stopped talking and took in another breath. "The extra time I will need to spend wouldn't be good for a new marriage, and I will not do that to Brandon." She gave a slow shake of her head. "It wouldn't be fair."

Brandon's mother looked at Andrea with a watery gaze. "What if you never find your birth mother? You can't expect our son to wait for you indefinitely."

Brandon's muscles became rigid. "Mother, please! This is between me and Andrea, and we will work things out."

She blinked rapidly. "Of course. I'm just concerned about both of you."

"So am I," Evelyn put in. "I don't think putting your marriage off is the answer."

"What is the answer, Mom?" Andrea asked.

"I don't know, dear, but this is something we all need to pray about." She looked over at Ray. "Don't you agree?"

"Yes, I do," he responded, "but in the end, it's Andrea and Brandon's decision."

"I concur," Brandon's dad spoke up. "We all need to pray and then let the bride- and groom-to-be decide what's best for them."

Brandon reached for his glass of water and took a drink. He'd thought he had known what was best for him and Andrea until she'd brought up the topic of putting their marriage on hold. Now he wasn't sure about anything.

Chapter 28

Jennifer sat at the kitchen table, massaging the back of her neck. "Our poor son. I can't believe Andrea wants to postpone their wedding. Didn't you see the hurt expression on his face when she made the announcement? He still appeared to be upset when they left here a short time ago."

"Yes, I'm aware." Larry got up and went around to stand behind Jennifer and take over her neck rub. "Try not to worry so much, Jen. Brandon is a grown man, and we can't shield him from situations that are not in our control."

"I realize that, but he needs our full support right now. What Andrea is putting him through is just not fair." Jennifer grimaced as Larry hit a tender spot on her neck. "If she's more interested in finding her birth mother than marrying Brandon, then I think he should break up with her."

"You're kidding, right?"

"No, I'm not. I am still dazed about Andrea wanting to postpone their wedding in February, and I don't understand why she couldn't give us a new date. Andrea can't expect Brandon to wait forever."

"Maybe she'll find out something soon in regard to her adoption. Evelyn did mention before Andrea and Brandon got here today that Andrea had sent away for a DNA test. That could be the ticket to learning who her biological parents are."

"You can stop massaging my neck now. It feels better," Jennifer said, making no comment regarding her husband's last statement.

Even if Andrea found her birth mother tomorrow, it didn't change the fact that the young woman had postponed her wedding to a man she was supposed to love. Brandon deserved better than that—if not with Andrea then with some sweet woman more deserving of him. *And maybe,* Jennifer thought, *if this whole thing with the search for her blood parents goes on much longer, Brandon might decide she's not the right woman for him and find someone else.*

~

"Ray, would you please slow down? The roads might be icy." Evelyn glanced nervously out the front window of their car as they headed home.

"It's warmed up, and I seriously doubt we'll find any patches of ice."

"Well, go a little slower anyway, please. I'm really on edge tonight." She could see the speedometer and felt relieved when her husband slowed their vehicle.

"I'm not surprised you're feeling anxious. When Andrea told us that she and Brandon had postponed their wedding, from that point on, you were wound up tighter than a clock."

Evelyn tried to calm herself on the ride home by looking out the passenger's side window at homes decorated with colored lights and yard displays for Christmas. But the views did nothing to relieve her anxious thoughts. *I had hoped my daughter could juggle the adoption business and still prioritize things for her and Brandon's future. I don't believe she's thought this through.* Evelyn shifted in her seat, letting out a deep sigh.

"I can't help feeling wound up," she stated, glancing in Ray's direction. "All these months we've been planning for the wedding, and now we have to cancel everything, including the use of our church." Evelyn twisted the ties attached to her coat collar around her fingers and frowned. "What are we supposed to tell everyone now? There are so many people who know about the wedding plans."

"We will tell them the truth—that the wedding's been postponed until a later date. Nobody has to know the reason."

Evelyn drew a deep breath and released it with a huff. "I wish Andrea's well-meaning cousin had never said anything to her about being adopted. Nothing has been the same for anyone in this family since she found out, and now it's affected her relationship with Brandon."

"I don't think you have anything to worry about, dear. Andrea and Brandon love each other, and they'll work things out."

I can't help having regrets about what the past is doing to us now. If only Ray and I had been honest with our daughter when she was a child, things might be different right now. She glanced at some more Christmas decorations as they went past. *If we'd been up front with her a long time ago, Andrea might not have chosen to look for her birth parents at all, or she might already know who they are and that would be it.*

Evelyn thought about the promise she'd made to herself to help Andrea find out who her birth mother was. She'd been so busy with other things that she hadn't done much of anything to help her daughter find out what she deserved to know. *I need to get busy on that,* she told herself. *My first order of business will be to find out if the state of Pennsylvania has altered their law about not releasing original birth certificates in closed adoptions. If the law is still in place, then maybe the adoption agency Ray and I used will be able to help.*

The ride back to Andrea's house Christmas evening was quiet. She couldn't think of anything nice to say because she felt like Brandon had thrown her under the bus by insisting that she be the one to tell their folks about the decision to postpone the wedding. From the moment Andrea had announced it, the atmosphere in the room changed. At first it seemed as though everyone was in shock, and then came the questions and concerns raised by Brandon's parents and hers. Andrea was fairly certain that no one understood her reasons nor did they seem to care whether she found her biological parents. *I had hoped someone would understand my situation and back me up 100 percent. I thought family was supposed to be there for you—especially at a time like this.*

Andrea rubbed her throbbing forehead. She'd felt a nagging headache coming on soon after they'd eaten their meal, but she had toughed it out until they'd eaten their dessert a few hours later. Finally, when the throbbing increased, she'd told Brandon that she had a headache and needed to go home. After he'd agreed to her request, she'd said a hasty goodbye to everyone, put on her coat, and hurried out the door, forgetting about the gifts she'd received from his parents and hers. Brandon hadn't forgotten, though, for he'd hauled the box full of gifts out to his SUV and put it in the back.

Andrea was thankful that the temperature had warmed up some and the roads were wet, not icy. That was one thing she didn't have to worry about as they continued driving.

When they approached her house, Brandon put the blinker on and pulled his rig onto the driveway. "I'll get the box from the back and carry it into the house for you." It was the first thing he had said to Andrea since they'd left his parents' house.

"Okay," she responded. "I'll take the gifts out that are mine, and you can take the box with your gifts to your house."

Brandon just got out of the vehicle and went to the back to get the box.

Andrea got out too and hurried up the front porch steps to open the door. She stepped into the hall and noticed that Brandon was right behind her. "You can take the box into the living room," she said. "I'll take my gifts out there and place them under the tree for now." Putting their open presents under the tree for a day or so after they'd received them was something Andrea's parents had done ever since she could remember. Her mother had said many times over the years that it was fun to look at what they'd received for a while until it was time to take down the tree and put everything away.

Brandon did as Andrea had asked, and after she'd removed her presents and placed them under the tree, he turned to her and said, "We need to talk."

Andrea grimaced. "Brandon, you know I have a headache."

"I'm aware, but you took two aspirin before leaving my folks' house, and what I have to say is important, so I'd appreciate it if you would hear me out."

"All right." She gestured to the couch. "Let's have a seat."

They'd no sooner sat down when Lady darted into the room and leaped onto Andrea's lap. The cat's soothing purr and the feel of her sandpapery tongue as she licked Andrea's hand helped her feel a bit more relaxed.

"What do you want to talk about?" She turned her head to look at Brandon.

"You. Me. Our relationship that seems to be on pretty shaky ground."

Andrea couldn't miss the hurt in his eyes. "It doesn't have to be if we just give it some time."

"How much time?"

She shrugged. "I—I'm not sure. At least until—"

"Oh, there we go again. I'm supposed to wait patiently until you find the woman who gave birth to you. Right?"

"I've explained this to you before. I need to find out about my true heritage." Andrea stroked Lady's ears, hoping the feel of the cat's silky hair might make her feel calmer.

"How about concentrating on us for a change?" The tension she heard in Brandon's voice let Andrea know how frustrated he felt.

She forced herself to look at him. "You're not being fair."

A muscle in his jaw twitched. "I'm the one not being fair? You said you loved me, and you were eagerly planning our wedding until your cousin revealed your family's secret that you were adopted."

"I still love you, Brandon," Andrea murmured. "I just can't commit to marriage right now. It wouldn't be fair to either of us."

"Speak for yourself." He heaved a sigh and pulled his fingers through the back of his hair. "I love you, Andrea, and I want you to be my wife, but I get the feeling that you think finding your birth mother is more important than me or anything else right now." He paused and then stood. "I think it would be better if we didn't see each other anymore."

Her eyes widened. "Are. . .are you breaking up with me?"

"Yeah, guess I am." His expression was as solemn as an unyielding mask. "If you ever change your mind about us, let me know."

She blinked slowly, trying to let his words set in. "I haven't changed my mind. I just. . ."

He held up his hand. "I can't deal with this anymore, Andrea. It's not fair to expect me to sit around waiting for you to find what you're looking for, knowing it might not happen at all. You may spend the rest of your life searching for something you'll never find. I'm sorry, but if I'm not at the top of your list, then I'd rather not be on the list at all." He picked up the box with his gifts and headed for the front door.

The words "Brandon, wait!" were on the tip of Andrea's tongue, but he went out the door before she could speak them.

"Maybe he's right," Andrea murmured, as her tears dripped onto Lady's back. "He's better off without me since I don't know what my future holds." She touched the engagement ring on her left hand. *I'll need to see that he gets this back. Maybe Colleen would be willing to return it for me.*

~

The phone rang the next morning, pulling Andrea out of a deep sleep. She looked at the clock beside her bed and realized that she'd slept until 10 a.m.

"Oh boy." She rubbed her eyes and reached for her cell phone. "Hello," she rasped, barely able to find her voice.

"Hey, friend. How'd your Christmas go? Did you have a nice dinner at Brandon's parents?"

"The food was good, but that's about all." Andrea sat up and dangled her feet over the edge of her bed.

"What do you mean?" Colleen asked. "Did something upsetting happen yesterday?"

"You could say that, and it didn't end at the dinner table."

"Sorry to hear it. Can you fill me in?"

Andrea spent the next several minutes telling Colleen how she'd announced to her parents and Brandon's parents that she and Brandon had decided to postpone their wedding."

"You're kidding."

"No, I'm not."

"What made you and Brandon do that?"

"It was my idea. I'm really tied up right now with trying to search for my birth mother, and I didn't think getting married in February would be a good idea since there's a good chance I won't have the answers I seek by then."

"I guess that makes sense, but I bet everyone was disappointed."

"Yes—especially Brandon. He's not supportive of my endeavors to find my biological parents, and if I married him before I found answers and kept on with my search, it would be bound to affect our marriage."

"You might be right, but you both love each other, and I'm sure Brandon would help with your search if you asked him to."

"I would never ask him to do that. He's too busy with his clinic." Andrea's eyes filled with tears, and she grabbed a tissue to blow her nose. "You haven't even heard the worst of it yet."

"You mean there's more?"

"Yeah. When Brandon brought me home last night, we broke up."

"What?" Colleen's voice was practically a screech. "Why would you do that?"

"It was his choice. He's convinced that I care about the quest to find my birth mother more than I do him, so he basically said we should call it quits." Andrea swallowed around the constriction in her throat. "I still love him, but maybe breaking things off is best for both of us."

"You can't mean that. Surely, there's some way you two can work things out."

"I don't know what it could be, short of me giving up the search that involves my adoption." Andrea paused to reach for another tissue. "I have a big favor to ask of you."

"Anything. Just name it."

"Would you be willing to return my engagement ring to Brandon? I should have done it while he was here, but I was flustered. I didn't think about giving the ring back to him."

"Don't you think that's something you should do yourself?"

"I can't. It would hurt too much. Please, Colleen. It's really important to me."

Her friend was quiet. Finally, she said, "Okay. I'll come by later today and get the ring."

"Thank you."

"I only agreed to do it because you're my best friend, but it doesn't mean I agree with your decision, because I think you're making a mistake."

Andrea didn't respond to that. Instead, she posed another question. "If I do find my birth mother, do you think Brandon would take me back?"

"I don't know. It might be too late by then." Andrea heard the sound of Colleen's finger snap. "Say, I have an idea. Why don't you write another letter to the Dear Caroline column? She gave you good advice before, and maybe she will again."

"I'll give it some thought." Andrea glanced at the clock. "In the meantime, I'd better get dressed and try to get something done today. I went to bed with a splitting headache last night and slept much longer than I'd planned."

"Okay, I'll come by around two o'clock. Would that work for you?"

"Yes, and thanks again for agreeing to take the ring to Brandon."

"As a good friend, I don't see I have any other choice. I'll see you later, Andrea. Bye for now."

Andrea clicked off the phone and went to the window to look out. No snow on the horizon, but the ground was still white from what had fallen before. She reflected on what a day she'd had yesterday. It still bothered her that neither his folks nor hers had said they understood and supported her need to keep searching until she found her birth parents. Worse yet, at the end of an already difficult evening, her fiancé had broken their engagement.

I'm glad Colleen is in my corner, even if she doesn't think Brandon and I should have broken up. At least she cares about me and supports my decision. Andrea felt the familiar bumping of a tail about knee height as she continued to stare out at the snow, trying to ignore her determined cat. It was a new day, and Andrea was free to do whatever she needed to get done. But having Brandon out of her life was not what she wanted or intended to have happen. Her chin trembled. *I thought he loved me as much as I love him.*

She looked down at Lady, who continued rubbing against Andrea's legs. "Okay, girl, I'm coming. I know you want to be fed."

Andrea put on her slippers and robe, then plodded out of the room. She felt an uncomfortable heaviness in her chest and limbs. *Why can't things be different right now? I wish I'd never found out that I was adopted. After I've had some breakfast, I'm going to take Colleen's advice and write another letter to Dear Caroline.*

Chapter 29

Brandon left the first examining room and headed down the hall for room 2 with a sense of determination. It had been nearly a week since his breakup with Andrea, and he dreaded tomorrow evening and spending New Year's Eve alone.

Of course, he reasoned, *I could always go over to my folks' place and join the little gathering they have planned with my brother Joe and his family. Mom did invite me, after all.* He pursed his lips. *I think she felt sorry for me and wanted to cheer me up after I told her and Dad that Andrea and I broke up.*

He paused in the hallway to let his thoughts sink in. It was hard for Brandon to concentrate on his animal patients when all he could think about was his broken engagement with Andrea. Despondency clung to him like a wet garment, only he couldn't take it off. Had he done the right thing? Could they ever get back together? Maybe, if she either found her birth mother or gave up the search. But that was doubtful since she seemed so determined to proceed. *And what about my dog and her cat? Now that Andrea and I aren't seeing each other, Duke won't be spending time with Lady anymore.* He frowned. *What good did it do for Andrea and me to work so hard at getting our pets to like each other?*

A dog's bark coming from the second examining room reminded Brandon to keep walking in that direction. No matter what happened in the future, Brandon's clinic was his responsibility and a job he enjoyed. He owed it to his animal patients and their owners to give them the best care possible, so that's what he would do.

Andrea had said goodbye to one of her younger piano students when the mailman stepped onto the porch.

"Here you go." He handed her a stack of mail along with a larger, padded envelope. "I hope not too many of them are bills. You know how it is. . . . Before Christmas it's lots of ads, and after the holiday, the bills come in."

"Thank you." She forced a smile, gave a brief nod, and stepped back inside.

After placing the mail on the table inside the entryway, Andrea discovered that the padded envelope was from AncestryDNA.

"Oh good, it's finally here!" Her pulse quickened. "I'll take this right away, then send it back in the mail. Hopefully, I'll know something soon." Andrea wanted to find out everything possible about her lineage. She hoped the test would bring to light her nationality and shed some light on who her birth parents were.

Andrea was about to go through the rest of the mail when her cell phone rang. She'd left it in the kitchen while she taught piano lessons this morning, so she hurried to grab it before it went to voice mail.

"Hi, Mom." Andrea recognized her mother's number right away. "Guess what? I have good news."

"Are you and Brandon getting back together?"

"No, it's not that."

"I'm sorry to hear it. When you called the day after Christmas and said Brandon had broken things off with you, I really felt bad. You two are a special couple, and I'd really hoped that—"

"Mom, my DNA test kit came in the mail today. I'm excited to take it and can't wait for the results to see if there might be a match."

"That's wonderful, dear, and I have some good news too."

"What is it?"

"I did some checking on an adoption website for the state of

Pennsylvania and discovered that a law they'd previously made had been changed back in 2017. Sure wish I would have had knowledge of that sooner."

"What law was that?"

"The one that said birth certificates from closed adoptions could not be available to anyone. Under the new law, adoptees over the age of eighteen can apply for their original birth records for the first time in thirty-three years."

Andrea's thoughts were scattered. "Let me get this straight— you said the law's been changed. Does that actually mean I can gain access to my original birth certificate now?"

"Yes, Andrea. You can apply to the state Department of Health for a copy of it. There is a twenty-five-dollar filing fee, and applications are expected to take about forty-five days to be processed."

Andrea's senses heightened. "Oh Mom, that is such good news. I don't know why I didn't think to check on that myself. It should have been one of the first things I did in my quest to search for the woman who gave birth to me. I just thought since it was a closed adoption that there would be no way I could acquire a copy of my original certificate."

"And now you can." There was a brief pause. "I'm happy for you, Andrea, and I hope that once you discover the name of the woman who gave birth to you, you'll be able to locate her."

"Thank you, Mom." Andrea felt good knowing that her adoptive mother had been helpful in the endeavor to discover her true heritage.

Walnut Creek

Lois shivered and went to the living room to stoke the fire in their free-standing woodstove. They'd had a cold snap two days ago, and the frigid temperatures had frozen their neighbor's pond. So as soon as school let out for the day, several children from their neighborhood had gotten out their ice skates and headed for the ice. Orley, with all the exuberance of a teenager, had found his old skates and informed Lois not to start supper too soon because he'd probably be gone a few hours.

She opened the stove door and saw that the fire had burned up most of the wood. She picked out a couple nice-sized logs and carefully added one at a time to the hot embers. She moved the logs in farther with the metal poker that rested nearby and then closed the door. The heat she longed for wouldn't take long to begin warming the room. *I'm thinking by the time Orley comes in from frolicking on the ice, this front room should be warm and inviting.*

Lois took a seat in one of the recliners. She couldn't believe that her husband, who had recently recovered from a sore back, would risk reinjuring it while skating—and in such cold weather, no less.

"But I shouldn't be surprised," Lois murmured. "Even when Orley's body is hurting, he never stays down very long. He's been a go-getter all the time I've known him." She could only imagine what her enthusiastic husband must have been like as a child. Probably not much different than he was right now, only Orley had been able to do a lot more foolhardy things back then.

For supper, Lois had put a small ham in the oven an hour ago, and she would serve it along with some boiled potatoes and peas. While the ham baked at a low temperature and she waited for Orley to come home, she would try to get some Dear Caroline letters read.

Lois felt the room beginning to warm up, along with the inviting popping and crackling coming from the wood-burning stove. She had always liked the warmth of a real fire and the heat it gave. Not that electric heat wasn't good, like in her English neighbor's place, but a good wood fire seemed to warm a person clear to the bones. Lois had placed a manila envelope full of letters on the small table beside her chair, so she picked it up and pulled out the first letter.

Dear Caroline,

I've written to you before, after learning that I was adopted, and I'm currently in the process of trying to find my biological parents. The man I was planning to marry doesn't understand why this is so important to me. When I told him I wanted to postpone our wedding, he was upset, and last week he broke up with me. What can I do to get him to be more understanding and take me back? Do I need to stop the search for my birth mother, or am I better off without a man who doesn't support my endeavor?

—*Brokenhearted*

Lois held the letter against her chest while closing her eyes in prayer. *Dear Lord, please give me the right words to share with this distraught woman. I can only imagine how much she is hurting. May my words be Your words when I respond to her desperate-sounding letter.*

As Orley limped home from the neighbor's place, he thought about what Lois would say when she heard that he'd fallen several times, leaving him with two very sore knees. No doubt she would say something like "You're getting too old for ice-skating. You should leave that kind of sport to the younger ones who have better balance."

"You're only as young as you feel," Orley muttered. "Course, right now I don't feel so young."

When Orley reached his home, he grabbed hold of the handrail and made his way slowly up the stairs. Upon entering the house via the back door, he was greeted with the tantalizing aroma of baked ham. It would feel good to eat but even better to get out of his cold, wet clothes and put something soothing on his sore knees.

Maybe I can sneak into the bathroom and take a shower before Lois sees me, Orley told himself as he hobbled down the hallway, gritting his teeth.

No such luck, however. His wife must have heard him come in, for she stepped into the hallway from the living room as he was going by. "I'm glad you're back, but why are you limping so badly?"

Her brows drew together.

He turned to face her. "I fell on the ice. More than once, I might add." Orley pointed to his knees. "I didn't break any bones, but I think my *gnie* must be bruised. On top of that, I'm so cold, my teeth are chattering."

She placed her hands against her hips. "You'd best get a warm shower and put some of that arnica cream on your sore knees. It's on the second shelf in the medicine cabinet."

He looked at her through half-closed eyes. "Aren't ya gonna say, 'I told you so'?"

Lois shook her head. "What would be the point? You've no doubt figured out that you should have stayed home where it's nice and warm and let the young people take their chances on the ice."

"Jah, but you know me—once my knees feel better, I'll probably grab my skates again and head right back out to that frozen pond."

Lois moved closer to him and reached up to stroke his cold cheek. "I guess some things never change."

Exhausted and hungry, Brandon entered his kitchen to fix something to eat. He wasn't in the mood to cook and wished now that he'd stopped at Lem's to get a pizza to bring home, but he was here now and may as well make the best of it.

Before checking the refrigerator for something easy to fix, Brandon poured dog food into Duke's dish.

The Brittany spaniel looked up at him and barked.

"Go ahead, buddy, eat your supper. After we've both finished eating, I'll take you out for a walk. I'll look at the neighbors' Christmas lights that haven't been taken down yet while you pull on the leash and sniff your way along, wagging your tail."

Duke ran over to the door and barked again, a little louder this time.

Brandon thumped the side of his head. "Oh, right. . .you want to go out right now. Well, that means no walk outside of the yard till after supper, but I will let you roam free in the yard."

Woof! Woof!

Since Brandon hadn't removed his jacket yet, he opened the door and stepped out onto the front porch. Duke zipped between his legs, raced down the steps, and into the yard.

Brandon shook his head. *Wish I had half as much energy as my dog does tonight.* He leaned on the porch railing and watched as Duke made his way around the yard a couple of times. Although the front of Brandon's property was fenced in, he'd forgotten to shut the gate. So rather than close it now, he would remain on the porch and watch until the dog was ready to come back inside. Duke never left the yard as long as Brandon was nearby, keeping a close watch on him.

Brandon observed his own breath as he blew out several puffs of air. As he continued to wait for Duke to do his business, he let his thoughts wander.

I wonder what Andrea is doing this evening. Does she miss me as much as I miss her, or is she so engrossed in searching for her birth mother that she hasn't even given me a thought today? I wonder if she's made any plans for New Year's Eve. Last year they'd gotten together with some other unmarried couples from church for an evening of games and refreshments. This year Brandon had made no plans. He'd probably veg out in front of the TV with a movie, his dog, and a bowl of buttery popcorn.

Woof! Woof!

Brandon looked down, surprised to see Duke sitting at his feet looking up at him. He hadn't even realized the dog had come onto the porch.

"Ready to go inside?"

Woof! Duke made a beeline for the door.

Brandon had to smile despite his melancholy mood. It was a pleasure to own a dog like Duke—always eager to please and wanting to be near his owner.

Back in the kitchen, Duke went to work on his dog food while Brandon hung up his jacket and took out the ingredients to make a ham and cheese sandwich. He had just taken a seat at the table when the doorbell rang. His heart beat a few extra beats. *Could that be Andrea?* He shook his head. *It's not likely that she'd be coming to see me, but I guess I'd better go see who rang the bell.*

When Brandon opened the front door, he was surprised to see Colleen on his porch.

"Sorry to show up unannounced, but I figured I'd probably find you at home around this time. I hope I'm not interrupting your supper."

"It's okay, I haven't eaten yet. Come on in out of the cold." Brandon held the door open wider and waited until Andrea's friend came fully into the house before asking the question on the tip of his tongue.

"What brings you by here on this cold night?"

"I came to see how you're doing and to deliver this." Colleen reached into her purse and withdrew a small green velvet box. "Andrea asked if I would return this to you."

Brandon didn't have to open the box to know what was inside. It was the beautiful engagement ring he'd carefully picked out for her. He took the box and set it on the entryway table. "I'm guessing she didn't have the courage to give it to me herself."

"Right." Colleen touched Brandon's arm. "I was sorry to hear about your breakup with Andrea. You have to know how much she loves you."

"Yeah, right. Andrea loves me so much that she has put finding her birth mother ahead of marrying me." He looked down and gave the green box a tap. "She's the one who called off our wedding, you know."

Colleen shook her head. "She didn't call off the wedding, just decided it would be best to postpone it until—"

"I'm aware." Brandon couldn't keep the disillusionment he felt out of his voice. "Andrea cares more about that than she does me."

"So you ended your relationship with her." Colleen's words were not posed as a question. She'd stated a fact.

"Yes, I did," he admitted. "Under the circumstances, it seemed like the only sensible thing to do."

Colleen's brows furrowed as she looked up at him. "So you're not willing to wait until Andrea finds the answers she's seeking?"

He shook his head. "She might be searching indefinitely and never find closure, which would mean that marrying me would never happen."

"Does that mean you'll be looking for someone to replace my dear friend?" At the end of her sentence, Colleen's lips pressed together.

His muscles tensed, and he gave a huff. "I am in no hurry to find a replacement for Andrea. I'm still in love with her, but I can't be expected to wait forever, and if she really loves me as much as she says, then I should come first, not a biological parent she's never even met. A woman who may not want to be found," he added with emphasis.

"I understand why you would feel that way, but I'm bothered by the fact that you aren't more understanding of how Andrea feels. If you really love her, shouldn't you stand beside her in all this and maybe even take part in the search for her mother?"

Brandon stood with his hands clasped tightly together. "I'm not an insensitive man. As I'm sure you must know, my veterinary practice keeps me very busy, so I really don't have time to begin a hunt for Andrea's blood relatives."

"No one's asking you to, but you could have been more support-ive of Andrea in all this. The fact that you broke up with her was like a slap in the face. She's deeply hurt and misses you very much."

"Did Andrea tell you that?"

"Yes." She placed her hand on his arm again. "Did you pray about this matter, or did you break up with Andrea because you were angry?"

"Not angry but hurt that I seem to be the last item on her list these days." He pressed one hand against his chest. "You're right about one thing, though. I have not prayed about this, so thanks for pointing that out."

"I hope you will spend some time in prayer." Colleen turned toward the door. "I'll let you get back to whatever you had planned this evening. I need to head for home. Shawn graciously agreed to fix supper for us this evening so I could come over here. I'm sure the meal is about ready by now, and I don't want to keep my family waiting."

Brandon opened the door for her. "Thanks for sharing your thoughts with me. I know you have Andrea's best interest at heart. She's fortunate to have a good friend like you."

"I have your interest at heart too, and I'm praying for both of you," she said before going out the door.

Brandon watched until Colleen had gotten into her car and pulled out of the driveway. Then he shut the door and returned to the kitchen, where he sank into a chair at the table. *I do need to pray about this. I need to seek the Lord's will and ask for His wisdom in deciding what is best for my life as well as Andrea's.*

Chapter 30

Walnut Creek

Orley wandered around Memory Keepers with a clipboard and paper in one hand and a pencil in the other. It was that time of the year when he and Lois did inventory of the stock on hand for tax purposes and also to determine what else they would need to acquire for the new year. Lois had been helping him this morning and had already finished one side of the store, but she had letters to mail, so Orley said he would finish the job while she went to the post office.

His thoughts went to how he and Lois seemed to have an eye for finding the right objects to sell in their business. Orley liked to see the happy faces of customers who found special treasures in their store. The other day a married couple had come in looking for nostalgic old advertising signs. They'd seemed pleased when they discovered one hanging on the store wall that featured an old soda pop product.

Orley moved on to one of the other shelves and counted the crystal pieces, making note of them on his clipboard. *I know a couple of these have sold lately and a few brass items as well.*

Orley paused from his work to look out the front window. He had heard from one of the customers earlier that the weatherman said Walnut Creek might see more snow this evening—maybe up to a few inches. Orley had not noticed any sign of it so far and wondered if their driver would be coming to pick them up for the trip home before any snow fell. He'd only seen a few people out shopping today, but they were two weeks into the new year already, and it wasn't unusual for people to do less shopping after the holidays. Besides, the weather in this part of Ohio was still plenty cold.

Normally, Orley would have enjoyed the lower temperatures, but he had not taken advantage of the colder temperatures to go ice-skating again or even taken his sled out on the hill. Since he'd bruised both knees so badly, Orley had temporarily lost interest in all outdoor games that could cause some sort of an injury. He'd been content to spend his free time with Lois, putting puzzles together, playing board games, or blowing on the mouth harp she'd given him for Christmas. Although he enjoyed outdoor fun, he was not about to risk getting hurt again. Next time he fell, it could be something more serious, like breaking a bone or falling through a section of thin ice.

Orley thought about an entry in *The Budget* last week, where one of the scribes from Wisconsin had written about a young boy from their community who had fallen through the ice and drowned. *How sad*, Orley thought. *My heart goes out to that child's parents. I wonder if the boy had gone skating alone or if there were others around who had witnessed the accident. I'm sure if there had been other people at the pond, they would have done all they could to try and save him.*

Continuing to gaze out the window and forcing aside his sad thoughts, Orley spotted the veterinarian who had visited the shop before Christmas and noticed that the young man seemed to be heading this way. Sure enough, a few minutes later the bell above the front door jingled and the man stepped inside the store.

"Well, hello there." Orley extended his hand. "It's Brandon, right?"

"Yes. I was here a few weeks ago." He gave Orley a hearty but cold handshake.

"I remember. You bought a vintage coffee table for your fiancée."

Brandon gave a nod. "Only we're not getting married after all."

"That's too bad. I hope it didn't have anything to do with the gift you gave her." Orley moved toward the front counter and placed the clipboard and pencil on it.

"No, she liked the coffee table. It's me she doesn't like very much anymore." Brandon dropped his gaze to the floor for a few seconds and then lifted his head and looked back at Orley with a grim expression. "She's in the process of trying to find her biological parents and said she wanted to postpone our February wedding because she's so wrapped up in her quest."

"Did you agree to that?"

"No, not really, but she insisted. I tried to reason with her, stating that we could still get married and she could keep looking for her real mother. Andrea refused, saying that as soon as things settled down in her life that we could sit down together and set a new date for our wedding. I was hurt that she had made up her mind on this and that my feelings didn't seem to hold much weight in this final decision. Then later, on Christmas Day, while we were eating dinner at my parents' house, Andrea told them that we had decided to wait to get married." A film of sweat erupted on Brandon's forehead, and he reached in his pocket for a hanky, which he used to wipe it off. "Of course, that's partly my fault, because when she first brought up the topic of postponing our plans to get married, I said that she should be the one to tell both sets of our parents."

"I see."

"The more I thought about Andrea putting the search for her mother ahead of marrying me, the more upset I became. So after I brought her home that evening, I told Andrea that we should go our separate ways."

Orley gave his beard a tug. "You broke up with her?"

"Yeah, and she gave me the engagement ring back. Well, she didn't have the courtesy to do it herself. Instead, Andrea asked her friend to bring it to me, which I also found upsetting."

"How come?"

"Because she should have given it to me herself."

"How do you feel about the decision you made to break up?"

"Terrible, but I can't be expected to wait around forever while she goes on a hunt for parents she may never find."

"Have you prayed about this matter?" Orley questioned.

"Yes, I have, but nothing has come clear to me yet."

"Do you want my advice?"

"I would appreciate it. That's why I came in here today. I could tell from my last visit that you're the kind of person who cares about people and has good advice to offer."

"I do my best, but I can't take the credit for my suggestions."

"Oh, why's that?"

Orley pointed upward. "Everything I say that is worth anything comes from what God lays on my heart."

"That makes sense." Brandon leaned one arm on the counter. "So what is God asking you to tell me now?"

Orley placed one hand on Brandon's shoulder. "If I were in your situation, I'd ask myself one very important question."

"What would that be?"

"How much do I love the woman I was engaged to marry? Can I picture myself spending the rest of my life without her being a part of it?"

"And if I can't see myself without Andrea in my life?"

"Then get down on one knee, if that's what it takes, and ask her to marry you again."

Brandon shifted his stance. "I'll give it some thought."

"And prayer?"

"Yeah, that too. I was alone on New Year's Eve except for my dog, and I tried to keep occupied by watching TV until midnight, but all I could think about was Andrea and how much I missed her."

"That says a lot, and it might be your answer."

"Could be, but I still have some doubts."

Orley was on the verge of saying more, but two customers came into the store, which interrupted their conversation.

"I'd better go and let you take care of business." Brandon shook

Orley's hand. "Thanks for taking the time to listen and also for your advice."

"No problem. Anytime you need a listening ear, you know where to find me."

"Thanks, I appreciate that."

As Brandon left the store, Orley turned to the English couple who had come in. "May I help you?"

~

Lois hurried toward Memory Keepers, adjusting the scarf that her sister Rebekah had knitted and sent to her for Christmas. One of their customers had said they'd be in for a few more inches of snow this evening, and she thought they might be right.

Lois looked up at the thick gray clouds hovering overhead, but so far there wasn't any sign of flakes. She couldn't help longing for warmer weather, but the cold was likely here to stay until winter ended. Even though the post office was only a few blocks away, it had been a chilly walk to and from, and she looked forward to the warmth of their store.

Inside the cloth bag Lois carried were more letters she'd received for her Dear Caroline column. Sometimes she wished she could take a break from answering all the letters that came in on a regular basis. At other times it gave her a good feeling to know she might be helping people with the answers she gave. Of course, unless Lois met someone in person who had written to her and she revealed her true identity, she would never know for sure if anything she'd said had made a difference in anyone's life. Even so, she planned to keep writing under the name of Dear Caroline until, and unless, God directed her to stop.

"How'd it go while I was gone?" Lois asked when she entered the store and joined Orley where he stood with his clipboard near a shelf full of old canning jars.

"A few people came into the store, which is why I haven't

finished inventorying this side of the building." He gestured to the old jars.

"Did you make any sales?"

"The English woman who came in with her husband bought a few pieces of vintage jewelry." Orley chuckled. "She said it was a late Christmas gift from her to her."

Lois smiled. "I'm glad she found something she liked. Was she the only one who purchased something?"

"Her husband seemed interested in one of the old tools, but I think he was just looking while his wife checked out the jewelry." Orley paused and made a notation on his clipboard. "Oh, and Brandon Prentice came by."

She tipped her head in question. "Who?"

"He's the veterinarian who came in before Christmas and bought that nice old coffee table for his fiancée." Orley frowned. "Only she's not his future bride anymore."

"How come?"

Lois listened as Orley shared with her what Brandon had said during his visit.

"That's a shame."

"It sure is."

"Did you offer him any advice?"

Orley nodded. "I suggested that he get down on one knee and ask her to marry him again, because it sounded to me like he still loves the girl. Oh, and of course I also said he should be praying about the situation, which is the most important thing anyone should do when faced with a serious decision."

"You're absolutely right." Lois's brows pulled downward in concentration. Hearing the things her husband had shared reminded Lois of the Dear Caroline letter she'd received from a woman whose fiancé had recently broken their engagement. She wondered if Brandon might be that man and thought about her response to that letter. Lois pursed her lips. *I hope what I said to the woman may have helped.*

When her stomach rumbled, reminding Andrea that she hadn't eaten lunch yet, she left the piano, where she'd been playing one of her favorite hymns, and went to the kitchen. There she found Lady rolling around on the floor with her new Christmas toy filled with catnip.

"Okay, little Lady, you've had enough of that for now." Andrea bent down and took the toy.

The cat looked up at her and gave a loud *meow!*

"I know you want to keep playing with it, but more than fifteen minutes is not good for you, and it's been that long at least." Brandon had given Andrea this information when she'd first gotten Lady and asked about letting the cat play with catnip. He'd also stated that failure to take the catnip-filled toys away after a few minutes of playtime would likely cause her cat to become bored. Additionally, Brandon had mentioned that if a feline exceeded the recommended amount of catnip consumed, they could experience some mild adverse effects, like nausea or vomiting. Andrea certainly didn't want that to occur.

Reflecting on Brandon's instructions caused Andrea to feel sad. She missed him, and it had been especially lonely on New Year's Eve when she sat home alone with Lady, thinking about how she and Brandon would have spent a wonderful evening together if their relationship hadn't gone sour. No doubt he would have brought Duke along so that he and Lady could enjoy each other's company.

She reflected on last New Year's Eve, when she and Brandon had spent the evening with some other couples from church. It was fun playing board games and chatting with others their age. At least Andrea had those happy memories to look back on and soothe the sadness she felt right now. *At that time, things were normal to me since I was still under the impression that Ray and Evelyn were my biological parents. I was happy in my relationship with Brandon, and my focus was on having a future with him. But now everything's drastically changed.*

"Maybe it's not God's will for us to be together," Andrea mumbled as she opened the refrigerator and perused the contents. She saw a cheeseball her mother had brought by the day before New Year's, when she'd invited Andrea to join her and Dad at their house for open-faced sandwiches that evening. Andrea had politely explained that she appreciated the invitation but felt tired and preferred to stay home and rest. She figured her mom must have thought Andrea would turn down the invitation. Why else had she brought the cheeseball along?

Andrea took the cheeseball out and retrieved a package of crackers from the cupboard. It would not be a filling lunch, but she didn't feel like going to the trouble of making a sandwich or even heating a can of soup. Her appetite had suffered ever since she and Brandon had broken up. At least she hadn't been the one to push for them to end their engagement. After all, he could've been more understanding to her needs and not given up on them. *I've always appreciated the fact that the man I still love is a devoted Christian, but apparently he's not devoted to me.*

Andrea's eyes burned with unshed tears, and she blinked a couple of times to keep them from spilling over. *I will not give in to more tears.* She'd already spent enough time crying, and where had that gotten her? Tears hadn't brought Brandon to her front door to apologize and say that he'd been wrong. Tears wouldn't change the fact that he obviously didn't care whether she found her birth mother or not. In the years she had known Brandon, Andrea had never thought of him as the insensitive type. He'd certainly shown compassion where his animal patients were concerned. Up until Andrea had learned of her adoption, Brandon had been loving and supportive of her endeavors to paint and teach piano lessons. Why couldn't he have done the same when it came to Andrea's need to spend time on the internet in search of her biological parents?

She grabbed a knife and dipped it into the cheeseball, then slathered some on a cracker. *Guess I'd better get something to drink.* Andrea found some eggnog in the refrigerator that was due to expire in two days, so she figured she ought to drink the rest of it. After filling a glass to the rim and putting more crackers and cheeseball on a plate, she took them into her studio and sat down at the desk, where she had turned on her computer before deciding to play some hymns on the piano.

As always, Andrea went first to her email box to see if she'd received any word from Ancestry. She scanned through the junk mail and deleted all that she didn't want. Hope welled in her chest when she found the message she'd been watching for in regard to her DNA test. The email stated that Andrea's DNA sample had been received, but unfortunately no matches were found in their data base.

Andrea frowned. *That's sure odd. Surely at least one of my blood relatives, either on my mother's or father's side, must have had a DNA test done at some time or another. This makes no sense.*

She sat stoically, staring at the computer screen. *If there is no match, which seems unlikely to me, what am I supposed to do next? I can't give up.*

Another thought flashed into Andrea's head. *I'm not at the end of the line at all, because as soon as the birth certificate I sent for arrives, I'll know my birth mother's name. Then all I will have to do is find out where she lives. Since she gave birth to me in Pennsylvania and may still live in that state, I'll start there.*

Excitement, mixed with a bit of trepidation, welled in Andrea's soul as she contemplated what might lie ahead. If she found her mother and made contact with her, would she be welcomed or would her birth mother prefer to have no contact with Andrea at all?

She leaned forward so that her head nearly touched the computer screen. *Since my mother gave me away, it must mean that she didn't want to raise me, but I need to know why.* Tears rolled down her cheeks. Even though it was likely that she and Brandon would never get married, if necessary, she would spend the rest of her life trying to uncover the truth that surrounded her birth. It was that important to her.

Chapter 31

After supper one evening toward the end of January, Andrea picked up the newspaper and took a seat on the living room couch. As she had done every night for the past three weeks, the first thing she looked at was the Dear Caroline column. She'd begun to think that her latest letter either hadn't been read or was not going to be answered due to lack of space in the column. There had to be some letters that Dear Caroline would never see or chose not to respond to at all. Tonight, however, Andrea was pleased to discover the letter she'd written as well as Dear Caroline's answer, which she read out loud.

> "*Dear Brokenhearted:*
>
> *When a couple breaks up, it can be difficult for one or both of them. It would be especially hard to accept when a person is on the brink of marriage. If you feel passionate about finding your birth mother, don't let anything stop you from pursuing that goal. If your fiancé really loves you, he should be more understanding and offer his support and help in locating your mother. There's really nothing you can do to make him more supportive. He needs to come to that realization himself. You might express to him, if you haven't already, that although you love him, you are not willing to give up the search for your biological mother.*"

Andrea placed the newspaper on the couch beside her and pondered Dear Caroline's suggestions. *I have already told Brandon that I love him. Would he be receptive if I said it again?* Her mouth felt dry, and she poured herself a glass of water and took a drink. *If I did talk to Brandon again, I would have to let him know that I can't give up the search for my biological parents even if we do get back together, and that's where the problem is.*

She bowed her head, and with her eyes closed tightly, Andrea prayed out loud. "Dear Lord, please guide and direct my life, and if it's meant for Brandon and me to be together, let us both know it and show us the way."

When he heard an odd clicking sound, Brandon glanced up from the newspaper he'd been reading while eating a late soup-and-sandwich supper. He was surprised to see Duke prance across the kitchen floor, walking backward.

Brandon chuckled. "You crazy little mutt. You sure know how to keep me guessing what kind of silly thing you'll do next." Last week Brandon had walked into the living room one evening and found Duke's back end on the couch with his head resting on one of the end tables.

Brandon watched in fascination as Duke went full circle around the kitchen, still walking backward, and then, with an undignified grunt, plopped down on the throw rug in front of the sink.

Maybe now I can read in peace. Brandon put his concentration back on the newspaper. After reading the local news, sports, and a few ads, he noticed the Dear Caroline column, which he normally skipped. One of the letters caught Brandon's eye, however. "Dear Caroline," he read aloud, "I've written to you before, after learning that I was adopted, and I'm currently in the process of trying to find my biological parents. The man I was planning to marry doesn't understand why this is so important to me. When I told him that I wanted to postpone our wedding, he was upset, and last week, he broke up with me."

Brandon took a deep breath. *I'm almost sure Andrea wrote that letter. She has to be talking about me, and I guess she doesn't care about keeping our relationship private. Anyone who knows us and reads this column is bound to figure out that the letter to Dear Caroline was written by my ex-fiancée.* Brandon's jaw clenched. *Why doesn't she just contact the local radio and TV stations too? She could run an ad that would let the whole world know about our breakup.*

He folded the newspaper and slapped it against the table without even bothering to read Dear Caroline's response. Brandon couldn't help feeling a sense of betrayal on Andrea's part. *If Andrea loves me as much as she has said in the past, then she should have come to me and tried to work things out instead of contacting a perfect stranger who writes for a newspaper column that I am certain many people who live in our area must read.* Warmth crept up the back of Brandon's neck and traveled around to his face. *I don't see how anything can ever be resolved between me and Andrea now.*

Brandon sat a while longer, staring at Duke, who slept peacefully on the rug, emitting doggie snores. "That dog of mine doesn't have a care in the world," he muttered. "He knows I'll take care of his needs and doesn't have to worry about whether I'll feed him or not."

Brandon finished the rest of his nearly cold soup and ate the last half of his sandwich. He felt stunned by Andrea's written comments and wished she hadn't done it. "I would never have written or sent a letter like that to the newspaper! What was she thinking? I would have gone to our pastor for advice first. At least that's confidential."

Duke's eyes popped open, and he looked toward his owner. Apparently, Brandon's ranting must have awakened the dog.

Brandon rose from the table, and after sidestepping Duke, he put his dishes in the sink and stormed out of the room. This whole thing bugged him to the core—especially after realizing how much the situation had escalated. "It all started with Andrea's cousin revealing the truth, and now it's all about her finding her birth parents, with nothing for me."

After taking a seat in his recliner, Brandon reflected on what Orley Troyer had said to him a few weeks ago. *I need to pray,* he told himself. *It's not good to get so worked up that anger and resentment sweep in, and it is certainly not very Christlike.*

He leaned his head back and closed his eyes. *Lord, what should I do? I need some kind of a sign to let me know if I should approach Andrea again. Do I tell her that I read the letter I believe she wrote to Dear Caroline? Should I apologize and say that I was wrong to break up with her?*

If I offered to help Andrea in the search for her biological parents, Brandon asked himself, *would that make a difference?*

The following morning, Andrea bundled up and went outside to get the mail. Seeing a manila envelope postmarked from Lancaster County, Pennsylvania, a sense of excitement welled in her soul. She felt sure the envelope contained her original birth certificate.

Back in the house, Andrea hung up her jacket and scarf. Then she went to the kitchen table to open the mail. As suspected, inside the manila envelope, she discovered her birth certificate. Her fingers trembled as she held it in her hands and read the most important parts out loud. "County of Birth: Lancaster. Name: Ruth Ann Miller. Sex: Female. Father's Name: Unknown. Mother's Name: Mary L. Miller."

Andrea's forehead creased as she continued to study the certificate. *The name Miller sounds kind of Amish to me, but then there's a family from our church whose name is Miller, and they aren't Amish.* Her fingers twitched as she held the document. *Since my father's name is listed as not known, it indicates that my mother must have been unwed. And there's no way for me to know who he was unless I'm able to contact my birth mother and get that information from her, because she must know who fathered her baby.*

She sucked in a quick breath and covered her mouth. *My birth mother named me Ruth Ann. Did my adoptive parents know that I had already been given that name when they got me? If so, why didn't they keep Ruth Ann as my name? Another question for me to ask Mom and Dad. Oh boy. . . I can hardly wait to tell them that the birth certificate issued when I was a newborn arrived in my mailbox today. I hope they will share in my joy over this and be willing to answer more questions.*

Something else popped into her head. *How do I go about finding Mary Miller? If she was single when she gave birth to me and has since married, which seems likely, then her last name would no longer be Miller. I am thankful to have my original birth certificate now, but am I any further along in the search for my mother than I was before?*

Walnut Creek

"This is sure a lot of work, but it'll be well worth it when we dig a big spoon into your tasty vanilla ice cream." Orley leaned closer and kept cranking the handle on their old-fashioned ice-cream freezer, which they had set up in the barn. Whenever they made homemade ice cream during the summer months, he usually set it up and did his cranking on the front or back porch. But it was too cold for that, and he didn't want to bring it inside the house, where spilled rock salt or ice could make a mess on his wife's clean floors.

Lois smiled at him from a wooden bench nearby and winked. "You're right, Big O. The ice cream will be a nice treat for us. I thawed some strawberries to put on top, and there's also some chocolate syrup in the cupboard I can open if you like."

Orley licked his lips in anticipation. "Sounds good. I can hardly wait." He looked over at her and grinned. "I kinda like it when you call me by the nickname I acquired when I was a teenager."

She winked again. "I know you do."

"Say, I just remembered to tell you about a message I found on our answering machine when I went out to the phone shed while you were mixing the ice-cream ingredients."

"Who was the message from?" Lois questioned.

"Paul Herschberger. He called to let us know that Lisa gave birth to a baby boy early this morning."

"Oh my!" Lois's eyes opened wide. "I thought she wasn't due for a few more weeks. Is she okay? Is the baby all right?"

"Paul said in his message that Lisa and the little guy they named Andrew Paul are both doing fine."

"I'm so glad. How happy they must be." Lois glanced away, then looked back at Orley. "Were there any other messages?"

He shook his head. "Not on our answering machine, but one of the customers who came into our store this morning asked if I heard about the accident our bishop and his fraa had yesterday," Orley said, taking their conversation in a more serious direction.

Her brows furrowed. "What happened?"

"They'd left the home of an elderly woman from outside our church district who has been laid up with a broken leg. On the way back to their home, the horse pulling their carriage somehow managed to get its tail under the lines. The buggy ended up tipping over."

"Oh dear! Were either of them seriously hurt?"

Orley shook his head. "The bishop's wife got a bump on the head, and he had a few bruises, but they're both okay. The Lord was watching out for them, because it could have been much worse. Either one of them could have been killed in the accident."

"You're right about that," she agreed. "So often when a buggy topples over, the occupants end up with serious injuries."

"On a different topic," Orley said, switching arms to do the cranking. "I read your Dear Caroline column this evening while you were mixing the ingredients for our ice cream."

"Oh?" She tilted her head to one side. "What did you think of it?"

"I was interested in the letter from the woman whose boyfriend broke things off with her because she's been too busy trying to find her biological parents. It made me think about Brandon Prentice. In fact, I have to wonder if it was Brandon's ex-girlfriend who wrote the letter."

"I suppose that's possible." Lois rubbed the bridge of her nose.

"Did you think the answer I gave her was all right?"

He bobbed his head. "You always give good answers."

"I hope so. I pray about each of the letters I receive before writing my response to their questions."

"Jah, prayer is always a good thing. That's what I told Brandon when he came into our shop a few weeks ago." Orley stopped cranking. "I do believe this is done. It won't crank anymore, so I'm sure it's as frozen as it's gonna get."

"Good, and as cold as it is, there's probably no need to let it set for a while with ice over the top of the container, like we often do during the warm summer months."

"Right."

"Would you like me to carry the container into the house?"

"No, that's okay. I'll do it."

"All right then, I'll go ahead and get our bowls set out along with the berries and chocolate syrup." She rose from the bench and left the barn.

Orley knocked some ice off the top of the container, and with his gloved hands, he lifted the container out and headed to the house.

As he made his way, his boot hit a patch of ice. The next thing he knew, he was lying in a pile of snow. The impact had caused the lid on the container to come off, and some of the ice cream oozed out. Although not hurt, Orley was embarrassed by his fall. He looked about the yard and to the street, hoping no one was outside and had seen him take a tumble. He didn't feel much like Big O at the moment, but he was relieved that this incident had gone unnoticed. About that time, two of their bigger barn cats ran out of the barn and began lapping up the ice cream that had escaped from the can. Orley quickly put the lid back on, scrambled to his feet, and headed toward the house, this time walking carefully with each step he took. He was glad slipping on the ice and landing on the ground hadn't injured him. He thanked the Lord for sparing him from injuring his back again—or any other parts of his body, for that matter.

When Orley entered the kitchen a few minutes later, he set the container in the sink and told Lois what had happened.

"Oh dear. . .I hope you weren't hurt."

"No, I'm fine, and don't worry, there's still plenty of ice cream in the container." He laughed. "I was glad when the *katze* came along 'cause at least the ice cream that ended up in the snow didn't go to waste."

Lois shook her head. "Sometimes, I can't believe you, dear husband. Only you could make a joke out of falling in the snow."

"But you still love me, right?"

She kissed his cold cheek. "Absolutely."

~

Their dessert was tasty, and Lois enjoyed each bite of the creamy delight. She had added some berries and a bit of chocolate syrup into the vanilla in her bowl and blended it all together. "Mmm. . . this is so good."

"Did you want a second helping before I put the rest of the ice cream in the freezer?" Orley called from the kitchen.

"I still have plenty in my bowl, but thank you for asking," she replied.

A couple of minutes passed before Orley returned to the living room with his second helping. "You know me—I can never be satisfied with just one bowl of delicious ice cream. The berries you froze from our garden add a nice touch too."

"I'm glad we had a big crop to freeze and make jelly."

"Jah, and eating those berries makes me long for spring."

"I hear you," Lois replied. "This cold weather gets tiresome, but the warm season will return before we know it." She placed her spoon in the empty bowl. "I wish we could take a trip to someplace warm and sunny, like some of our friends do this time of the year."

He smiled. "Maybe you and I should plan a vacation. We just need to figure out where we'd like to go."

Lois tapped her chin. "There are lots of places I'd like to visit.

I've heard some interesting things about California, Texas, and Florida, but they are all quite a ways from here, which would mean we'd probably need to be gone a few weeks."

"Those states you mentioned are a lot warmer this time of the year, and a couple of them are tropical."

"The only problem is, what would we do with our business if we took an extended vacation? Could we find someone to fill in for us, or would it be best to close Memory Keepers while we're gone?" Lois picked up her spoon and licked the little bit of ice cream that remained.

"That's a good question, and we should do the best thing."

"What's that?"

"Pray about it, and see what the Lord guides us to do."

"I agree," Lois said, "but meanwhile we're stuck dealing with this cold, sometimes icy, winter weather."

"True, but if we can figure out where to go and a way to keep the antique store open while we're gone, we can travel like you want to, away from this chilly place."

Lois nodded. "It would be nice to be somewhere warm right now. And it would be fun to see some unusual places, but unless the good Lord opens the door for us to go, we'll need to be content to stay put."

"Jah." He put another spoonful of ice cream in his mouth.

Lois figured with the good amount he'd eaten already, when her husband finished this second bowl, he'd probably close his eyes and take a nap. It had been nice talking about taking a trip together, but right now it seemed unlikely.

Soon after Orley had set his empty bowl on the coffee table, he fell asleep in his favorite chair as she'd predicted.

Lois scooped up their bowls and took them to the kitchen. After washing and drying the dishes, she headed for the desk in her sewing room. She needed to read and hopefully answer more letters that had been sent to her Dear Caroline column, but for some reason, she wasn't in the mood.

Although they were nearly a full month into the new year already, Lois began to reflect on the previous year, and she asked herself a few questions. *What did I do during the past twelve months that was of value in God's eyes? Have I done enough when it comes to helping others who need food, clothing, or financial assistance?* While Lois and Orley often attended benefit auctions and the like, and they always made a contribution, she sometimes felt that it wasn't enough.

Lois leaned forward with both arms resting on her new desk. *And what about my newspaper column? Have the words I shared helped anyone to make a change for the better? Have I prayed when I should have? Read my Bible often enough? Told others about the love of Jesus our Redeemer when I was given the opportunity? Orley and I have been so blessed—with our business, our health, and the precious moments we've had together and with friends. To list all of our blessings would be impossible.*

Lois paused and took a sip of the apple-cinnamon tea she'd brought into the room with her. She had lost her father this past year, and that had been difficult. But at least she'd been with him when he died, and the letter he'd written to her, which had been found in his Bible, had helped to heal a lot of Lois's emotional wounds from her childhood.

"God's will be done," she murmured, then closed her eyes. *Help me and Orley to be thankful every day of this new year for our many blessings. And please show us when and what to say whenever You bring a hurting soul our way.*

Chapter 32

Apple Creek

"How are things going with the search for your birth parents?" Colleen asked when she stopped by Andrea's house the following day.

"In some ways, good. In other ways, not so much," Andrea replied as Colleen removed her outer garments and did the same for her son, Tyler.

"What do you mean?"

Andrea gestured for her friend to take a seat in the living room. Colleen sat on the couch and tried to coax Tyler to join her, but the rambunctious two-year-old took off after Andrea's cat.

"Tyler, come back here." Colleen cupped her hands around her mouth.

"It's okay. Lady will find a place to hide if he bothers her too much." Andrea took a seat beside Colleen. "Would you like a cup of coffee or some tea?"

"Maybe later. Right now I'm more interested in hearing how your adoption search has been going."

"My original birth certificate came in the mail yesterday. Would you like to see it?"

"Yes, of course. You must be excited about that."

"Yes, and I'll be right back." Andrea left the room. She was almost to her bedroom when she heard a crash coming from within. Upon entering the room, Andrea saw that her nightstand lamp wasn't where it should be. Tyler stood near the bed with his eyes wide open and tears on his cheeks. The lamp was on the floor, and the bulb had broken. Meanwhile, Lady, who'd been under the bed, darted out the door in a blur. Andrea did not want Tyler to go near the shards of glass, so she took his hand, led him out of the room, and shut the door behind them. "How about you play with the kitty out here?"

The little boy looked up at her and nodded.

"I'll be right with you. I have a little cleaning up to do in my bedroom," Andrea called to Colleen from the kitchen a few minutes later.

It wasn't long before her friend came in. "What's going on?"

"The bedroom lamp got knocked over, and there's broken glass from the lightbulb on the floor." She removed the broom from the storage closet. "There's a spare bulb in here, which I'll take care of putting in the lamp later on."

Colleen looked down at Tyler, who had followed Andrea and her cat into the kitchen. "I'm guessing my son was responsible for knocking over your lamp?"

Andrea shrugged. "I believe Tyler went into my room, chasing after Lady, but he may not have been responsible for the lamp toppling off the nightstand. Lady could have knocked it over trying to escape."

"I'm sorry it happened. My son should not have been chasing the cat or gone into your room." She reached for Tyler's hand. "Please settle down and stay close to Mommy."

"It's okay. It was just the bulb. The lamp is fine." Andrea went to her room to clean up the broken glass. Afterward, she unplugged the lamp and carefully removed the guts of the bulb. *Tyler's a cute little guy, but I think I've gotten a taste of what it would be like to have a child. I have to say, they do keep things lively, and you can't let them out of your sight for long.* Andrea heaved a sigh. *If only Brandon and I could work things out, then one day we might have a child.* She pushed that thought aside and opened her top dresser drawer to get the birth certificate.

Andrea put the broom away and then went to the living room, where Colleen sat with Tyler on the couch. Andrea removed the certificate from the manila envelope and handed it to her friend. "I'm eager to know what you think."

Colleen studied the document before handing it back to Andrea. "So your biological father is unknown, and all you have is your birth mother's name, which was most likely her maiden name. That's not much information, but it's better than nothing. So now where do you go?"

Andrea shrugged. "I'm not sure. I talked to my folks yesterday, and Mom suggested that I should visit a website called Spokeo that she'd discovered. She said it's a place where a person can confidentially search more than fourteen billion publicly available records and other information. She also mentioned that from the basic search, you can discover locations, age, and relatives." Andrea's words were rushed. "So I may try that."

Colleen smiled. "I hope it works out for you. I'm sure this must all be pretty stressful."

"It is—especially since my desire to locate my birth mother caused Brandon to end our relationship, which was something I never thought would happen. He's always seemed so devoted to me."

"Have you heard from him lately?"

"No, and I doubt that I will."

"Have you considered making the first move in an effort to get back together?"

"Yes, and I've prayed about it too. The trouble is, I'm afraid nothing I could say, except that I'd be willing to give up my search, would satisfy him." Andrea shook her head forcibly. "I can't do that. Finding my birth mother is too important to me."

"I would have to say that you've had more time to focus on locating your birth mother since you've parted ways. Just look at what you have done already. Little by little, you are getting closer to your goal." Colleen glanced at Tyler. He'd gotten off the couch and now lay on the floor with Lady sleeping beside him.

"Do you really think I'm getting closer?" Andrea questioned. "It hasn't been easy turning over every stone I can think of, but there seems to be a driving force that is propelling me on." She took a seat on the couch beside Colleen. "I still love Brandon, and I wish things could be different, but at this point, it seems doubtful."

Colleen leaned close and gave Andrea a hug. "Guess if I was in your shoes, I would feel the same way. Even so, I wish you and Brandon could get back together. You always seemed like such a happy, well-suited couple."

Andrea sniffed, trying to hold back tears. "We were—until I found out that I'd been adopted. Then everything changed."

Evelyn sat quietly at the kitchen table, eating the taco salad she'd fixed for lunch. Since Ray was at work and she'd be eating alone, it was a good opportunity to enjoy some of her favorite hot sauce, which her husband didn't like. In fact, Ray didn't care for anything spicy. Whenever he indulged in spicy food, he'd end up with heartburn.

We may not always have the same taste in foods, she thought, *but Ray and I agree on so many other, more important things.* They had both agreed that they should support Andrea's decision to search for her birth mother. It had nearly broken Evelyn's heart to witness their daughter's reaction when she'd first learned of her adoption. Since then, with Andrea postponing her wedding and then Brandon breaking things off, Evelyn had been quite distressed. She hoped that if Andrea could locate her birth mother soon, she and Brandon might get back together. But with her daughter being so focused on locating the woman who'd given birth to her, Evelyn couldn't help worrying that this could drag on for a while. The thought of seeing her daughter lose a nice fellow like Brandon saddened Evelyn. And she felt odd—like she wasn't as important to Andrea anymore and could be replaced by the biological mother. It was hard not to feel a little jealous.

Evelyn thought about her husband. She figured with Andrea's biological father's name having been left off the birth certificate, Ray wouldn't feel any concern about the possibility of another man taking his place in their daughter's life. *Of course*, she mentally added, *for all we know, Andrea's birth mother may not be living anymore.*

Evelyn finished the last of her salad and placed her dishes in the dishwasher. *What I need to do now is haul the last of the boxes full of Christmas decorations up to the attic*, she told herself. *None of them are heavy, and I've put this off long enough.*

Evelyn left the kitchen and went to the spare bedroom at the end of the hall, where she had temporarily put the decorations. She picked up the first box and headed upstairs, being careful not to trip and fall. As she passed Andrea's old bedroom on the second floor, a lump formed in her throat. *I miss the days when our daughter lived here and life seemed so simple and joyous.* Andrea had always been a pleasant child, never disrespectful or defiant like some kids could be. Evelyn wondered if their daughter would have been any different as a child if she'd known about her adoption. *Would she have been just as happy and content, or would knowing the truth at a young age have caused her to feel insecure—not sure where she belonged?*

I need to stop dwelling on this and focus on the here and now. Evelyn shifted the box to her hip and opened the attic door with her free hand. Taking her time and being careful with each step, she made her way up to the third floor. When Evelyn reached the top and entered the dark, dusty attic, she clicked on the overhead light and set the box down on the squeaky floor. Instead of going back down for another box, Evelyn paused to look around. The first thing she spotted was Andrea's old toy box, filled with many of the things she had played with during the early part of her childhood. Dust particles danced in the shaft of light coming in through one of the small windows. Some old board games, a rolled-up rug, and a number of picture frames had been stacked against one wall. Several storage tubs filled with outdated clothing adorned another wall. So many memories and keepsakes were stored up here. Evelyn wished she had time to comb through each one and dwell for a while on the past.

She rubbed her chilled arms while standing in the middle of the room. The winter chill seeping in was not comfortable. *I should have thought to put on a sweater before coming up here.* She moved back near the attic entrance, where she felt some warmth coming in from the heat rising through the house.

Her gaze traveled to the opposite side of the unfinished room, where her grandmother's old trunk sat. Over the years, Evelyn had put some family heirlooms in there. *I think I'll just open it and take a peek. It won't take long, and then I'll go back downstairs for the next box of decorations.*

Evelyn knelt on the floor in front of the vintage trunk and opened the lid. Peering inside, she spotted Ray's old uniform from when he'd served in the military before they were married. She also discovered a box of letters he had written to her when they'd been dating. He'd always said that he could put down on paper the way he felt about her easier than saying it to her face.

Evelyn smiled. *That husband of mine is such a romantic. I wonder if he truly realized how much those letters meant to me.* Evelyn was tempted to sit in the old rocking chair nearby and read some of Ray's love letters, but if she got started, it would probably be time to start supper when she got back downstairs. *I'll look through a few more things and then go after the next box to bring up.*

Half an hour later, she reached down to the bottom of the trunk and felt something soft. She grasped the item between her fingers and pulled it out. "Oh my, I can't believe I forgot all about this until now."

Evelyn held the cloth doll against her chest as the memory of the day she'd been given it filled her mind. When she and Ray had gone to the hospital to get their adopted daughter, a nurse had handed Evelyn the doll and said, "This belonged to the baby's birth mother. She wanted her little girl to have it."

Forgetting about the rest of the boxes downstairs still needing to be brought up, Evelyn closed the trunk lid and got up from the floor. *I am going over to see Andrea right now. She needs to see this doll.*

Andrea had been so involved in painting a picture of the adorable Amish child she had seen during a shopping trip the other day that she had lost track of time. It wasn't until her stomach rumbled that she looked at the clock and realized it was almost time to start supper.

I'll finish working on the little girl's hair and then go make myself something to eat.

Andrea was surprised when she heard the doorbell ring. She didn't have any piano students today and wasn't expecting company.

She set her paintbrush down and left the studio to answer the door. When Andrea opened it and saw her mother on the porch, she felt concern. Mom rarely came by without calling first to see if Andrea was home or in the middle of a lesson. To drop by unannounced and so close to supper must mean that something was wrong.

"Mom, are you all right?" Andrea reached out and touched her mother's arm.

"I'm fine. Why would you ask? Do I appear to be sick?"

"No, not at all, but since you rarely come by without calling first, I thought something might be wrong."

"No, I'm fine, and so is your dad."

"Oh good. I'm glad."

Andrea opened the door wider. "Come on in out of the cold. Would you like something warm to drink?"

"Maybe later. First, we need to talk." Her mother stepped in, and Andrea hung her coat on the coat tree in the entryway.

"So to what do I owe this pleasant surprise?"

"Not what but who." Mom moistened her lips with the tip of her tongue. "Can we go in the living room and sit down?"

"Of course." Andrea led the way. Once they were both seated on the couch, she leaned closer to her mother and asked, "Who do I owe this visit to?"

"Your birth mother."

Andrea's eyes widened, and her mouth dropped slightly open.

"You know where she is? Have you spoken to her?" The mere thought of it seemed too good to be true.

Mom shook her head. "It's nothing like that, but I found something in the attic today that she wanted you to have."

"Seriously? What is it?"

"This." Mom reached into her oversized handbag and withdrew a small cloth doll with no face dressed in Amish girl's attire.

Andrea's ribs tightened, and her lips quivered when she spoke. "How do you know it was her doll and that she wanted me to have it?"

"Because when your dad and I went to the hospital to pick you up, a social worker, along with a nurse, brought you out of the maternity ward to us. The nurse said the woman who gave birth to you wanted you to have the doll. She said it had been her own doll when she was a child."

Andrea's hand shook as she reached out and took hold of the doll with no face. "It's an Amish doll; I've seen others similar to this in some of the gift stores in our area as well as those in Holmes County." She pursed her lips. "So my birth mother's last name, Miller, must be Amish, which means that—"

"That the woman who gave birth to you was Amish." Mom finished Andrea's sentence.

Andrea's head moved slowly up and down while she tried to digest everything. They sat staring at each other as Andrea struggled not to give in to the sob rising in her throat. *No wonder I've always been so intrigued with the Amish way of life. And that's the reason I've chosen so many Amish buggies, houses, barns, and children to paint.*

"If you've had the doll since I was a baby, why'd you wait so long to give it to me?" Andrea looked directly at her mother.

"When we came home with you, I put the doll in my grandmother's trunk, along with other mementoes," her mother replied. "I had intended to give it to you when we felt you were old enough to be told about your adoption, but. . ." Tears gathered in the corners of Mom's eyes.

"But then you and Dad decided not to tell me, so you just left the doll there, believing I would never find it and ask where it had come from?" Andrea couldn't keep the resentment she felt from her tone of voice. She'd thought she had forgiven her parents for keeping the truth from her all those years, but now a feeling of bitterness was creeping in, and she had to do something to stop it before it took hold.

"I didn't leave it there on purpose, Andrea." Mom spoke quietly but in a sincere tone. "Your dad and I were caught up in the joy of raising you, and we really did forget the doll was in the trunk."

"Okay." Andrea placed the doll in her lap and lowered her head. A strange feeling came over her as she gazed at the faceless doll. It was hard to believe that she could actually be holding a doll that her biological mother wanted her to have. While the feeling was exhilarating, it didn't answer the big question on Andrea's heart, mind, and soul. *Where is this Amish woman who gave birth to me nearly thirty-three years ago?*

She leaned her head heavily against the back of the couch and closed her eyes. *Dear Lord, how am I ever going to find the woman who gave birth to me? Since I was born in Lancaster, Pennsylvania, would a trip there be the best place to start?*

Chapter 33

I hope Memory Keepers is open today and that Orley Troyer is in the store, Brandon thought after he left his clinic and headed across the parking lot to his vehicle. *I need to speak with Orley before I make any contact with Andrea. I've gotta be sure I say and do the right things and don't let my emotions get in the way of good judgment.* Brandon regretted that he had broken things off with Andrea. Doing it hadn't helped him feel any better—in fact, he felt worse. He kept asking himself if it would have hurt to have supported Andrea instead of thinking only of himself. Now the road to getting back with his girl seemed long and humbling. Brandon was amazed by how one wrong decision could have such consequences in a person's life. He wasn't happy and felt lonelier than ever. Brandon grimaced. *Why did I let my pride lead me to break things off with her?*

For the past few weeks, Brandon had been praying about his relationship with Andrea as Orley had suggested. He'd finally reached the point where he thought he could talk to her but needed some reassurance before he plunged ahead.

As Brandon stepped through patches of snow approaching his SUV, he noticed that the parking lights were on. "Oh great," he mumbled. "I hope it didn't drain my battery." He touched the button of his key fob, and the door unlocked for him. *Maybe my rig will start.*

Brandon climbed into his cold vehicle, closed the door, and turned on the ignition. He frowned when it didn't start. "What's up with this?" He tried again. Still nothing. He made a couple more attempts and finally gave up. He hoped it was just a dead battery and nothing more serious.

Brandon pulled his cell phone from his jacket pocket to call for roadside assistance, which was one of the benefits included with his insurance policy. After speaking with the person on the other end, he was told that someone would be out to assist him within the hour.

That's just great. By the time I get to Walnut Creek, the antique store will probably be closed. Brandon massaged his temples. There was nothing he could do except wait, but it was too cold to sit in his vehicle. He got out and went back to the clinic where he could at least stay warm.

Both Brandon's receptionist and his assistant had already gone home, so the clinic was dark and quiet. He flipped on the light in the waiting room and took a seat. It seemed strange to be sitting where the owners of his animal patients usually sat.

He glanced around the room, wondering if the things set out in this room were pleasant enough and offered the people who came here a comfortable, relaxing place to wait. The posters of various breeds of dogs and cats were interesting. Pet supplies displayed on one side of the room and ready for purchase made it easy for people to see what was available at Brandon's clinic.

As he sat there, Andrea came to mind. *I sure miss her pretty face and being able to spend time together like we used to.*

In an effort to clear his head, Brandon glanced at the clock on the wall. It was close to dinnertime, and his stomach gurgled at the thought. *I'm getting hungry, and there's nothing here to eat unless you're a dog or cat.* He looked over at the reading materials on the end table. *I should've put an extra bag of chips in my lunch box today, but how was I to know this would happen? Oh well, maybe I can find something interesting to read in one of the magazines here on the table.*

He picked up a pet-centered magazine and thumbed through it, stopping when he came to an article titled "How to Tell If Your

Dog Loves You." Brandon chuckled. *I have no doubt whatsoever that Duke loves me. He wags his tail and barks when I get home and likes to curl up beside me on the couch or drape himself on my lap when I'm in my recliner. He also follows me around the house and paws at my leg to get my attention. Yep—my dog loves me a lot, and I love him.* Brandon thumped his head. "Course, not nearly as much as I love Andrea. I just wish that she—"

A horn honked out in the parking lot, jolting Brandon out of his musings. He put the magazine down and went to open the door. Roadside assistance had arrived, to his relief. If they couldn't get his vehicle started, though, he'd need to have it towed to the nearest mechanic.

~

Andrea held the faceless doll in her hands as she carried on a phone conversation with Colleen. Just seconds ago, she had told her friend about the doll.

"Wow, that's amazing." Colleen gave a little whistle. "I can only imagine the excitement you must have felt when your mom presented you with it and said your biological mother had wanted you to have it."

"It was quite a shock, and at first I was a little peeved that Mom hadn't given it to me sooner, but then she explained she'd forgotten the doll was in that old trunk in the attic."

"Know what I would do if I were you?"

"What?"

"I'd take that old doll to the antique store in Walnut Creek to get an appraisal."

"How come?" Andrea asked. "You should know that I'm not going to sell it. This doll is precious to me. It's all I have from the woman who gave birth to me."

"I wasn't suggesting that you sell it, Andrea. I thought you might think it was interesting to find out how much the doll is worth, and in the process of asking, maybe the Amish couple who own the store could shed some light on what Amish community the doll might be from."

Andrea's fingers traced over the doll's empty face. "I doubt that a doll such as this would be any different from one community to another. Except for the fact that my doll looks well-used, she's not much different than the ones I have seen for sale at some of the gift shops in our area."

"Maybe you're right, but I still think it'd be a good idea to take it in for an appraisal. You never know, you might have been given something quite valuable."

"I doubt it, but maybe I will take it in. I'll do it tomorrow since I'm going to be in Holmes County anyway."

"How come?"

"There's a Christian bookstore in Berlin, and I want to get something for my mom there. Would you like to come along?"

"Normally, I would, but I have a dental appointment tomorrow, and since my mother will be watching Tyler, I promised to take both of them to lunch afterward. I'll call you tomorrow evening, though. I'd like to hear what you found out about the old doll."

"Okay, I'll talk to you soon. Have a good evening."

"You too."

When Andrea ended the call, she took the doll into her studio and placed it on the desk next to the computer. *I wonder if my birth mother made this doll.* The longer she studied the cloth memento, the more Andrea wondered what her mother was like. Since the faceless doll had come into her life, Andrea almost felt like a little girl again. No matter what room she was in, she brought the doll with her so she could see it. Every time she looked at the doll, Andrea tried to imagine what her birth mother looked like. *Does she have auburn hair like me, or do I take after my biological father?* So many unanswered questions swam in Andrea's head it almost made her feel dizzy. One thing was sure: as soon as the weather improved, she was going to make a trip to Pennsylvania with the hope of finding some answers.

Walnut Creek

Since Brandon had no farm calls to make on this cold Saturday afternoon, he was on his way to Memory Keepers Antique Store to speak with Orley. Thankfully, he hadn't needed a new battery yesterday. The jump start had been sufficient, but by the time the man had taken care of the problem, it was too late to make it to Walnut Creek before the antique store closed. That was okay, though. Going there earlier in the day gave Brandon more time to speak with Orley if he wasn't busy with other customers.

Brandon found a parking spot close to the store and made sure his lights had been turned off before he got out. Although no new snow was in sight, the wind had picked up, hitting Brandon's face with a blast of cold air. He hurried toward the store and quickly opened the door, causing the little bell overhead to announce his arrival.

Brandon glanced around and was pleased to see Orley behind the front counter next to Lois.

"Nice to see you again!" Orley smiled and motioned for Brandon to come over.

He didn't hesitate and greeted the bearded man and his soft-spoken wife with hearty handshakes.

"If you're not too busy, I was wondering if I could talk to you for a few minutes." Brandon directed his question to Orley.

"Of course. Lois and I were just going over our inventory list, but I think we're about done with it, so I have time to talk." Orley pointed toward the back of the store. "Why don't we go into the office? That way we won't be disturbed if a customer comes in."

Brandon hesitated before nodding. He hoped Orley's wife didn't feel like they were leaving her out. *But then*, he reasoned, *someone has to stay up front to greet any customers who might come in.*

Brandon followed Orley to a small room at the back of the building. Besides a vintage-looking desk and two chairs, the only other things in the room were two tall filing cabinets and an old manual typewriter sitting on a metal cart. Brandon wondered how they got by without a computer, but from the little he knew about the Amish, he figured most of them were probably old-school when it came to the way they lived and worked.

"Please take a seat." Orley gestured to the chair sitting near the desk. Brandon sat down, and Orley took a seat on the other side of the desk. "How are things going with you?" the kindly Amish man asked. "Has anything changed between you and the woman you'd planned to marry?"

Brandon shook his head. "I've been praying about it, and I do want to get back with her, but nothing has come clear to me yet. If only God would give me a sign."

"Sometimes when I've prayed about something, I didn't receive any specific kind of sign." Orley placed both hands on the desk and leaned slightly forward. "What I did receive, however, was a deep sense of peace once I made up my mind to do something. I took that to mean that it must be God's will, so I moved forward with what I thought I should do."

"Guess my trouble is that I'm full of self-doubts where my relationship with Andrea is concerned."

"What are you feeling doubtful about?"

"I'm afraid that I hurt Andrea so deeply when I broke things off that even if I went to her now and apologized, she would not take me back."

Orley's glasses had slipped down almost to the middle of his nose, and he pushed them back in place before responding. "I can only say this: if you want to resume your relationship with Andrea, then you should go to her and say what's on your heart. The fact is, you won't know unless you try, and if it's meant to be, then you will feel God's peace."

Brandon sat quietly, letting Orley's words sink in. Then he offered a quick, silent prayer. *Lord, whatever way it goes between Andrea and me, please grant me Your peace.*

When Andrea drove her car into the town of Walnut Creek, she began to have second thoughts about going to Memory Keepers. As she had told Colleen when they talked on the phone, there was no valid reason to find out how much the faceless doll might be worth since she had no intention of selling it. Furthermore, it was highly doubtful that the Amish couple who owned the antique store would know what Amish community it had come from.

But I'm here now, Andrea told herself as she pulled up to the curb in front of the store. *So I may as well go inside and show them my doll.*

Lois put the inventory list away and was about to open a box Orley had brought in from the storage room earlier, when the bell above the front door jingled. She turned to see who'd come in and was surprised to see the auburn-haired woman who had been in the shop several months ago. As Lois recalled, her name was Andrea. Lois assumed the young woman might have brought something in that she wanted to sell or leave on consignment, for she held a small box in her hands.

"Welcome back." Lois greeted the young woman near the door. "May I help you with something today?" Lois had hoped she would have an opportunity like this to find out where Andrea stood spiritually.

Andrea gave a slow shake of her head. "I. . .uh. . .have an old doll in this box, and I was hoping you'd have the time to take a look at it."

"Certainly. Are you wanting to sell the doll?"

Andrea shook her head again. "I'm wondering what it might be worth and whether you would have any idea of where it may have come from—like what Amish community, perhaps."

"If you'll bring it on up to the counter, I'll take a look." Lois headed in that direction and Andrea followed.

When Lois set the box on the counter and opened the lid, she squinted over the top of her smudged glasses. "It's a faceless doll—an old one at that, from the looks of the faded dress and yellowed skin-colored material. "Do you mind if I have a closer look?"

"Please, help yourself."

Lois picked the doll up and continued to squint as she studied its arms, legs, and face.

"I'm guessing the doll's not worth much, right?"

Lois gave no response. Instead, she turned the doll over and pulled the snaps off the backside of the faded blue dress. She studied it, and her mouth quivered a bit. "Where did you get this doll? Did you find it or buy it somewhere locally?"

"No, it was a gift." Andrea paused, wondering how much she should share with this woman she barely knew. After a few seconds' deliberation, she said, "I was adopted as a baby, and my adoptive mother found the doll recently in an old trunk in her attic." Andrea stopped talking and reached out to stroke the doll's arm. "She said it had belonged to my birth mother, and that when she and my dad came to the hospital to get me, a nurse gave them the doll and said the woman who'd given birth to me wanted me to have it." Andrea paused once more and looked at Lois. She was surprised to see that the Amish woman's face had turned paler than the snow outside. The next thing Andrea knew, Lois gasped, and then she collapsed onto the floor.

Andrea's heartbeat quickened, and she had the sensation of things moving too quickly to process. She took a few deep breaths to calm herself and thought about what she'd learned when she'd taken a CPR class. Andrea didn't know for sure, but she thought the poor woman could have had a heart attack. Should she call 911 for help, try to revive Lois herself, or see if Lois's husband was somewhere in the store?

Andrea's sensibility kicked in, and she rushed to where Lois had fallen and dropped to her knees. She called out Lois's name, and when there was no response, Andrea clasped the woman's cold wrist and took her pulse. It didn't seem irregular, but Lois's eyes were still closed. Andrea remembered from the class she had taken that she should have a person who has fainted lie down with their feet elevated. This would make more blood flow to the brain, causing most people to recover quickly after fainting.

Before Andrea had a chance to look for something to put under the woman's feet, Lois opened her eyes. She looked at Andrea, and in a voice barely above a whisper, Lois said, "*Dochder.*"

Chapter 34

Andrea turned when she heard footsteps. Orley and Brandon were heading toward them. *Brandon? What's he doing here?*

Lois moaned, and Andrea turned her attention back to the poor woman, who was attempting to sit up.

"Please, you must lie still," Andrea instructed.

Orley rushed forward and dropped to his knees. "Lois, what happened? Did you slip on something and fall?" Andrea heard the depth of Orley's concern as he leaned close to his wife and touched her face. "Lie still while I get you some water to drink and a wet paper towel to put on your forehead." He looked at Andrea. "Please keep an eye on her while I run into my office for some water and paper towel."

She nodded.

When Orley returned a short time later, he knelt beside Lois again. After placing a dampened folded towel beneath her head, he gave her a few sips of water. "What happened that caused my wife to fall?" Orley directed his question to Andrea.

"I was telling her about the doll my mother found in her attic and explained that it had belonged to my birth mother, and she wanted me to have it. When she looked at the doll, she had a strange expression, and then after looking at the back of the doll, under its dress, she fainted." Andrea's words were rushed and spoken before Lois had a chance to respond to her husband's question. "After she came to a few minutes ago, Lois whispered some word that I didn't understand."

"I said *daughter*." Lois sat up and looked at Andrea with eyes wide, and then she gave a disbelieving shake of her head. "I—I don't know how this could be possible, but that doll was mine when I was a girl. I gave it to a nurse at the hospital to give to my baby girl before she was given to strangers."

Andrea listened to all that was being said, letting it slowly sink in. Even though her ex-fiancé was there with them in the room, she focused on what Lois was saying. It wasn't that she intentionally excluded him, but she had been searching for news of her birth mother for months.

Orley looked up at Andrea with eyebrows squished together. "I think my wife must be delusional. We have no daughter—no children at all."

Andrea wondered why the woman would say *daughter* if she didn't have one.

Lois pointed at Andrea with a shaky hand. "I—I believe that you are my daughter."

Before Andrea could form a response, Orley spoke again. "You're not thinking straight, Lois. We do not have a daughter."

She pointed at Andrea again. "I am almost certain that Andrea is the daughter I was forced to give up nearly thirty-three years ago."

"What?" Orley looked at his wife with a dazed expression. "I have no idea what you are talking about. I believe when you fell and bumped your head, it messed up your thinking."

Brandon stepped forward and pulled his cell phone from his jacket pocket. "Should I call 911? Lois could have a concussion and need to be examined." He looked at Andrea. "Wouldn't you agree?"

Unable to think clearly or form a response, Andrea bit down on her bottom lip. She wanted to know what Brandon was doing here, but now was not the time to ask. The one thing Andrea needed right now was answers to questions she had for Lois.

Lois released her stiff white head covering and reached up to finger the bun at the back of her head, where some of her auburn-colored hair had come loose. "I'm fine; there are no lumps or pain, and I can see clearly. I was so stunned when I saw the doll and heard Andrea's story, that everything started closing in on me and I passed out." She looked over at Brandon and shook her head. "I'm fine, and I won't be needing any medical help."

"Okay." He glanced at Orley and returned his cell phone to his pocket.

"Let's get you up and into a chair." Orley helped Lois to her feet and over to one of the antique rockers that was for sale. Once she was seated, he situated her head covering, then pulled up a straight-backed chair and sat beside her. Lois smoothed the wrinkles in the skirt of her olive green dress and glanced back toward the counter.

Andrea wasn't sure what to do, so she stood off to one side with her arms crossed and heart pounding. Brandon joined her but said nothing.

"Now what's all this talk about Andrea being your daughter?" Orley looked at his wife with concern. "Were you thinking what it would be like if we had a daughter who looked like her?"

Lois shook her head. "No, I was thinking, as I am now, how much she looks like me when I was her age. She has the same auburn hair and brown eyes I do."

Andrea had never thought about it until now, but she and Lois did share those similarities. Even so. . .

"I suppose if she was dressed in Amish clothes and had long hair pulled up into a bun, she would resemble you in some ways."

Andrea could tell by the gentle way Orley spoke to his wife that he didn't believe what she had told him and was merely going along with it to keep Lois from becoming upset. The truth was, Andrea didn't believe Lois either. How could she? It would be too much of a coincidence if Lois was truly her birth mother. Besides, Andrea was born in Pennsylvania, and Lois lived here in Ohio.

"Where's the doll? What happened to it?" Lois tried to leave her chair, but Orley reached out and placed his hands on her knees. "You need to stay seated, Lois. At least till your head is clear and you can think straight again." He looked up at Brandon as though seeking his help. "I'm still thinking that my wife should see a doctor."

Before Brandon had the chance to retrieve his cell phone again, Lois shouted, "Could someone please find the doll and bring it to me?"

"It's over there behind the counter. You dropped it when you fell." Andrea hurried over and picked up the doll. In her concern for Lois, she hadn't thought about the faceless doll until now. She walked to where Lois sat and handed it to her. "I was telling you how I recently learned that a nurse at the hospital where I was born had given this doll to my adoptive parents, saying that my birth mother wanted me to have it."

Tears pooled in Lois's eyes and ran down her cheeks. "Look here." She pointed to a place on the doll's back, where the name Mary L. Miller had been written in black ink.

"Mary L. Miller is the name of my birth mother," Andrea said. "It says so on my original birth certificate, which I also recently acquired."

Lois placed a hand against her chest. "I am Mary L. Miller. That doll used to be mine, and I'm the one who gave it to the nurse and asked her to give it to my daughter."

The shock of what Lois had said surged straight through Andrea, making her dizzy. Brandon must have seen that she was shaky on her feet, for he quickly grabbed another chair and instructed her to take a seat.

"But. . .but isn't your name Lois?" Andrea could barely get the question out as she spoke through trembling lips.

"My given name was Mary Lois, but everyone called me Lois because one of my cousins was also named Mary and my mother didn't want there to be any confusion." Lois touched the spot on the doll's back where the writing was located. "I wrote here what had been written on my baby's birth certificate."

"Oh my!" Andrea clasped both hands over her mouth. "Is it really possible that you could be my birth mother?"

"Yes, I am certain of it."

"But I was born in Lancaster, Pennsylvania, and you live here."

"I didn't always live in Ohio. I grew up in Mifflin County, Pennsylvania, and when my father found out I had gotten pregnant out of wedlock, he sent me to live with my aunt, whose home was in the village of Bird-in-Hand, which is just outside of Lancaster." Lois paused and drew in a shaky breath. "No one knew about my pregnancy except for my father and aunt. It was kept a secret because Dad was embarrassed by what I'd done, and he didn't want to bring shame on our family."

Andrea felt the comfort of Brandon's warm hands on her shoulder. Did he understand the way she felt? Did Brandon realize how overwhelming this was for her?

⁓

Orley sat in stunned silence as Lois continued to talk with Andrea about her past. *Doesn't my wife realize what a shock this is for me to hear? Why has Lois never mentioned any of this to me? It makes no sense at all.*

Slowly, Orley pulled his fingers through the ends of his beard as he tried to process everything that had been said. It was hard to fathom that during all these years of being married to Lois she had kept such a shocking secret from him.

Orley's muscles tensed as he thought about her deception. Apparently, his wife must be the kind of person who tried to keep things hidden from him. Lois had done it previously, when she'd been quiet about her job for the paper writing the Dear Caroline column. He'd had no idea she'd been involved in that until she confessed it later on. But Lois had apologized, and they'd worked it out. Some time ago, Orley had forgiven her for keeping him in the dark.

He looked at his trembling wife again. *I need to say a quick prayer about how I should address this topic concerning Andrea to my fraa.* He wanted to confront her about this right now, but not in front of two people they barely knew. The issue was between him and Lois, and they needed to talk about it privately.

Orley cleared his throat. "Umm. . .there are some things my wife and I need to discuss." He looked at Andrea, then Brandon. "Would you two mind leaving us alone for a while? Perhaps you could come by our house later this evening." This statement he directed to Andrea. "It will give you a chance to ask Lois more questions and get better acquainted."

Tearfully, Andrea nodded her head. "I would like that very much."

Orley got up and went over to the counter, where he wrote his and Lois's address on a piece of paper. He came back to where Andrea sat and handed it to her. "Would seven o'clock be too late?"

"No, that'll be fine." Andrea smiled at Lois and clasped her hand. "Finding you has been an answer to my prayers. I am eager to know more about you and look forward to talking with you later this evening. I'd like to find out about my biological father, who was listed on my birth certificate as 'unknown.'"

"I will tell you all that I can." More tears filled Lois's eyes and dripped onto her flushed cheeks. "For a good many years, I too have prayed, and now, at long last, God has answered that prayer."

"I'll see you later then. Goodbye for now." Andrea rose from her chair and looked down at the doll Lois still held in her lap. "Would you mind if I take the doll with me?"

"Of course not. It's yours and was always intended for you." Lois handed it to Andrea.

"Thank you."

"You're welcome."

~

Brandon was at a loss for words, but if he was going to speak, it had better be now. He couldn't believe he'd just witnessed the woman he loved finding out who her birth mother was. And Brandon couldn't have been more shocked to learn that it was Lois Troyer. He said a hasty goodbye to Orley and Lois, then hurried past Andrea and opened the door, holding it for her to walk out.

"Thanks."

"You're welcome." He walked beside Andrea as she headed for her car. It felt so good to see her again. He had missed that pretty smile of hers and so many other things. Though it was quite chilly outside, with ice dotting the walkway, Brandon thought he could melt like a snowman in warm weather while he was in Andrea's presence. "I was wondering if you'd like to grab a bite to eat with me," he questioned.

"Right now?"

"Yeah."

"I'm not hungry at the moment, and I'd rather not go to a restaurant with my eyes all red from crying." She reached her vehicle and was about to open the door on the driver's side when Brandon stepped in front of it. "Besides, I'm going over to my parents' house to tell them that I found my birth mother."

"We need to talk, Andrea." His tone had become solemn.

She tipped her head back and looked up at him. "You think so?"

"Definitely." Brandon struggled with the urge to take Andrea into his arms and kiss her soundly, but it might not be appreciated since they hadn't worked things out. Right now, Brandon wanted to resume their engagement, but he would have to be the one to fix things since he was the one who'd ended their engagement. But what if he'd blown it and she didn't want to reestablish their relationship?

"How about this—you can go see your folks before going home, and around five o'clock I'll stop by Lem's and get a pizza to go. Then I'll pick up Duke and come over to your place. I'm sure he'd like to see Lady again, and the two of them can get reacquainted while we talk and eat. Would that be okay with you?"

Her forehead wrinkled and she dropped her gaze. Brandon felt sure she was going to say no.

"I. . .I guess it would be all right. I think Lady's missed hanging out with Duke."

Not nearly as much as I've missed you. Fearful that Andrea might change her mind, Brandon didn't say the words on his heart. He didn't deserve a second chance with her, but oh how he longed for one.

He gave Andrea's arm a little tap and stepped away from the car. "I'll see you at your place in a few hours."

"Okay. Bye for now."

As he headed for his SUV, Brandon prayed. *Lord, please pave the way, and give me the right words to say when I get to Andrea's house. I'm truly sorry for not offering her the support and encouragement I should have when she was searching for her mother.*

Chapter 35

Orley left his seat, walked over to the front window, and flipped the OPEN sign over so it said CLOSED. Then he shut the blinds and locked the front door.

"What are you doing? It's not time to go home yet," Lois said, looking toward the battery-operated clock on the wall. "Our driver won't be here for at least another hour."

"I'm well aware, but it's time for us to have a serious discussion." Orley moved the chair he'd been sitting in so that it faced Lois and sat down. "I'd like to know more about this secret you've been keeping from me all these years and why you've kept this very important information to yourself."

Lois shed a few more tears and dabbed at them with a tissue she'd pulled from inside the band on her apron. "I'm so sorry, Orley. I was wrong not to tell you, but there were two reasons I never said anything about the baby I had out of wedlock."

Orley leaned slightly forward. "I'm listening."

She held up one finger. "I was ashamed of what I'd done and thought you would think less of me if you knew, like my father did." Her chin trembled. "He was very upset when he found out that I was pregnant, and he would have done just about anything to keep those in our church district from finding out."

"What's the second reason?" Orley questioned.

"I knew how badly you felt about not being able to have any children of our own, and I thought if you knew I had given birth to a child and then gave her up for adoption, it would have caused you even more emotional pain."

Orley's lips pressed together in a slight grimace. "I thought you knew me better than that. I love you, Lois, and I've always believed our relationship was strong enough that you would feel free to tell me anything. But now that the truth has come out, I want to understand your thinking and try to help mend this emotional wound for both of us." He paused briefly as though trying to gather his thoughts. "So now I will listen carefully as you explain everything to me."

"My father was very upset and angry with me when he discovered I was expecting a baby. He couldn't deal with his daughter's mistake and feared that those in our community would look down on him as well as his wayward daughter."

"May I ask who the father of your baby was?" Orley leaned closer to Lois. "I need to know."

"His name was William Hostettler, and we were just a couple of lovesick teenagers when it happened."

"Why wasn't his name on Andrea's birth certificate?"

"Because I never told him I was pregnant, and while I was living with my aunt Eva in Bird-in-Hand, Pennsylvania, I read in *The Budget* that William and his entire family had been in a tragic van accident and everyone died, including their driver." Lois paused and sucked in a deep breath. "No one except for my daed and Aunt Eva, who as you know, are both deceased, knew about my pregnancy. I was instructed not to tell anyone else. Dad contacted an adoption agency in Pennsylvania, and they set things up with an English couple who wanted to adopt a baby." Lois lowered her head and let the tears flow freely. "It's been difficult to keep this secret buried in my heart all this time." She sniffed and blew her nose on the tissue Orley had handed her. "I've lived with my guilt every day, wondering if I should have told you the truth and trying my best to help others who were hurting."

"Helping others is a fine thing, Lois." Orley put his hand under her chin so she was looking directly at him again. "But you can't find true peace in your heart by helping others when you should be seeking your own inner peace, which has apparently been lacking. I believe you have tried to hide the pain of your past by doing good things and trying to help people with their problems."

"I. . .I thought I had succeeded in putting the past behind me until Andrea revealed who she was by showing me her doll. I never would have known where my daughter was if it hadn't been for that." Lois swallowed against the pain in the back of her throat. "Instead, all I've managed to do is make a mess of things, and now I've lost your love and respect." She blinked several times. "I wouldn't blame you if you asked me to leave your home."

Orley gave a brisk shake of his head. "That will never happen. We've worked too long and hard for our relationship to end that easily. When we got married, it was for life, and my home is your home, plain and simple." His features softened as he clasped both of her hands and gave them a tender squeeze. "Although I am disappointed that you didn't feel you could share your secret with me, I'm thankful that it's finally out in the open and pleased that you have been reunited with your dochder." His eyes glistened with tears of his own while he spoke in a gentle voice. "It looks like our little family has just grown, and now we both have a daughter."

Struggling to find the right words to convey her gratitude, Lois murmured, "Danki, my dear husband. I love you so much."

"And I love you."

Apple Creek

"Come on, boy!" Brandon slapped his leg. "Wanna go for a ride with me to see Andrea and your furry friend Lady?"

Arf! Arf! Duke ran for the front door with his tail wagging, and he looked up at his owner as if to say, "Hurry up, let's go."

Brandon chuckled. "Hang on. Let me get your leash."

He felt really good about seeing Andrea again. It was great

that she had discovered who her birth mother was, but it had been a shock to find out that it was Lois Troyer. Brandon liked Lois and Orley, and from what he could tell, they were a caring couple. Andrea couldn't have picked a nicer woman than Lois to be her biological mother.

Brandon had spent some time praying after arriving home from Memory Keepers. He had thanked the Lord for working things out for Andrea and for creating an opportunity for the two of them to talk this evening. He'd changed clothes, brushed his teeth, and combed his hair, and then he inspected himself in the mirror to make sure he looked presentable. Things needed to be perfect for this evening, when he hoped to win Andrea back into his life.

Brandon moved away from the mirror and went to get his dog's leash. After clipping it to Duke's collar, he and his little buddy went out the door.

A short time later, they were in Brandon's vehicle, heading for the pizza place to pick up the order he'd called in. From there, it would be on to Andrea's, where he would apologize. Brandon hoped then they could start with a clean slate. He patted his jacket pocket and sent up a prayer.

Chapter 36

As she finished setting out paper plates and napkins, Andrea hummed one of her favorite choruses that they often sang at church. Soon after arriving home from her parents' house, she had freshened up and changed into a new top. Today had been good but quite emotional. She was glad to have found her biological mother. It would be the start of a new chapter in her life.

She'd taken out the glasses when the doorbell rang. *That must be Brandon.* She looked around for Lady and saw the cat sleeping in one corner of the room. Andrea hoped this evening would go well between her and Brandon. Several weeks had passed since they'd exchanged any words, and she was worried that things might be too awkward.

Andrea left the kitchen and went to the front door. The minute she opened it, Duke darted in, pulling against the leash in Brandon's gloved hands.

"I think he's as eager to see your cat as I am to see you."

"Lady's asleep in the kitchen right now, but you can let Duke loose if you want to." Andrea made no reference to Brandon's statement about being eager to see her.

"Here's the pizza I got at Lem's." Brandon lifted the box he held. "Where would you like me to put it?"

"I'll take it to the kitchen while you release Duke's leash from his collar. You can hang your jacket on the coat tree here in the hallway."

"Okay." Brandon leaned down, and the minute his dog was free, Duke took off down the hall and nearly ran into the wall as he rounded the corner and disappeared into the kitchen.

Brandon rolled his eyes. "I told you he was eager to come over here."

Andrea couldn't resist smiling. In fact, smiling had come easy to her since she'd left Memory Keepers earlier today. When Andrea had stopped by her folks' house, Dad was still at work, but she'd been glad to find her mother at home. Andrea could still see the look of surprise on Mom's face when she'd told her what had taken place at the antique store and about the miracle of finding her birth mother in such an unexpected way. Mom had hugged Andrea and said she was happy for her. She'd even said she would like to meet Lois sometime soon to get acquainted and share pictures of Andrea taken when she was a child.

Andrea's father had called her after he'd left the bank and heard the news from her mother. He too said it would be nice to meet Andrea's biological mother and fill her in on some of Andrea's childhood experiences.

Redirecting her thoughts, Andrea entered the kitchen and placed the pizza box on the table. The mouth-watering smell that escaped from the box made her appetite grow. Duke was in the same room, wagging his tail near the cat's food dish. She wasn't surprised to see that Lady was not only awake but sharing her bowl of water with Duke.

"Those two were meant to be together, don't you think?" Brandon asked when he came into the room.

"Well, I'd have to say they think so." She shook her head. "One would never know that Duke used to be afraid of Lady."

Brandon laughed. "Yeah, my dog was sure a big chicken when it came to your cat."

"I think she has him buffaloed."

Brandon took a few steps toward Andrea. "I want you to know how sorry I am for not being there when you needed me the most.

I should have realized how desperate you were to find your birth mother and been more understanding."

"I'm sorry too," she said. "I was not considerate of your needs either."

"I love you, Andrea, and I will do everything I can to prove it." He moved closer and dropped down on one knee, then opened his hand. "Will you marry me, please?"

Her eyes filled with joyful tears as she gazed at the beautiful engagement ring she had foolishly sent back to him, which was now cradled in his hand. "Yes, Brandon, I will marry you, and this time there will be no postponing or canceling the wedding."

"Agreed. We will, however, have to choose another wedding date, because February 14th is just a week away." He slipped the ring on Andrea's finger and stood. Gathering her into his arms, Brandon kissed her so tenderly that Andrea didn't want it to end. She'd had many happy times in her life, but nothing as joyous as today. In addition to the thrill of meeting her biological mother, she and Brandon were together again.

"After we finish eating, would you like to go over to the Troyers' house with me?" Andrea asked, stroking her fiancé's cheek.

"Most definitely. If I'm going to become part of your family soon, then I'd like to get better acquainted with your birth mother and stepfather, Orley, who has also been a big help to me."

"Really? How's that?"

"I'll tell you while we eat our pizza." Brandon gave Andrea another kiss and pulled out a chair for her.

Before they took slices of pizza, they held hands and Brandon prayed. "Heavenly Father, thank You for the food we are about to eat, and bless the hands that prepared it. We are thankful for all that You have done in our lives and are especially thankful for Lois Troyer and the wonderful announcement she made today." He squeezed Andrea's fingers as they both said, "Amen".

During this special moment, Andrea's mind emptied of all

concerns as a warm tingle infused her body. She quietly thanked God for answered prayer.

When Andrea opened her eyes and looked at Brandon, a wide smile spread across her face. "I just thought of something."

"What is it?" he asked.

"When I sent my DNA sample in and got the results, the only thing I learned was that I'm of German descent. Now I know why." She spoke in a bubbly voice. "I believe that the reason I've always had an interest in the Amish way of life and painted so many pictures of horses and buggies, barns, and Amish children and was so excited by that old Amish quilt is because of my true heritage." She placed one hand against her chest. "Somewhere deep inside, I must have known that I had been born to Amish parents. And if they had raised me, I'd most likely be wearing Plain clothes and driving a horse and buggy myself."

Brandon gave her a tender smile. "But then, since I am not of Amish descent, you would never have met or agreed to marry me, which in my opinion would not be a good thing."

"You're right, but it didn't happen that way, and I believe that God worked it all out according to His plan."

~

Walnut Creek

"You were sure out there in the phone shed for a while," Orley said when Lois entered the kitchen and took a seat at the table across from him. "What took so long?"

"I called my sisters and half-brothers and left them all messages. I decided that it was time for Elizabeth, Rebekah, Benjamin, and Jacob to hear that they have a niece none of them have known anything about."

"Did you explain the circumstances of your pregnancy?"

She nodded. "I can't deny that I was not married when my baby was born, and in the messages I left on their answering machines,

I gave them the details and told how I was miraculously reunited with my daughter today."

"Do you think they will understand and not judge you the way your daed did?" Orley asked.

"Although I'm sure they won't approve of my actions as a teenager, I believe they will not condemn me."

"I doubt that any of them have lived perfect lives, because we are all born into sin and make mistakes."

Lois swallowed against the lump in her throat. "I asked my heavenly Father to forgive me a long time ago, and I believe He did."

"Of course. Psalm 86:5 says: 'Thou, Lord, art good, and ready to forgive; and plenteous in mercy unto all them that call upon thee.'"

"I am thankful that God loved the world so much that He sent His only Son, Jesus, to the earth as a baby. And I'm even more appreciative that Jesus, after He became a man, bore the sins of the world when He died on the cross."

"Jah," Orley agreed, "and all people have to do is ask His forgiveness and accept Him as their Lord and Savior."

"Absolutely." Lois smiled in spite of the tears she felt behind her eyes that at any moment could spill over.

Lois took out a loaf of bread and placed it on the table. Then she opened the refrigerator and removed a package of lunchmeat and cheese, along with some mustard, mayonnaise, and pickles. "If you don't mind, Orley, I'd like to keep this evening's supper simple so we can eat it before Andrea and Brandon get here. I'm almost certain he will be with her."

"That's fine with me."

Andrea's stomach tightened when Brandon pulled in front of an older-looking but well-built farmhouse. "According to my GPS, this is the Troyers' place," he announced.

"I'm suddenly nervous," she said. "I am about to see my birth mother's home for the first time, and I'm not sure how to act."

"Just be yourself. Amish folks aren't really that different from you or me. They just live a distinctive lifestyle."

"Yes, one that doesn't involve all the modern conveniences we English people have, such as electricity in their homes, which means no televisions, computers, dishwashers, or electric lights."

"I've visited a few Amish homes around Apple Creek when I've been called to treat a sick or injured animal." Brandon set the brake and turned off the ignition. "Some homes were very simple, with the barest of necessities, while others had a more progressive feel but without all the modern things we are used to." He reached across the seat and took hold of Andrea's hand. "Try to relax and enjoy this evening as you get to know Lois and Orley. And be sure to take the opportunity to ask any questions you may have."

Andrea smiled. "Thank you for coming with me. I really appreciate your support."

He gave her fingers a tender squeeze. "I should have been more supportive from the beginning, when you first told me you wanted to search for your biological parents."

"It's in the past," she said. "Let's just focus on the future we're going to have together."

"Yes," he murmured with his mouth close to her ear. "And we will make sure that Lois and her husband are a special part of our lives. I think it would be good if we introduced the Troyers to both of our families so they can get to know them too."

Feeling content and quite hopeful, Andrea leaned her head on his strong shoulder. "I love you, Brandon."

He put his hand on her forehead and lifted her bangs. "I love you, too, and here's the proof." Brandon pulled Andrea into his arms and gave her forehead and both cheeks feathery kisses. Then his lips captured hers in a tender but firm kiss. "Ready to go knock on the door now?" he asked when the kiss ended.

"Yes, I am." Andrea got out of his SUV, and when he joined her, they walked up the porch steps together. Andrea reached out her hand to knock, but the door opened before her knuckles made contact with the wood.

"Come in. Come in. . . ." Orley greeted them both with a warm handshake and took their jackets. "Lois is in the kitchen, taking a pan of brownies from the oven. We can either join her there or wait for her in the living room."

"I'm fine with going to the kitchen," Andrea was quick to say.

"Alrighty then, you can follow me." Orley led them halfway down the narrow hall, turned left, and entered a warm, cozy kitchen.

Lois quickly set a pan of brownies on a cooling rack that had been placed on a counter near the sink. "I'm so happy to see you again," she said, giving Andrea a welcoming hug. Following that, she shook hands with Brandon. "Did you have any trouble finding our home?"

"Not a bit." He smiled. "I just typed the address Orley gave Andrea this afternoon into the driving directions on my phone, and it brought us right here."

"Oh good." Lois gestured to the brownies. "These need to cool a bit, but while we are waiting, let's go into the living room, where it's more comfortable and we can visit."

Andrea and Brandon followed the Troyers across the hall to a living room that was larger than Andrea had expected. It was furnished with a good-sized couch, two leather recliners, a wooden rocker, and two straight-backed chairs. Lois suggested that she and Andrea sit on the couch, and the men could have the recliners.

Once seated, Andrea noticed two battery-operated lights hanging on hooks from the ceiling. Their brightness illuminated the entire room.

"Have either of you ever been in an Amish home before?" Orley asked.

"I've been in a few, when I made calls to treat some Amish people's animals," Brandon spoke up.

"And you?" Orley looked at Andrea.

She shook her head. "This is my first time."

Lois reached across the space between them. "I hope you will visit here and at Memory Keepers many times in the years to come. I want us to take every opportunity to get to know each other well."

Tears welled in Lois's eyes, which put Andrea on the brink of tears too. "I'd like that," she said with feeling.

"Would you like to know a little bit about my family?"

"So you have no other children?" Andrea asked.

Lois shook her head. "No, we don't, but I do have four siblings, although none of them live in Ohio. Someday, if we can work it all out, I'd like you to meet them and their families."

Andrea glanced at Brandon, engrossed in a conversation with Orley that involved the weather; then she looked back at Lois and smiled. "I would like that very much. Having grown up as an only child and only having one cousin, I've never known what it was like to be part of a large family. Not that I'm complaining," she quickly added. "My parents and I have always been close, and we've done many fun things together."

"I'm sure you have." Lois twirled one finger around the narrow ties of her head covering. "I look forward to meeting your mother and father someday."

"I stopped by their house after leaving your antique store today and told my mother how we found each other and I came to realize that you were the woman who gave birth to me in Lancaster, Pennsylvania, almost thirty-three years ago."

"Was she surprised?"

"Yes, and Mom said she was happy for me. Dad called me when he got home, and he seemed pleased too." Andrea scooched down on the couch so she was a little closer to Lois. "They want to meet you and Orley, so maybe we can pick you up some evening or weekend when you are free, and we'll eat supper at my folks' place."

"You'd all be welcome to come here if you like," Lois said. "I would be pleased for the opportunity to cook a meal for you and your parents." She looked over at Brandon. "You're invited too, of course."

He grinned. "That's good, because I proposed marriage to Andrea before we came here, and since she said yes, I will soon be part of the family."

Orley got up from his chair and went over to give Brandon a few thumps on his back. "That's good news. I knew everything would work out for you two."

Andrea assumed from his remark that Brandon must have told Orley about the problems they'd had. But she didn't mind. Everyone needed someone to talk to when they were going through a troubled situation. She'd shared things with Colleen and had even written a few letters to Dear Caroline, which gave her the assurance someone cared and wanted to help.

"Would you mind if I asked you a personal question?" Lois asked, leaning a bit closer to Andrea.

"No, not at all."

"When you and Brandon were going through a difficult time, did you by chance write a letter to the Dear Caroline newspaper column?"

Andrea blinked several times. "Why yes, I did. I'm confused though—what made you ask me that question?"

A crimson flush crept across Lois's cheeks. "Since we are telling the truth while sitting here on this sofa, I must admit to you that I am Dear Caroline."

"Really?" Andrea's mouth dropped open. "Wow, that is a surprise, and no wonder you gave such good advice. Now may I ask you a question?"

Lois bobbed her head. "Anything, Andrea. Anything at all."

"How do the Amish say *mother* in Pennsylvania Dutch?"

"Well, there's *mudder* for mother. Or *mamm* for mom."

"Some children call their mothers *mammi* or *memm*," Orley interjected.

Andrea let those words roll around in her head for a minute. Then she looked at Lois and said, "Would it be all right if I called you Memm?"

Tears filled Lois's eyes and dribbled down her cheeks. "Oh, I would like that very much."

Andrea nodded. "And so would I, my dear memm." Her gaze went to Brandon again, and she was pleased when he grinned at her and held up both thumbs. Through all the days of worry and searching the internet for answers, in her wildest dreams, Andrea never could have imagined that she would end up with two very special mothers.

Epilogue

Three months later

"You look radiant, Andrea, but you need to stop fidgeting so I can make sure your veil is on straight."

"Sorry, Mom, but this is my wedding day, and I can't help feeling nervous." Andrea turned to look at her mother. "Weren't you nervous when you and Dad got married?"

"Of course, dear, and I'm sure your groom is as nervous as your father was on our wedding day. Marriage is a huge milestone in a person's life, and you want everything to go perfectly."

"Yes, but life's not perfect, and I know there will be bumps in the road."

"You've got that right—especially when you start having kids," Colleen interjected as she looked at her reflection in the full-length mirror Andrea had brought from home. They'd been told that the bridal party could use any of the Sunday school classrooms to get ready for the wedding, but the room lacked mirrors.

Andrea smiled as she looked at her stunning matron of honor wearing a lovely rose-colored dress. "Even if there are days when we're faced with challenges, I'm excited today about becoming Brandon's wife, and I look forward to whatever time God gives us here on earth as husband and wife."

A rap sounded on the door. "Are you ready in there, ladies?" Dad called. "It's about time for my wife to be seated and for me to walk my daughter down the aisle."

Andrea's mother opened the door. "Come in, Ray, and see how lovely the bride looks in the satin dress I wore on our wedding day."

Andrea's father entered the room, and when he walked over to Andrea, tears pooled in his eyes. "You're as beautiful in that dress as your mother was the day she became my bride." He leaned close and kissed her cheek. "This is probably the most important day of your life, and your mother and I are pleased that you chose Brandon to be your mate for life. He will not only be a good provider, but he's a kind and generous man."

"I agree," Mom said, slipping her arm around Andrea's waist.

"Do either of you have any advice for me before I take that walk down the aisle?" Andrea asked.

"Just be loving, kind, and honest," Dad said. "And remember to keep God at the center of your marriage. Pray about everything, and seek the Lord's will concerning every aspect of your life."

Mom nodded. "I'm in complete agreement with what your father just said."

"Same here." Colleen stepped forward and handed Andrea her delicate white rose bridal bouquet. "Now it's time for us to leave this room because there's a church full of family and friends who are as eager to see you and Brandon get married as I am on this beautiful sunny day in May."

Moments later, following Colleen, Andrea walked down the aisle with her hand in the crook of Dad's arm. As they approached the front of the sanctuary, she spotted her birth mother's white head covering and smiled. Orley stood beside Lois, looking quite dapper in his Amish-styled suit. How wonderful it was that Andrea's new family could be there to witness her marriage to Brandon.

Andrea's gaze went to her groom, dressed in a black tuxedo and standing beside his brother, Joe, whom Brandon had chosen to be the best man. Andrea had a feeling of weightlessness as the minister asked, "Who gives this woman to be wed?" and her father replied, "Her mother and I do."

A comforting warmth radiated throughout Andrea's body as

she slipped her hand from the crook of Dad's arm and sought the hand of her groom. It felt as if she'd been waiting for this special moment all of her life.

Tears, like silver, glistened in the corners of Brandon's eyes. Andrea felt moisture in her eyes as well. *Dear Lord, thank You for the blessings I've received in the last few months—for bringing my birth mother and me together and for helping me realize how important Brandon is to me. Please guide and direct us both as we begin our new life,* Andrea silently prayed as she and the handsome, smiling man who would soon be her husband turned to face the minister in preparation for saying their vows.

⁓

"Did you ever see a sweeter-looking bride?" Lois whispered to Orley from their front-row seat, where they sat next to Andrea's adoptive parents.

He smiled and gave a brief nod.

Lois's heart swelled with joy as she watched her newly found daughter recite vows to her groom in this church full of people. Although it would have given her the greatest pleasure to have raised Andrea herself, Lois felt thankful that her daughter had been brought up in a Christian home with parents who loved her and had provided for Andrea's needs. Rather than feeling bitter because she'd been robbed of the right to watch her daughter grow up, Lois felt grateful that God had provided a miracle and brought Andrea back into her life. Since that day in their antique store, when Lois realized who Andrea was, she and Orley had been given the opportunity to meet and get to know Evelyn and Ray Wagner. From their first meeting, which had taken place a few days later, Lois had known her daughter was loved and cherished by the man and woman she'd grown up to call Dad and Mom.

Although this was quite different from a traditional Amish wedding, Lois found herself enjoying each moment. When the minister prayed for Andrea and Brandon, read some passages of scripture, and spoke about the importance of good communication and remembering to speak the truth to one another, Lois felt a twinge of guilt creep back in. *Even before we were married, I should have told Orley about my pregnancy and the adoption of my baby. I did us both a disservice by keeping the birth of my child a secret.* But Orley had forgiven Lois, and for that, she also felt thankful.

Looking ahead to the future, she anticipated being included in her daughter and son-in-law's lives. If they were blessed with children someday, Lois would have the privilege of being a grandmother.

Lois shifted on the pew. She had to admit that the padded benches with backs were more comfortable than the backless wooden benches that were used in Amish church services. Even so, Lois wouldn't trade her way of life to become part of the English world.

A smile played upon Lois's lips as she thought about the vacation she and Orley would be taking next week. While Andrea and Brandon spent their honeymoon in Hawaii, Lois and Orley would be getting plenty of sun in Sarasota, Florida. They had heard that the month of May was a good time to go there because the people the Floridians referred to as snowbirds would have returned to their northern homes by then. This meant that the Sarasota beaches and other places would be less crowded. Lois hadn't been to the beach in a good many years, and she looked forward to walking barefoot in the sand, looking for unusual shells.

Lois's thoughts were redirected when the minister told the groom that he could kiss his bride. Although this was definitely not something one would witness at an Amish wedding, Lois found it to be quite endearing. Following the kiss, the minister looked out at those in the audience and said in a loud, clear voice: "I would like to introduce to you Mr. and Mrs. Brandon Prentice." Harmonious organ music filled the room as Andrea put her hand in the crook of her husband's arm and they stepped off the platform. When they walked past the pew where Lois, Orley, Evelyn, and Ray sat, Andrea looked over at them and smiled.

Smiling in return, Lois wiped tears from her cheeks. This was one of the happiest moments of her life. She closed her eyes and prayed: *Heavenly Father, once again I thank You for the miracle that You provided and for this opportunity to witness my daughter's marriage. Please bless the happy couple in the days ahead, and continue to guide and direct Orley's and my life. Remind us daily to set a good example to those we meet, and if it be Your will, send more people into Memory Keepers who need a touch from above as we speak the words that You will place upon our hearts.*

RECIPES

Lois's Egg Drop Soup

INGREDIENTS:

2 cups chicken broth

2 teaspoons soy sauce

2 large eggs

Pinch of salt

Pinch of garlic powder

1 large green onion, chopped

Heat broth and soy sauce in saucepan. While broth is heating, whisk eggs with salt and garlic powder in a bowl or larger measuring cup. When broth starts to boil, use a wooden spoon to stir the soup. Slowly drip egg mixture into broth, stirring continually in the same direction. As soon as egg mixture has been poured in, remove soup from heat. Pour into soup bowls, garnish with chopped onion, and serve. Makes two servings.

Andrea's Tangy Potato Salad

INGREDIENTS:

4 potatoes, cooked until tender and diced

4 hard-boiled eggs, chopped

¼ cup diced onions

¼ cup dill pickles, cut into small pieces

½ cup mayonnaise or salad dressing

¼ cup brown mustard

1 tablespoon apple cider vinegar or pickle juice

Salt & pepper to taste

Cook potatoes and boil eggs in separate saucepans. When they are done, transfer to a bowl of cold water until both are cooled. Dice potatoes and eggs and place in large bowl. Mix onion and pickles into potato-egg mixture. Stir in mayonnaise, mustard, vinegar, and salt and pepper. Mix gently until evenly coated. Refrigerate for fifteen minutes to half an hour before serving.

DISCUSSION QUESTIONS

1. Lois and Orley Troyer felt called to mentor people who came into their antique store with problems. Like this Amish couple, how can we mentor others who are hurting or need guidance and counsel?

2. What problems have you faced recently? How has God provided for you? Did you find guidance from reading the Bible, talking to a friend, listening to a pastor's message during church, or in some other way?

3. Ray and Evelyn had not told Andrea the truth about her adoption, which created a problem when she found out accidentally. Was it wrong for them to keep their daughter's adoption from her for over thirty years? Why do you think they chose not to say anything? Is there ever a good reason for an adoptive parent to keep a child's adoption from them?

4. Andrea was quite upset after her cousin informed her that she'd been adopted. She felt betrayed by her adoptive parents, and it put a wedge between them for a while. Have you ever been in a similar situation where you felt betrayed by someone you had trusted? How did you work through those feelings?

5. Andrea's adoptive father, Ray, trusted God and reassured his wife that their daughter would come around and forgive them for not telling her that she'd been adopted as a baby. What should a person do if someone they hurt is not willing to forgive?

6. Andrea's adoptive mother, Evelyn, was concerned that if Andrea found out who her birth mother was, she might bond with her, and the relationship Evelyn had established with her adopted daughter could suffer. Have you or someone you

know ever been in a situation similar to this and worried about how things would turn out? What could Andrea have done to assure her adoptive mother that their relationship wouldn't change if she located her birth mother?

7. When Andrea began a search for her biological parents, her fiancé, Brandon, felt left out because she had less time to spend with him, and when they were together, all she talked about was her need to find out who had given her up for adoption. When Andrea suggested that they postpone their marriage, Brandon was so upset that he broke up with her. Do you think that was a wise decision, or should he have been more understanding and tried to work things out?

8. Andrea was deeply hurt when Brandon broke their engagement. She needed his support and didn't understand why he couldn't wait until she had located her birth mother to get married. Have you ever been in a situation where you needed encouragement and support from someone you love, but they did not provide it for you? What would you have done if you'd been in Andrea's position? Should she have been willing to marry Brandon even though she was still searching for her biological parents?

9. Although Brandon was not as supportive as Andrea needed him to be, her friend Colleen encouraged Andrea to follow her quest to find her birth mother. How important is it for friends to support each other during difficult times? What does the Bible teach us about friendship?

10. Lois had chosen not to tell her husband that during her teen years she had given birth to a baby and put the infant up for adoption. Many years later, when the truth came out, Orley was deeply hurt because Lois hadn't told him about this significant event from her past. Is there ever a time when a

secret such as the one Lois had should be kept from a spouse?

11. Orley forgave Lois for not telling him about the child she'd had out of wedlock. Why do you think he was able to forgive? What does God's Word tell us about forgiveness?

12. As an artist, Andrea enjoyed painting pictures of Amish barns, buggies, and children. She had also been intrigued by an old Amish quilt. Do you think the reason Andrea was drawn to the Plain people's way of life was because of her heritage that she knew nothing about until she discovered who her birth mother was?

13. The importance of prayer is mentioned several times in this book, as the characters asked God for guidance and help with various situations. Prayer time was also necessary when the characters thanked God for His many blessings. How important is it for a Christian to pray? When a prayer is answered, does it strengthen your faith?

14. Did any of the scriptures mentioned in this book reinforce your faith or help in some spiritual way? How can reading the Bible and memorizing verses help us deal with life's problems?

15. While reading this story, did you learn anything new about the Amish who live in Apple Creek or Walnut Creek, Ohio? Have you had the privilege of visiting either of those towns? If so, what were your favorite things to see or do there?

A NOTE FROM THE EDITORS

We hope you enjoyed *The Apple Creek Announcement* by Wanda E. Brunstetter, published by Guideposts. For over seventy-five years, Guideposts, a nonprofit organization, has been driven by a vision of a world filled with hope. We aspire to be the voice of a trusted friend, a friend who makes you feel more hopeful and connected.

By making a purchase from Guideposts, you join our community in touching millions of lives, inspiring them to believe that all things are possible through faith, hope, and prayer. Your continued support allows us to provide uplifting resources to those in need. Whether through our communities, websites, apps, or publications, we inspire our audiences, bring them together, and comfort, uplift, entertain, and guide them. Visit us at guideposts.org to learn more.

We would love to hear from you. Write us at Guideposts, P.O. Box 5815, Harlan, Iowa 51593 or call us at (800) 932-2145. Did you love *The Apple Creek Announcement*? Leave a review for this product on guideposts.org/shop.

Your feedback helps others in our community find relevant products.

Find inspiration, find faith, find Guideposts.

Shop our best sellers and favorites at

guideposts.org/shop

Or scan the QR code to go directly to our Shop